Art Education:

The Development of Public Policy

Art Education:
The Development of Public Policy

Charles M. Dorn

ART EDUCATION:
THE DEVELOPMENT OF PUBLIC POLICY

by

Charles M. Dorn

Library of Congress Cataloging-in-Publication Data

Dorn, Charles M.
Art education : the development of public policy / by Charles M. Dorn
p. cm.
ISBN 0-9715402-9-2 (alk. paper)
1. Art—Study and teaching (Elementary)—United States. 2. Art—Study and teaching (Secondary)—United States. 3. Art and state—United States. 4. Education and state—United States. I. Title.

N353.D66 2005
707'.1'273- -dc22   2005048193

Printed in the United States of America.

Barnhardt & Ashe Publishing, Inc.
Miami, Florida
www.barnhardtashepublishing.com

To all our K–12 American art teachers who genuinely believe in the children and youth they serve and in the power of art to transform the life of the mind, and in memory of Melville Dorn, my father, who always believed that anything was possible.

Credits

Front Cover Art:
Charles M. Dorn, artist; Tallahassee, Fl.; 54 x 44 in.; *Presence Two;* oil; 2003.

Page 72:
Designed by William Morris; Panel of tiles; 160.0 x 91.5 cm V & A C.36; 1972. William Morris Gallery, Walthamstow; Linda Parry (ed.) *William Morris;* London: Philip Wilson Publishers, Ltd.; 143-149 Great Portland Street; London WIN SFB; 1996; p. 193.

Page 78:
Artist unknown; location unknown; 91.5 x 63.5 cm., 36 x 25 in. The eagle and palette logo of the Federal Art Project was never standardized. This poster illustrates one of the many variations created. *Posters of the WPA,* Los Angeles, Ca. 90068; 1987; p. 41.

Page 80:
Beniamino Bufano (in striped trousers) at work in the WPA/FAP sculpture studio; San Francisco, Ca.; statues of (left to right) *Louis Pasteur, Mother of Races, Dr. Sun Yat-sen* (a red granite head), and *St. Francis* (a model for his head); (NCFA: Cahill) *Art for the Millions;* Greenwich, Ct.: New York Graphic Society; 140 Greenwich Ave. 06830; 1973; p. 108

Page 87:
Boy Painting at Phoenix, Arizona, Community Art Center; (NCFA: Cahill); *Art for the Millions;* Greenwich, Ct.: New York Graphic Society; 140 Greenwich Ave. 06830; 1973; p. 207.

Page 88:
Charles Louff; Riverside, Rhode Island; © 1890; Carousel Giraffe. Painted wood, leather, and metal. Rendered by Henry Tomaszewski, 1939. *Index of American Design;* National Gallery of Art; Washington, D.C.

Table of Contents

Preface

INTRODUCTION

Upon reflection, our recent research efforts in K–12 portfolio assessment (Dorn 2002, 2003; Dorn, Madeja, and Sabol 2004) were mainly responsible for my decision to write this text on art education and public policy. What required us to look at the process of student K–12 art assessment in the first place were the new national and state policies driving the need for student assessment and the need for public accountability in the nation's schools.

Our efforts thus far have been limited to the assessment of student artwork in part because artistic activity remains the primary goal of most K–12 school art programs. At the same time we are also aware that our art programs today provide a much broader range of cognitive learnings than we are currently looking at. This includes learnings the art teaching profession over time has decided to embrace including a myriad of critical, historical, aesthetic, and social behaviors especially in the multicultural, interdisciplinary, environmental, and cultural domains.

The addition of these newer studies to the artistic, creative, and aesthetic goals already present have considerably expanded the breadth of the art curriculum. As a result, some in our field believe we have become a school subject without a curriculum, where in reality we may have only reached a point where the curriculum has become broad enough to confuse the art teacher as to which goals they should pursue and which behaviors they most need to evaluate.

Art teachers are, as a result of their vocation, fiercely independent in their choice of curricula and learning goals that are further exacerbated by a field without standardized texts and one that accepts an open concept as to what students should know and be able to do. Without any agreed-on curriculum sequence and scope, and even fewer rules and guidelines to follow, many art programs still offer a random array of nonsequential activities that, in effect, offer almost as many different curricula options as there are art programs.

What has contributed to this lack of agreement on the art curriculum are the changing values that have occurred in both the art discipline and the educational programs of the nation's schools. We are, as a field, guided by many competing and sometimes contradictory aesthetic and educational values that interact with and are influenced by the changing social values of legislators, bureaucracies, and special interest groups who make government policies designed to achieve school reform and accountability. Teachers usually out of the loop of the policy formation process largely have to depend upon their national government and state legislatures to form these newer educational policies designed to exercise the right of government to interfere with private choice.

As a result of these new laws, art teachers are not only confused about what they should teach but also challenged by laws requiring them to teach even language and math courses in order to assist the schools in meeting state-mandated curriculum goals. This provides even less time for art instruction and, in some cases, loss of the art room and even the school itself. At present we have good reason to expect in at least some lower- performing schools that we may even lose art teaching positions due to art teacher morale and their frustration teaching in areas other than art.

Policy issues in art education today more or less show the effects of at least two somewhat different policy interventions in K–12 schooling enacted by Congress in the 1990s. These include (1) the Goals 2000 and National Standards legislation that emphasized the needs for school accountability and a populist-oriented education policy and (2) the No Child Left Behind (NCLB) Act, fostering both school choice and accountability. As a result, today's education policies are directed toward achieving both the populist reforms outlined in Goals 2000 and the models of school accountability advocated in the NCLB legislation. These 1990s federal government interventions into K–12 school policy have also encouraged two quite divergent art curriculum initiatives in K–12 art education programs, one focused on the need for the art education curriculum to become more responsible to the public interest and the other on how art education can be used to reconstruct the current American social and political system. This book will address both these points of view and offer alternatives through examining government educational policies promoting both a populist approach to school accountability and the postmodernist ideologies of social reconstruction.

GOVERNMENT REFORMS

Over the past two decades, education in the United States has undergone significant changes. Fueled by both internal and external forces, challenges arose to previously held humanistic values. Political, economic, social, cultural and technological concerns have combined to drive the changes. Cycles of educational reform precipitated by publication of *A Nation at Risk: The Imperative for Educational Reform* (National Commission on Excellence in Education 1983) and *Toward Civilization: Overview from the Report on Arts Education* (National Endowment for the Arts 1988) continue today. By focusing national attention on the scope of public education, these and other reports stimulated intense examination of its nature and quality.

CURRENT FEDERAL LEGISLATION

Legislative concerns about improving the quality of education led to successive sets of federal goals (U.S. Department of Education 1994), and those set by Congress (U.S. Congress 1994). For the first time the national education goals of 1994 included the visual arts. Earlier, in 1969, Congress mandated the National Assessment of Educational Progress (NAEP), whose purpose was to survey and monitor changes in the educational accomplishments of all U.S. students. The NAEP has traditionally assessed learning in mathematics, reading, science, writing, world geography, U.S. history, civics, social studies, and the arts (Calderone, King, and Horkey 1997).

Goals 2000

The first federal effort to initiate social equality and equity began with the national Goals 2000 (CNEA 1994) effort, which defined the goals of schooling in order to make sure that:

1. All children in America will start school ready to learn.

2. The high school graduation rate will increase to at least ninety percent.

3. All students will leave grades 4, 8, and 12 having demonstrated competency in challenging subject matter including English, mathematics, science, foreign languages, civics and government, economics, the arts, history, and geography, and every school in the United States will ensure that all students learn to use their minds well, so they may be prepared for responsible citizenship, further learning, and productive employment in our nation's modern economy.

4. United States students will be first in the world in mathematics and science achievement.

5. Every adult American will be literate and will possess the knowledge and skills necessary to compete in a global economy and exercise the rights and responsibilities of citizenship.

6. Every school in the United States will be free of drugs, violence, and the unauthorized presence of firearms and alcohol, and will offer a disciplined environment conducive to learning.

7. The nation's teaching force will have access to programs for continued improvement of their professional skills and the opportunity to acquire the knowledge and skills needed to instruct and prepare all American students for the next century.

8. Every school will promote partnerships that will increase parental involvement and participation in promoting the social, emotional, and academic growth of children.

Goals 2000 was directed toward achieving equality of opportunity among the races and toward schools accepting responsibility to educate every child regardless of his or her color and economic status. Although it did—at the same time—also provide a basis for establishing achievement standards, it did not specify them.

Educational Standards

A second federal educational reform effort focused on creation of standards. This occurred as a result of increased dissatisfaction with school performance and the realization that educators and other stakeholders showed only minimal support for numerous issues central to the education of students, including content, knowledge, skills, and processes. The content of disciplines became a source of disagreement, encouraging in arts education the movement called discipline-based art education (DBAE). In the field of art education, content was said to be idiosyncratic and lacking uniformity. According to the federal government, numerous factors accounted for the divergences, including differences in local resources, needs and values of the community, funding, facilities, and staffing. In addition, art education teaching content was frequently accused of reflecting the art teachers' individual interests or skills and the lack of quality in teacher pre-service training.

National Content Standards

With the emergence of the Getty Trust funding of DBAE in the mid-1980s and publication of the national fine arts standards (Music Educators National Conference [MENC] 1994), the federal government, state departments of education, and local school districts supported various visual arts curriculum initiatives. The goal was to promote consistent and assessable curriculum content, and the result was to restructure state visual arts proficiency guidelines and frameworks and local curriculum guides in order to ensure compliance. The national content standards in art (MENC 1994) included:

1. understanding and applying media, technique, and process
2. using knowledge of structures and function

3. choosing and evaluating subject matter

4. reflecting on and assessing the merit of artworks

5. making connections between the visual arts and other disciplines

Art teachers in public education in the 1980s, although primarily committed to a child-centered point of view, also knew that in the modern schooling climate, the products of instruction that cannot be evaluated become products that, for all intents and purposes, do not exist. The choice for art teachers was to either find a way to assess arts instruction or possibly witness its eventual elimination from the school curriculum. The political argument as advanced in the Goals 2000 legislation concerned looking at assessing art in terms of its usefulness in solving a variety of school problems, including keeping students in schools, improving graduation rates and academic performance, and offering positive alternatives to juvenile crime and drug abuse (Dorn 1999).

The National Assessment of Educational Progress

A third intervention from the federal government occurred in 1997 with the issuance of the NAEP test in art education. The NAEP first assessed visual arts achievement in 1974 and 1978, raising numerous issues and concerns about the nature of assessment in art education (Sabol 1990). The NAEP's findings prompted similar large-scale, state-level assessments in the 1980s (Sabol 1990; Shuler and Connealy 1998). The 1997 NAEP test in the visual arts consisted of items designed to measure historical, critical, and aesthetic knowledge and skills in creating and responding to art. The items were aligned with the national visual arts standards and with DBAE practices. Findings in *The NAEP 1997 Arts Report Card* (Persky, Sandene, and Askew 1999) and ongoing secondary analysis of the 1997 NAEP visual arts data by researchers (Diket, Burton, and Sabol 2000) have focused attention on national visual arts assessment, which in turn has contributed to examinations of local assessment issues in visual arts education.

A CHANGING POLITICAL CLIMATE

Those politicians who viewed the nation's educational systems as failing pointed to not only a lack of national content standards and assessments, but also the role of teachers. Questions about the quality of teachers and their instruction have traditionally been at the heart of the legislators' concern. With the support of DBAE, new efforts were focused on standards for art education pre-service programs and training and also for certification and licensure. DBAE supporters saw poor student achievement as being due to too much emphasis on student creativity and not enough emphasis on assessable cognitive learning in art history, criticism, and aesthetics.

As a result of the new standards, state professional teaching standards boards and other license-granting agencies have restructured licensure standards and procedures and made them more rigorous. Many state recertification programs contain career ladder mechanisms that require ongoing professional development. Some include mentorship programs and public-service requirements. Most include some form of assessment or accountability measures. Teacher and instructional improvements are the expected result of all these changes.

STATE DEPARTMENTS
OF EDUCATION

Beginning in 1999, some thirty-eight states began efforts to improve K–12 instruction. California, Delaware, Florida, Idaho, Kentucky, Michigan, Oklahoma, Oregon, Tennessee, Texas, Utah, Virginia, and Wyoming announced plans for new graduation requirements, new accountability models, new accreditation and graduation requirements, statewide tests in all subjects, performance accountability models, and instructional remediation (National Art Education Association [NAEA] 1999).

In Florida, the State Department of Education developed a new teacher-pay-for-performance development plan, a new school accountability plan (the A+ plan), and Senate Bill 2500, which requires school districts to have a State Department of Education–approved plan for curriculum and instruction improvement, supported by student performance data obtained from the students to whom the teacher is assigned. Art teachers in many Florida school districts are involved in formulating their own art teaching performance plans. Some school districts are now even offering teachers the opportunity to increase their salaries by five percent if they can show that the art instruction offered in their classroom does improve student art performance and, if not, the school district will lower school support, including teacher salaries.

Art teachers in all states are currently facing an arts assessment dilemma which is exacerbated by both the lack of standardized art tests and district-wide assessment plans which can economically and accurately assess the art instructional programs of the schools. In Florida, as well as in other states, art teachers were concerned that no art tests and no assessment plans for district schools were being developed. The general view in many state departments of education is that the art teaching profession remains too deeply divided on what should be taught and how it can be evaluated. Without adequate tests and realistic district assessment plans, it is quite probable that the arts in many states will never be assessed; with the current climate suggesting that what cannot be tested cannot be taught, the arts in the near future may face total elimination from the curriculum in U.S. schools.

TEACHERS AS REFORMERS

The answer to how we got to where we are differs according to what particular political interest group is asked. School reformers generally believe that U.S. schools are failing to provide a quality education for most American children, while public school interests believe most of the problems that can be identified are the fault of inadequate financing and increased regulation of schools and school programs.

Educators are all too familiar with an endless number of school reform efforts and those who have taught for a while find them long on rhetoric and short on effecting any important change.

Generally, most teachers believe that reforms are something they have to endure and that, if they are only patient, they can outlast them. For example, in the 1960s it was Jerome Bruner and behavioral objectives; in the 1970s, newer media; in the 1980s, school-based management; and in the 1990s, Goals 2000 standards and school assessment. Two recent examples of school reform efforts which reportedly have failed include the site-based management program that the National School Board Association recently called a failure (NAEA 1999), and the Getty Discipline Based Art Education Program whose former director now views it as a failed effort and a dead program (Duke 1999).

According to Philip A. Cusick (1994), reformers generally believe there is a power vacuum in the schools that must be filled with mandates and regulations to control teachers. They also think the teacher-centered classroom is to blame for educational problems and that teachers should accept reform or be regulated. Reformers also want more power at the state rather than classroom level, in part because reformers come from outside schools and often have little or no school experience.

Reform efforts, on the other hand, are usually rejected by teachers who are, in reality, the truly deciding element in any reform effort. Cusick also believes teachers should feel free to join or not join in the reform effort. Further, he believes that the reason teachers choose to teach is because they see personal interpretations and choices as central to their professionalism and that most of all they are individuals and not a collective force. What teachers need, he thinks, is not more regulation and control but rather the opportunity to voluntarily join in reform efforts without state-mandated compliance. This supports his view that teachers are quasi-autonomous individuals who are independent, self-reliant, and able to regulate and evaluate themselves and set their own standards.

POPULIST REFORM

The American public is generally growing uneasy with what some refer to as the arrogance of the public education bureaucracy. Parents want to be able to choose which school their children attend, and are turned off by institutions that still offer one-size-fits-all services. Entrepreneurial governments and schools thus have begun to offer their customers choices—of schools, recreational facilities, and even public services.

Schools influenced by total quality management approaches (TQM) such as were attempted in the 1980s in Minnesota, Wisconsin, California, Washington, Colorado, and other states have helped the American public see that schools are not necessarily synonymous with buildings, that children need not be assigned to buildings, and that choices in what school to attend are not out of the question. Many school systems today do give parents a choice of schools on the basis that school systems should embrace competition and choice as incentives to do better.

While school choice is still much debated in the educational community, many of public education's customers, i.e., the children and parents, are beginning to reject older notions of K–12 schooling that is centralized, top down, and rule driven, where each school has a monopoly, where customers have little choice, and where no school person's job depends on his or her performance.

K–12 education changed radically in the late 1980s when the President and the governors adopted restructuring schools as part of their agenda. This led to endorsing a number of the principles of entrepreneurial governance by giving greater choice for parents and students, a system of accountability that focuses on results rather than on compliance with rules and regulations, the decentralization of authority and decision-making responsibility to the school site, and a personnel system that provides real rewards for success and real consequences for failure.

As to whether all school systems will reach the utopian goals of individual schools competing for students, pursuing their own missions, developing their own budgets based on the number of students that they attract, and retaining the funds that they did not spend is extremely doubtful. What is possible, however, is that entrepreneurial K–12 schooling in the twenty-first century will offer its customers more choice as to where they send their children to school. Schools will have more freedom, be more accountable to parents, and focus on results rather than on rules and regulations.

The publication of the NAEA book *The Handbook of Research and Policy in Art Education* (Eisner and Day 2004) does suggest that the leadership in art education is beginning to recognize that much of what goes on in the art classroom is increasingly being driven by federal and state public policies. Although this new work is a welcome step in recognizing the importance of public policy in the shaping of the art curriculum, it is quite clear that many of its contributors lack familiarity with the art policy–making process. *Art Education: The Development of Public Policy* is therefore a timely attempt to acquaint the art educator with: (1) the public policies that have shaped the art education curriculum over time, (2) the policy problem-solving process that informs the public policy-making process, and (3) the ways in which art professionals can play a more constructive role in the policy-making implementation and evaluation process.

Finally, it should be noted that *Art Education: The Development of Public Policy* is not intended to serve as a crystal ball predicting the future of the art teaching profession. Its purpose is rather to provide a critical look at how the field today was influenced by the policy forces over time, such as changes in the art world and government policies including both market and government failures, the effects of laws affecting the democratic process both past and present, and their ultimate effect on the school art curriculum. Also presented are some different curricular alternatives and suggestions for what should be our most important program goals for the future.

ACKNOWLEDGMENTS

I am particularly indebted to Barbara Aleene Edwards, my assistant, for her diligence over several revisions of the manuscript, recording my handwritten copy, and organizing all this into manuscript form. I wish also to thank both Tom O'Brien, who initially edited the manuscript, and Joanna L. Lilly, who accomplished the final editing of the copy. I am also indebted to my Florida State University students who responded to the manuscript content in their graduate classes. Also, I want to thank "Rip" Harlan Hoffa for his review of the federal period and Stanley Madeja for his comments and suggestions. Finally, a thank-you to my editors and my publishers for having the confidence in what I have to say having value to the art teaching profession.

REFERENCES

Calderone, J.; King, L.M.; and Horkay, N.; eds. 1997. *The NAEP Guide* (NCES Publication No. 97-990). Washington, DC: U. S. Department of Education, National Center for Educational Studies.

Cusick, P.A. 1994. "Teachers regulating themselves and owning their own standards." In *The Future of Educational Perspectives on National Standards in America,* ed. Cobb, N. New York: The College Board.

Diket, R. M.; Burton, D.; and Sabol, F.R. 2000. Taking Another Look: Secondary Analysis of the NAEP Report Card in the Visual Arts. *Studies in Art Education* 41 (3): 202–207.

Dorn, C.M. 1999. *Mind in Art: Cognitive Foundations in Art Education.* Mahway, NJ: Lawrence Erlbaum Associates.

_____. 2002. The Teacher As Stakeholder in Student Art Assessment and Art Program Evaluation. *Art Education* 55 (4): 40–46.

_____. 2003. Models for Assessing Art Performance: A K–12 Project. *Studies in Art Education* 44 (4): 350–371.

Dorn, C.M.; Madeja, S.S.; and Sabol, F.R. 2004. *Assessing Expressive Learning: A Practical Guide for Teacher-Directed Authentic Assessment in K–12 Visual Arts Education.* Mahway, NJ: Lawrence Erlbaum Associates Publishers.

Duke, L. H. 1999. *Looking Back, Look Forward, Keynote Address.* Reston, Va: National Art Education Association, 13–20.

Eisner, E.; and Day, M.; eds. 2004. *Handbook of Research and Policy in Art Education.* Mahway, New Jersey: Lawrence Erlbaum Associates Publishers.

Music Educators National Conference (MENC). 1994. *The National Visual Arts Standards.* Reston, Va: MENC.

National Art Education Association. 1994a. *Dance, Music, Theatre, Visual Arts.* Reston, Va: Music Educators National Conference.

_____. 1994b. *The National Visual Arts Standards for Art Education.* Reston, Va: National Art Education Association.

_____. 1999. Student Achievement in the Arts Falls Short.

NAEA News. 41 (Feb 1999): 1–3.

National Commission on Excellence in Education. 1983. *A Nation at Risk: The Imperative for Educational Reform.* Washington, DC: U.S. Government Printing Office.

National Endowment for the Arts. 1988. *Toward Civilization: Overview from the Report on Arts Education.* Washington, DC: National Endowment for the Arts.

Persky, H. R.; Sandene, B. A.; and Askew, J. M. 1999. *The NAEP 1997 Arts Report Card: Eighth Grade Findings from the National Assessment of Educational Progress.*

Washington, DC: U.S. Department of Education, Office of Educational Research and Improvement.

Sabol, F. R. 1990. "Toward Development of a Visual Arts Diagnostic Achievement Test: Issues and Concerns." In *Working Paper in Art Education 1989–1990*, Zurmullen, M. Iowa City: The School of Art and Art History of the University of Iowa: 78–85.

Shuler, S.C.; and Connealy, S. 1998. The Evolution of State Arts Assessment from Sisphas to Stone Soup. *Arts Education Policy Review* 100 (1): 12.

U.S. Congress. 1994. *Improving America's Schools Act of 1994*. H.R. 6, 103rd Cong., 2nd sess.

U.S. Department of Education. 1994. *Goals 2000 Educate America Act*. Washington, DC: U.S. Government Printing Office.

The Public Policy Process

INTRODUCTION

For the purpose of this text I decided to use the definitions of public policy formulated in political-science literature, from which government bureaucrats trained in public management classes learn how to deal with the public policy problem. In the public management literature, policy is basically defined as the right of government to interfere in coercive ways with private choice. According to that literature, governments can interfere when public actions suffer from either "government" or "market" failures. Market failures occur in the arts through what Heilbrun and Gray (1993) call a "cost disease," something which is judged to occur when there is an economic imbalance in the ideal economy when supply and demand are not in balance. In the arts it is generally agreed that no such balance is possible, in part because there will always be more products than buyers and because artists will continue to produce creative products even when no one will buy them. In general, it is also believed that artists will produce work because they need to and will continue to do so even if it is free.

The Public Policy Process

Government failure comes into play when there is a market failure and when governments fail to assure markets for the broad consumption and enjoyment of artistic objects and events. To restore the balance between supply and demand, governments create rules that regulate trade, introduce monopolies, and regulate markets in ways that compensate for the imbalance. This regulation comes in the form of laws, rules, government grants to artists, art educators, and arts organizations through 501(c)(3) tax-free status, monopolies, licensure of art teachers, and tax deductions for artists' and donors' gifts to museums.

Market failures and government failures, in effect, provide the right for governments to control markets in order to restore the balance between supply and demand, but corrective policies also carry restrictions on how these assets and advantages are distributed. Given the general admonition that governments should do good and do no public harm, policies must be constructed in ways that ensure equity and access for all, achieving efficiency, recognizing the dignity of human beings, and distributing benefits in such a way that everyone benefits or at least no one is harmed. This needs to be accomplished even when two individuals receiving the same benefits do not benefit equally. Public policy is also developed in stages involving such things as policy research, the creation of policy alternatives, the process of choosing the right alternatives, and the process of deciding issues of political feasibility and potential success in implementation of new policy and policy changes.

Policy is then a process by which governments have the right to interfere with private choice and to coerce compliance through rules and regulations. Policy is also, therefore, not neutral, but rather implicitly aimed at achieving an equal distribution of benefits, in order to compensate citizens who are less powerful and restrict those who are economically advantaged and/or represent the ruling class.

Besides offering special benefits to those affected, public policy also assumes that the consuming masses are incapable of making decisions that will lead to balanced and equitable policy formation. Therefore, it is assumed that public policy requires government bureaucracies to both create and implement policies through a largely undemocratic political process, where policy is formed through so-called iron triangles involving trade-offs between legislatures, bureaucracies, and special interest groups. These trade-offs are decided mostly through special interest groups agreeing with one another about who gets what, and how, and where in the trade-off process everyone gets at least something and no one suffers too much.

The public policy–making construction process ideally pursues a series of steps including (1) the identification of the policy problem, (2) the modeling of the problem, (3) choosing and explaining goals and constraints, (4) choosing a solution, and (5) presenting recommendations. These steps provide for a logical analysis by the policy maker but do not necessarily occur in this order nor are always adhered to by all policy makers. The implementation and evaluation of the policy follows but is beyond the scope of this text.

Problem Analysis

Problem analysis requires that we understand the actual problem, frame it in terms of its probable impact on those affected, identify the variables, choose goals and constraints, and offer solutions. The policy problem is, of course, the most important part of the analysis because it determines how we proceed with the rest of the process. Problems in education occur where there are inequities in the ways we serve the teachers, the students, the profession, and the public where all these stakeholders are not treated equally. Problems largely occur as a result of changes within the society, the discipline, and the educational process. Because we can always expect changes in these variables, policy change over time is inevitable.

Choosing and Explaining Goals and Constraints

Goals and constraints are often multiple, conflicting, and vague but should include efficiency, equity, human dignity, and political feasibility. In education, goals relate to problems concerning the public, the teacher, and the student. In art education they would also involve the classroom environment, art, and art education disciplines, including what it is we want students to know and be able to do and the methods we use in evaluating the program and the student. Goals, it should be kept in mind, are not the actions or the policies we use but rather the means to be used in the evaluation of our policies.

Choosing a Solution Method

Choosing a solution method in government policy analysis would include formal benefit-cost analysis in answer to the efficiency problem, qualitative benefit-cost analysis involving what impact the policy will have on the school environment, and a modified benefit-cost analysis that defines the minimum levels needed to ensure personal dignity. At the school level, we would use a multi-goal analysis involving a systematic comparison of alternative policies in terms of three or more goals. In art education this involves changing the general goals to consider more specific requirements. These may include the goals of art, the art teacher, the student, the public, and the art teaching profession.

Specifying Policy Alternatives

Policy alternatives should be considered when establishing public policy at the state, district, school, and classroom levels. Alternatives provide choices to either maintain the status quo; adopt policies in place in other states, schools, and classrooms; use generic policy solutions, and use custom-designed alternatives. Policy changes are usually incremental and the alternatives should be considered in order to offer opportunities for policy changes that are the most productive and meld the familiar with the unfamiliar.

As a result, my approach to the text begins with the identification of various views on the function of art; second, I identify the nineteenth- and twentieth-century antecedents to present policy formation; third, I describe the various shifts in education between 1960 and 1997; fourth, I examine various art education alternatives; and finally, I examine the future of art education policy.

The policy effects on schooling were addressed first through the interventions, monopolies, and rules provided by government in order to ensure compliance with the policy and secondly through the effects this had on K–12 curricular change over time. Finally, the new art education curriculum initiatives now being used to frame future policies were analyzed.

Policy Windows

From the onset, it should be made clear to the reader that the art policies discussed in this work will be limited to descriptions of art education policy research, planning, journalism, and analysis, in part because the art education discipline itself has not adumbrated policies that have been formally implemented and evaluated in the school context. It should also be made clear that the art education policy research and planning discussed here has, for the most part, come in the form of field reactions to policy shifts determined mostly by external agents, especially government and private foundations.

The principal policy window that provided the greatest opportunity for most policy initiatives in American art education came with the launching of the Russian Sputnik in the late 1950s, which led to our government's energized commitment to an improved, space-age science education for America's schoolchildren. Although its effect in schools was generally first felt just through the "new science" and "new math" initiatives, this commitment eventually worked its way through the entire educational curriculum, including the arts. The two principal government programs shaping the "new" art education policies of the 1960s included a newly formed arts and humanities branch in the U.S. Office of Education's (USOE's) Research Division in 1962 and the creation of the National Endowments for the Humanities and Art in 1965.

GOVERNMENT INTERVENTIONS

Rationale for Intervention

American government policy interventions in the arts were justified as being necessary due to the problems of "cost disease" in art from market or government failures. This gave support to those who wanted to expand the interventionist and coercive powers of government in order to aid arts programs that serve the public interest but are unable to survive without government and private financial support. Government support of the arts brought to the art world several key public policy requirements involving (1) access, equity, and efficiency; (2) the Pareto principle, or equity in distribution of benefits; and (3) the effects of what I call the "policy iron triangle," a set of organizations and individuals who view policymaking not as a democratic process but rather as a process of trade-offs between bureaucracies, legislators, and special interest groups.

Government Interventions in the Sixties

In 1965, the art community expressed concern that government policy interventions in the arts would eventually lead to government censorship and the loss of artistic freedom. Such concerns were set aside because of the efforts of Congress to create an endowment separate from the executive, legislative, and judiciary branches and because Roger Stevens, the NEA's first chair, and Chuck Mark, his assistant, introduced the artist peer-panel review process, which gave assurance to artists and the art world that their policy views would always be heard. What could not have been predicted, however, was the eventual elimination of public funding for artists during the Jane Alexander era at the Arts Endowment, as a result of both congressional actions and struggles within the art community itself.

Several government agencies developed initiatives that have shaped policy goals in art education over the past thirty-five years. Many of the initiatives evolved from the NEA's Artists in the Schools (AIS) program and the Office of Education's sponsorship of a variety of meetings, seminars, and research support in the 1960s and 1970s (Central Midwestern Regional Education Laboratory [CEMREL] 1970). The Arts Endowment did, however, have less influence than USOE primarily because art educators were opposed to the NEA's AIS program (Madeja 1991), believing it to be both elitist and a covert effort to *replace* art teachers in order to introduce the unqualified to teach art in the schools. It seemed to be a jobs program for artists, not an education program for children. In the end, the AIS program was the last effort of its kind to advocate the artist as a model for the teaching of art in K–12 education.

In the 1960s the USOE generally adopted an empirical view of national art education. In the early part of the decade it provided art education grants mostly for data- driven empirical research with a decidedly constructivist view of art education rooted in the intellectual development of the child. At that time, a large number of art education researchers were given financial support to conduct experimental studies of K–12 children's artistic development. Funding was aimed primarily at providing statistical data in support of various cognitive approaches to curriculum and teaching. USOE also sponsored numerous seminars and meetings that encouraged the use of constructivist methodologies, newer media, and the study of children's art learning. In the 1960s USOE was partially broken up into regional centers. That effort shifted the agenda more toward demonstrations of curriculum reform and assessment and the introduction of a series of think-tank seminars on aesthetic education and cognition that, in turn, introduced a number of newer educational ideas into the art education profession.

Policy Interventions 1970–1995

In the late 1970s, government support for the USOE labs diminished and private support was carried on mainly by two foundations, including the JRD III Fund (Art for Every Child) (Madeja 1991) and the J. Paul Getty Trust (the Getty) DBAE (Getty 1987). These research initiatives focused on general education in art and were influenced by the notion that art production, artists, and art educators were not always essential to the success of the art education program. Although these philanthropic organizations were not official government agencies, they remained closely associated with public policy makers and constituted a kind of "shadow government." Their leaders were former USOE and NEA employees who maintained close ties to government. The relationships between the federal government and the Getty was particularly evident in the 1990s when the Getty and DBAE jointly funded national meetings on art education, and where the Getty curriculum in art production, art criticism, art history, and aesthetics provided the content for the National Standards in Art Education (MENC 1994) and support for the NAEP test on art achievement.

The Empiricist Argument

These interventions, along with others, led to the field pursuing a predominantly empirical path to policy formation in art education curriculum and teaching. The policy shifts were, of course, incremental and in the late 1980s and early 1990s, advanced mostly by art education scholars in support of the Getty program, which provided as much as $100 million for the training of art education generalists (elementary teachers) in K–6 art audience development.

7

The empirical model is based essentially on the notion that we cannot define what art is; it therefore rejects the notion of the artist as a creative "genius." For logical positivists, art is not an object but is rather something found in the language that one can use to discuss it. In such discussions, they claim, we are unable to say an object *is* art but only that certain things may be *called* by that name. Art, to the empiricist, is what we can collectively agree on as being worthy of discussing as art. The only valid activity, in this view, is the engagement of public discussions of art rather than our individual responses to it. In postmodern empiricism, we go even further. Art is seen not as an aesthetic object that can be observed and understood as embodying expressive forms of feeling but rather a basis for constructing socially framed statements about the struggles between rich and poor, haves and have-nots, and elites and common people. Further, it is assumed that people who participate in high-art events are really elitists who do so only to make fun of others or show off their superiority or contempt. In this view, so-called "high art" is, therefore, something understood only by elitists, the best educated, and the rich.

PHILOSOPHICAL FOUNDATIONS OF POLICY FORMATION

How art educators answer policy initiatives is critical. Answers should not be based simply on an uninformed choice or haphazard guess but rather on the premises that art educators choose to use in the process of determining the K–12 school art curriculum. The premises that support arguments on either side are basically philosophical ones and involve what *beliefs* we hold on how we come to know things in our world (epistemology), what the meaning of life is (metaphysics) and what has value (axiology). Unfortunately, too few art educators really think on such matters, and although they should know better they all too often avoid admitting or analyzing the premises that undergird their assumptions on how students learn, how they should be taught, and what they should be taught.

The philosophical issues which should shape the content of the art curriculum begin with questions such as what is art, what is its purpose, how do we decide whether it is or is not art, and what mental processes are used in making art. Philosophically, the answers depend mostly on whether the person accepts an idealist or empirical philosophical position, or aesthetically whether they accept either a formalist or postmodernist view of art.

Empiricist Theory

Empiricism, especially as influenced by John Locke, supports the notion that ideas can exist in things (objects and events). As an empiricist, he believed that we find ourselves through having experiences with the world's objects and events. As human beings, we are thus defined by the objects and events that we encounter in the physical world and not by the ideas developed only in the mind. Locke believed that the world is best understood through the language that we use to describe it, a notion that has influenced most empiricist thinking, especially in analytical philosophy, logical positivism, and postmodernism.

Idealist Theory

The philosophical system variously referred to as idealism, neo-idealism, or German idealism based its views on the ideas of Immanuel Kant (1729–1804). Kant's idea of art as "purposiveness without purpose" forms the basis for most traditional non-functional forms of art thinking today. This is, in part, due to the fact that his ideas also formed the basis for the thinking of such modern philosophers as Schopenhauer (1788–1860), Kierkegaard (1813–1855), Nietzsche (1844–1900)), and Hegel (1770–1831).

Immanuel Kant

Kant's philosophy combined the ideas of both the rationalist school of thought (as represented by Descartes) and the empiricist (represented by Locke); Kant claimed that ideas can exist independently in the mind but that experience also changes the way the mind thinks. This view conceives of the individual as both a subject and as an object, a view similar to what John Dewey (1934), the twentieth-century philosopher, described in both "doing and undergoing." Kant's claim (Scruton 1982) makes it possible for us to know that we exist without resorting to someone else or some thing outside of ourselves to confirm it, yet also recognizes that through *doing*, the self also engages in the process of changing. Thus when Dewey talks about "art as experience" he is referring both to the cognitive thinking involved in making art and how the process of making it changes our thinking, which is both to do something consciously while also changing oneself in the act of doing it (Dewey 1934).

Kant believed that knowledge is achieved through the synthesis of a concept and experience; thus, we can know *a priori* that our world must obey certain principles implicit in such concepts as substance, object, and cause and must fall under the general order of space and time. Kant also believed that there is more to the self than present self-knowledge can offer—hence the Kantian concept of self as subject presupposes the self as object.

Kant also viewed the world as a "world of appearances" in the sense that it exists in time, consisting of objects and processes that are either perceived by us or else causally related to our perception. This world of appearances marks a limit that he believed we cannot, given the nature of things, ever transcend. Knowledge is thus described in subjective terms as something generated by the understanding and the synthesis of concept and intuition.

The division of thinking between various art educators and policy makers who side with either the empirical or idealist view results in two different views of aesthetics: those who accept the formalist (Kantian) view of aesthetics and those who accept the Lockian view of art as language. In order to understand the basic difference between the traditional art-centered art education curriculum and one that views art education as language (the postmodern view), we must first explore in greater depth the difference between the formalist and postmodernist argument.

PHILOSOPHY AS POLICY

Although the shifts in art education policy over the past fifty years are linked (mostly) to an empiricist view of philosophy, it is also necessary that we distinguish among the various empiricist orientations to learning. Three different cognitive orientations, for example, are offered by Efland (2002), who defines cognitive process as (1) symbol processing, (2) having a socio-cultural perspective, and (3) individuals constructing their own view of reality. According to Efland, the *symbol processing view* assumes there is an objective reality that exists independent of the knower as represented in symbols formed and manipulated in the mind. The *sociocultural cognitive* theories assume that reality is socially constructed and transmitted through communicative transactions that individuals have with one another. The third orientation is that reality is a *construction of the individual* guided by his or her own knowledge-seeking purposes.

Efland considers all three cognitive orientations as being constructivist positions that are concerned with the structures of knowledge. His views are based on the idea that mental schemata, images, and concepts are symbolic entities and are created by the mind to represent different realities. Efland credits the Russian linguist Vgyotsky with the idea that there is a constructivist model of learning grounded in a social context; in his view, the higher levels of the mind are socially mediated or acculturated through language. The symbol processing view of Piaget (1952) and Lowenfeld and Brittain (1975) and the socio- cultural view are both based on the belief that the human mind is shaped by a strictly empirical view of the world where it is developed by only what one sees and attends to.

Policy Windows

The major policy shifts that provided the opportunity for the art teaching profession to adopt these empirical policy alternatives over the last half of the twentieth century came about through two major efforts—one by government to support a disciplinary shift from the personal interest theory to the symbol processing view, and the other by foundations to move the curriculum toward a more humanist perspective. Although both views accepted a predominantly constructivist view of learning, they differ in how they view the art object and the artwork as it relates to art instruction. Both systems are viewed by their proponents as yielding knowledge of both how children learn in art and how they should be educated.

The Education Policy Problem

Art educators today unfortunately have no clear criteria for analyzing art policy. The same holds true for those involved in arts and cultural policy formation in general. Academics who teach policy in schools of public administration argue that *policy* is "to inform some decision either implicitly (A will result in Y) or explicitly (support A because it will result in Y, which is good for your constituency, or your country" (Weimar and Vining 1999, 27). Policy decisions for the political scientist are public decisions informed by social values. The policy analyst using this point of view is implicitly placing a value on the welfare of others through holding a comprehensive view of consequences and social values. These social values include, for example, economic efficiency as a social value not only because it measures aggregate welfare fairly well but also because it tends to receive inadequate weight in political systems.

Policy Analysis

Policy analysis includes several related professions, including academic social science research, policy research, classical planning, and journalism. *Academic research* in the social sciences contributes to a better understanding of society. *Policy research* focuses on relationships between variables that reflect social problems and other variables that can be manipulated by public policy. As a general rule, policy researchers are less closely tied to public decision-makers and usually view themselves as members of an academic discipline who are often mostly concerned with the publication of their work in professional journals. A third area includes the process of *classical planning,* where the planner specifies goals and objectives that will lead to a better society and determines the most efficient ways of achieving them. From the working policy analyst point of view, the social science researcher, the policy researcher, and the classical planner are often irrelevant to the needs of decision-makers because they have difficulty translating their findings into action, and all too frequently ignore political realities.

Ideally, art policy analysis and formulation evolves over five major steps: (1) understanding the problem, (2) choosing and explaining relevant policy goals and constraints, (3) choosing a solution, (4) adopting and implementing the policy and (5) evaluation. In K–12 art education, however, policy is rarely formulated by administrators or teachers in such a formal way, partly because the nation's schools are predominantly *reactive* rather than *proactive* to political and social policy changes. College art educators, art policy researchers, and planners do publish and discuss arts education policy, offer various approaches to problem analysis, and choose and explain goals and constraints. Nevertheless, it is generally the task of federal and state legislatures and their educational bureaucracies to formally analyze, construct, and implement policy.

The curriculum concern, therefore, is with policy shifts that have, over time, moved the art education agenda from a curriculum focused on the child as artist to the current focus on the child as social activist. The narratives that follow assume also that there are real gaps between the time that policy analysts and planners make policy claims in the literature and the curricular shifts that actually go on in schools. Education reformers know only too well that teachers in general are independent and see their classroom as being under their control, an attitude reformers view as being an obstacle to change. Even when education policies are supported by government incentives or punishments, real change is slow and varies a good deal across the country, in part because schools, teachers, and students are resistant to change.

Given these realities, in the last analysis, art education policy shifts may be only specified as policy windows where policy researchers' suggestions for change are offered and over time come to be accepted as the *raison d'être* for teaching art in K–12 education during a particular period of time. Like the antecedents to present-day art education policy reported in Chapter 3, causality cannot be proven except to say if it looks like a duck and quacks like a duck, it may well be a duck.

As to the shifting policy agenda also noted in Chapter 3, it should be noted that the art world has also, over time, been undergoing a number of changes in regard to both how we view the artist and how we define what is art. Prior to the 1960s, the general view in art education supported the notion of the child as artist and art as being something more or less guided by the "spirit." In my view, it was the 1950s government interventions into education—inspired by the so-called space race—that fostered the two major shifts in twentieth-century art education policy. One of these moved art education from being considered as discovery and learning to being considered mostly as a cognitive activity, and one where the art curriculum sought to match the child's cognitive ability and learning style with various strategies of instruction. That match, for the most part, assumed constructivist forms of knowledge where the child's brain is considered to be wired into mental sets or schemas that can be unlocked in order to accept newer strategies, as long as they were pursued through the correct instructional match.

A second shift occurred as a result of constructivist influence. One result was a change in the content of art education instruction from art as a specialized form of individual knowledge to art as a contextualized message useful to all children rather than the few. In the latter view, true value was to be found in integrating various social elements into the school curriculum. The shift also challenged the idea of the child as artist primarily because its supporters feared the romantic concept of the artist and its related cult of individuality as an obstruction to the sociocultural progress. The main goal was to shape a concept of art instruction as ultimately useful to all children rather than to conceive of it as a subject which impacted only a talented few.

I place these interventions as occurring mainly over a thirty-five-year period between 1962 and 1997. Some interventions were inspired by the federal government in the period between 1962 and 1970 and others were sponsored by U.S. foundations, including the JDR III Fund and the Getty Trust between 1970 and 1997.

In this effort I tried to record the relevant facts as gleaned from a broad variety of reports on government art education activities in the 1960s. I also included a good deal of relevant historical data taken from both primary and secondary sources including various nineteenth- and twentieth-century art sociological experiments. Because of my active involvement in art education over the past fifty years, and because I was a participant in many of these government events occurring in the 1960s, some observations may be less objective than they should be. On the other hand, my participation and acquaintance with many of the government players in Washington, DC at that time may have provided me with additional insights unavailable to others in the field.

The three things that I wanted to accomplish in this effort were to (1) acquaint the reader with the effects of government policy on the conduct of art education in K–12 schooling, (2) identify in particular the effects of policy on how we now define art and the artists, and (3) specify how art educators can go about influencing the policy-making process.

In the pursuit of this effort I attempted to identify historically how art lost its aura in the eyes of the K–12 curriculum maker and how the artist as a social model was now being questioned in newer postmodern theory. In addition, I wanted to investigate how, over time, the progressive notions of the child as artist and art as experience were challenged by the notion that art is only another avenue for students to become political activists in a struggle among social classes. Moreover, I wanted to examine how creative artistic activity in the process of expressive forming is now being replaced by lessons in the use of political power as means for reconstructing the social order. My final goal was to delineate how concepts such as imagination, consciousness, and life of the mind are being challenged by the interest of overcoming what are currently perceived as the major social inequities of American life.

What can this effort contribute to the art education field and to U.S. government art policy? I only hope that this historical review of curriculum change derived from a policy approach will add to our understanding of the field and encourage further and more-comprehensive art education policy studies in the future. Understanding how policy works and how it changes over time may be more determinative than the study of the curriculum itself, and should help art educators get a clearer picture of how the field is evolving and how art educators themselves can play a bigger part in deciding what policies are needed in the future.

ORGANIZATION OF THE BOOK

In order to map these influences more completely, I have organized this work into six chapters. Chapter 1 introduces the policy process, the philosophical foundations of policy making, the policy window, and policy analysis, suggesting the content issues and the order in which they are addressed.

Chapter 2 addresses the aesthetic concerns which underlie modernist and postmodernist arguments about the functions of art, including how we define the artist and the artistic process and how we define the role of the viewer as interpreter of the art object.

Chapter 3 presents the antecedents to the current art education policy changes undertaken from 1880 to 1944. These include the discussion of four movements in art and art education that have characterized the shifts in thinking about the artist and the art object. These movements include William Morris and the arts and crafts movement, the U.S.-WPA federal arts project, the Owatonna Art Education Project, and the WPA federal art project.

Chapter 4 presents what I call the federalization of art education policy from 1960 to 1975 as a result of USOE research incentives offered art educators to research constructivist learning theories. In the view of the USOE, these offered the most promise in defining the subject matter content and learning strategies to be used in K–12 schooling in art. The discussion includes the goals of the various research initiatives, the activities that they sponsored, the outcomes that they achieved, and the policy arguments advanced by professionals in the field of art education.

Chapter 5 reviews and discusses the merits and limitations of a number of curriculum policy alternatives, including how these alternatives can be made available to the policy maker and guide the policy choice.

Chapter 6 examines the future of art education, the development of goals, and the case for a new art education policy encouraging the direct engagement of students and teachers involved with expressive creation of art and the study of art objects as individual objects of aesthetic value.

SUMMARY

The public policy process chapter has sought to point out that current policy shifts in K–12 art education have changed the goals of art education over time. It also delineates the factors affecting art creation and the changing of the art classroom from a laboratory for creative activity into a social studies class. This argument was supported by discussions of art being influenced by government interventions devoid of individual choice, which in turn have been fueled by empiricist values as promoted by American government educational policies. Also discussed were significant art education policy shifts of the last half of the twentieth century that have led to art education in the twenty-first century being seen more as an instrument of social change. Examined also were the issues attendant to policy formation in art education, including the philosophical and psychological issues that shape policy formation in the field.

The chapter concluded with a description of the order of presentation shaping the remaining chapters in the book. The next chapter will discuss the philosophical and aesthetic factors supporting art education as a creative activity and as a sociocultural construct.

REFERENCES

Central Midwestern Regional Educational Laboratory (CEMREL) 1970. *The Artist in the School: A Report on the Artist-in-Residence Project.* St. Ann: Missouri Central Midwestern Regional Educational Laboratory.

Dewey, J. 1934. *Art As Experience.* New York: G.P. Putnam's Sons.

Efland, A. 2002. *Art and Cognition: Integrating the Visual Arts in the Curriculum.* New York: New York Teachers College, Columbia University.

Getty Center for Education in the Arts. 1987. *Discipline-Based Art Education: What Forms It Will Take.* Los Angeles: Getty Center for Education in the Arts.

Heilburn, J.; and Gray, C.M. 1993. *The Economics of Art and Culture: An American Perspective.* New York: Cambridge University Press.

Lowenfeld, V.; and Brittain W.L. 1975. *Creative and Mental Growth.* 6th ed. New York: Macmillan Publishing Co., Inc.

Madeja, S., ed. 1991. *Kathryn Bloom: Innovation in Arts Education.* DeKalb: Northern Illinois State University.

Music Education National Conference (MENC). 1994. *National Standards for Art Education: What Every Young American Should Know and Be Able to Do in the Arts.* Reston, Va: MENC.

National Assessment Governing Board. 1994. *Arts Education Assessment Framework.* Washington, DC: The Council of Chief State School Affairs.

Piaget, J. 1952. *The Origins of Intelligence in Children.* New York: International Universities Press.

Scruton, R. 1982. "From Descartes to Wittgenstein." In *Short History of Modern Philosophy.* New York: Harper Colophon Books.

Weimar, D.L.; and Vining, A.R. 1999. *Policy Analysis.* Saddle River, NJ: Prentice Hall.

The Historical
Functions of Art

INTRODUCTION

As indicated in Chapter 1, policy shifts in art education come about as a result of the ever-changing social goals of society and the changing direction of education in art. Framing the policy problem requires that we understand the history of these changes in how we view the purpose and function of the arts in education. These changes include those social values that shape our attitudes toward the need for equity and access for all our citizens, the function of art in relation to achieving our national social goals, and the beliefs and values of the nation's educational system.

How we view the goals of education today is radically different from colonial times in regard to both race and gender equity, access to educational opportunities, and the need for human dignity. These paradigm shifts involve issues about who should be educated, how we should educate them, and to what ends. This chapter explores how our conceptions of art have changed over time with regard to what we believe are the social values of art and the artist in American society.

Mundy (2000) believes (1) that culture may provide the state with incidental but important contributions to its economic and social welfare, (2) that decision making at the local level brings a degree of ownership to public policy, and that culture is (3) both the most personal of concerns to a nation and (4) one of the most binding of international issues by helping individuals fulfill their own potential. Public cultural policy in support of the arts according to Mundy (2000, 84) should:

- help individuals fulfill their cultural potential
- slant policy toward the stimulation of creativity

- equip the population psychologically and physically to enjoy the results
- empower people to contribute to the cultural wealth of the nation through active participation whether amateur or professional; recognize the ephemeral and fluid boundary between the two
- ensure physical and social access for all
- preserve ancient and small-scale crafts
- keep the living element in culture and heritage not in an artificial theme park environment—especially in the case of minority or indigenous cultures
- aim to achieve a feeling of cultural security throughout the population

How we view the social functions of art has radically changed over time. Because both past and present views of the creativity and function of art never totally disappear, it is appropriate for us to look at a variety of new and past theories and to test their potential for realizing Mundy's claims.

MODERNIST THEORIES OF ART

Immanuel Kant (1729–1804) is generally considered responsible for generating the modernist view that the artist is someone who responds to the world intuitively and individualistically. Artists are, therefore, special people endowed with the gift of being able to produce visual forms capable of expressing states that, when interpreted by a viewer, translate the feelings of the artist into the viewer's own states of feeling. This implies that art does not communicate what the artist feels in the form of any direct message to the viewer. In this sense, art also does not encourage the viewer to take some kind of right action or offer any kind of information useful to achieving some specific end.

Kant argues for what is sometimes called the *aesthetic paradox*, by claiming that art involves both the objectification of subjective knowledge, and purpose without purposiveness—also known as *disinterestedness.* He takes this position because he accepts both the rationalist (from Descartes) position that we have a mind that thinks and the empirical (from Locke's) position that we are also shaped by the environment in which we live. As a result, we are creatures who know of our existence as self knowledge but also recognize that the knowledge of the self changes as we have commerce with the world. This idea was interpreted by John Dewey and reformulated through the concept that the individual is both *doing* and *undergoing.*

Post-Kantian thinking, especially that of G.W.F. Hegel (1770–1831), further developed the Kantian view through claiming that in art we are concerned with objects outside of our understanding, that we contemplate them for our own sake, that they are not objects that provide knowledge or encourage right thinking, and that the subjective values of both the artist and the viewer are objectified through making and understanding the art object.

Kant argued in the *Critique of Judgement* not that aesthetic values were objective but rather that we must think of them as objectively valid. Although he considered the pursuit of objectivity hopeless, he also considered it inevitable and indispensable to an aesthetic judgement grounded in critical understanding and never reducible to mere sensuous indulgence.

Aestheticians who support the Kantian, or idealist, theory, especially Monroe Beardsley and Harold Osborne, address both the question of what effects aesthetic objects have on us and also why some aesthetic objects vary in their capacity to engage us. Addressing the question of what is art, Beardsley (1958) admits that it means many things to many people. As to whether art is practical at least in the sense of improving plumbing, controlling disease, or improving automotive engineering, he admits concertos, watercolors, or lyric poetry experiences may be found wanting.

Monroe Beardsley

Beardsley believed there are at least seven effects aesthetic experience has on us: (1) relief from tensions and destructive impulses, (2) decreased self-conflicts in pursuit of harmony, (3) the refinement of perception and discrimination, (4) the development of imagination, (5) improved mental health, (6) greater mutual sympathy and understanding, and (7) providing an ideal for human life.

In support of his belief that aesthetic experience relieves tensions and quiets destructive impulses, he cites Bertrand Russell's belief that, if the love of excitement is a fundamental motive of man then art may be valuable because it gives scope to this tendency, reducing the warring tendencies of mankind. In addition, he notes Russell's contention that the excitement of artistic creation—and the discovery of new artworks—are two of the highest, purest, and most satisfying types of excitement.

Beardsley contends that art mediates self conflict and promotes personal interpretation and harmony. This, he argues, is due to the fact that when our attention is engaged with an aesthetic object we feel a kind of clarification that relieves a restless frame of mind, provides a sense of divided obligations, and helps us sort out our conflicts. Reading a good story, contemplating a picture, or hearing a piece of music will, when experienced at the same time as addressing a problem, help develop a different state of mind that is clearer and more decisive.

Beardsley's idea that aesthetic experience refines perception and discrimination is based on the claim that increased aesthetic experiences improve such things as the discrimination of color tones and musical practices; that is, one improves in his or her discrimination through continuous aesthetic experience. This improved sensitivity and perceptiveness will have a bearing upon all other aspects of human life including, Beardsley says, emotional relations with other people.

The development of imagination—and the ability to put oneself in the place of others as an outcome of aesthetic experience—comes from experiencing artwork that exposes us to new qualities and new forms. In short, Beardsley believes aesthetic experience provides a kind of training of the imagination, which results in an improved ability to think of original scientific hypotheses, find ways to resolve practical dilemmas, and improve our understanding of others.

Beardsley also believes that aesthetic experience, as a preventative measure, helps ensure good mental health. A world filled with harmonious shapes is, he believes, good for the eye and the spirit, especially for those who spend at least part of their day listening to or performing musical compositions of high aesthetic value and who love good language and/or use it for creating poetry and storytelling. In his view, these activities will prevent many common neuroses and psychoses at the start, as evidenced in the success of the music concerts staged in England during World War II.

Beardsley believes that aesthetic experience also fosters mutual sympathy and understanding among people. This comes about especially when people listen to the same music or view the same painting, which encourages similar responses through a shared experience. Shared aesthetic experiences help bring people together in friendship and mutual respect and in ways that other experiences cannot. This is due, in part, to the fact that aesthetic experiences are more portable and that they provide a distillation of certain qualities of experience that people can share.

Beardsley believes aesthetic experience also offers an ideal for human life. This is true, he believes, because in aesthetic experience means and ends are closely related, alleviating emptiness, monotony, frustration, lack of fulfillment, and despair which tend to cripple much of human life. Aesthetic experience also acts as an antidote for the repetitive and spiritually deadening consequences of the laborer who finds few meaningful connections between what he or she is doing and what the final product will be. Aesthetic experience offers the worker something more than a Saturday-night binge and early retirement, by bringing ends and means together and bringing hope into life by providing a clue into what a life of richness and joy can offer.

Although Beardsley argues for the utility of aesthetic experience, he also claims that not all objects of a given kind have the capacity to serve in a certain desirable way. He notes that there are members of a certain object class that can do what other members of the same class cannot. He describes a "good" as the capacity to function in what he calls a function class. Most of all, he notes, it is necessary to establish that an aesthetic object is in a function class, which requires that there is something that aesthetic objects can do that other things cannot do or do as well. He believes, therefore, one thing you can do with an aesthetic object is to perceive it in a certain way and allow it to induce a certain kind of experience, which in turn requires that we define what an aesthetic experience is.

For Beardsley, an aesthetic experience is first and foremost one in which attention is firmly fixed upon heterogeneous but interrelated components of a phenomenally objective field, i.e., visual or auditory patterns or the characters and events in literature. This requires that the experience has a central focus, the eye is fixed on the object, and that the object controls the experience. With respect to the object itself, Beardsley believes that it causes the experience as well as existing in the experience of a phenomenally objective field.

Second, he believes an aesthetic experience must be one of some intensity dominated by intense feeling and emotion. Such emotion is bound to the object and provides us with a concentration of experience with a segment of human life that is both noteworthy and significant.

Third, an aesthetic experience that is coherent; that is, one thing leads to another causing a continuity of development without gaps or dead space and providing an orderly accumulation of energy toward a climax. Even when this experience is disrupted or temporarily broken, a return to the activity requires only a few seconds to reestablish a connection to what went before that puts the participant back in the same experience.

Fourth, he believes it is an experience that is unusually complete in itself, counterbalanced or resolved by other elements within the experience. The experience further detaches and insulates itself from the intrusion of alien elements. Moreover, because it is concentrated and localized, it tends to mark itself out from the general stream of experience, thus remaining in memory as a single experience.

Beardsley also notes that aesthetic objects are not quite real, having attributes that prevent the status question of their reality from arising. They are, he notes, complexities of qualities and surfaces. This complicates the problem of determining whether some objects have greater aesthetic value than others but still does not deter Beardsley from making the claim that "X has greater aesthetic value than Y means X has the capacity to produce an aesthetic experience of greater magnitude (such an experience having more value) than that produced by Y" (1958, 53). The test of whether an object has aesthetic value is whether its presentations cause and enter into aesthetic experiences.

Beardsley also identifies certain requirements humans must

have to engage effectively in aesthetic experience, which range from the basic requirements that one must understand French in order to read Baudelaire. Similarly, one must not be tone-deaf to listen to music nor color-blind to see paintings. Further, Beardsley notes that even with such capacities assured, we cannot necessarily predict that one will, as a result, have an aesthetic experience with Baudelaire, with the music, or with a painting. Beardsley concludes that we can speak both of the capacity of the object to produce an aesthetic experience and the capacity of a person to be affected by the object.

Harold Osborne

Harold Osborne who, like Beardsley, embraces a Modernist or formalistic theory as a general concept, also accepts that art has social value at least in its intent to evoke and sustain aesthetic attention. This is based on the assertion that aesthetic experience has intrinsic value, that it is worth pursuing for its own sake, and that the appreciation of beauty is a worthwhile thing on its own account—even apart from all incidental benefits that may accrue from it. All these constitute the ultimate ground for all aesthetic evaluation.

Self-rewarding activities generally include (1) satisfaction of elementary human drives and basic needs such as food, shelter, sex, comfort, security, affection, and curiosity; (2) amusements different people pursue or, at the extreme, engage in—hobbies such as stamp collecting or bird watching; or (3) cultural values based on the social ethics of our day whose reward is their exercise and cultivation for their own sake—that is, without the utilitarian motivation of faculties that involve practical or biological ends. Unfortunately, idealist aestheticians also recognize that art as the cultivation of cultural values involves the active interests of a rather small minority group.

Aesthetic experience for the Modernist is concerned with intelligence exercised for its own sake, combined with a curiosity freed from utilitarian function; it is a non- utilitarian exercise for its own sake of perception. Aesthetic contemplation represents the freeing of perception from the domination of the practical.

After reading these definitions of the rationale of aesthetic experience, aesthetic interest, and aesthetic contemplation, it is not hard to imagine why so few citizens are drawn to disinterested art appreciation. Osborne notes:

> It must be borne in mind also that our appreciation of any work of art is necessarily limited by the extent to which we perceive it, and perception is limited by the degree of our understanding. There's no intuitive revelation in aesthetic appreciation as there may be in religious apprehension. We cannot perceive (in the wide sense of immediate apprehension) what we have not understood. Aesthetic experience is not understanding (1986, 337).

In spite of his claims of disinterestedness, Osborne (1986) also supports what he calls a formalistic theory, one that does not bind us either to believe that only the formal properties of things or artworks are of interest and importance, or to value them necessarily above other features. He claims those who adhere to formalistic theory will argue that although works of art may be valued for many other reasons, they may also be good or bad works of art by virtue of their formal properties alone.

According to Osborne, formalistic theory should never be confused with an "art for art's sake" philosophy, which maintains that works of art may not serve as vehicles for any other values except aesthetic values or that any function is a defect in a work of art. Formalistic theories, he believes, recognize the intrinsic value of aesthetic experience as a self-rewarding activity of aesthetic contemplation.

Appreciation is, for Osborne, a self-rewarding activity. In the case of fine art, it lies in its capacity to deliver a non-utilitarian perception or immediate awareness of the environment for the sake of such awareness. Osborne believes the theory explains a change of attitude toward the value of aesthetic experience that changes our appreciation of art and the role we ascribe to it. Unfortunately he notes that traditional education carries a bias toward purely intellectual skills, which should be corrected. Further, he reviews the righting of this imbalance as essential in the revival and development of atrophied powers of perceptiveness, which are regarded as valuable for their own sake and conducive to a more rounded personality.

Noel Carroll

Noel Carroll shares Osborne's formalistic theory, and agrees we do pursue aesthetic experience because we believe that art in itself has instrumental value. Her view, like Osborne's, is that the content of the aesthetic experience (i.e., the tracking of the formal structure of artworks, or design appreciation) is what attracts us to have an aesthetic experience. According to Carroll, an aesthetic experience is one that involves design appreciation and/or the detection of aesthetic and expressive properties and/or attention to the ways in which the formal aesthetic and expressive properties of the artwork are continued (2000).

Further, she very much agrees with Clive Bell's notion of significant form and with Beardsley's notions of aesthetic enjoyment as having unity, complexity, and intensity. She argues that experiencing the artwork through its aesthetic and expressive properties is sufficient for calling an experience aesthetic.

Her concern is that artists and critics today are overly concerned with a message rather than what is called the experience of the work. In her view, aesthetics is concerned with experience and with experiencing the artwork. Artworks are produced with religious, political, moral, and cognitive purposes and are not designed to be experienced disinterestedly as experience for its own sake. She believes the notion of valuing an experience for its own sake may be an explanation of why only humans, among living things, have the capacity for aesthetic experience and why humans value an experience for its own sake and not for the sake of bringing about something else.

Carroll believes in an evolutionary point of view where the human capacity for having an aesthetic experience is selected and sustained because of its instrumental value. The major modes of aesthetic experiences according to Carroll include (1) interpretive experiences in the search for meaning in the artwork, (2) pattern detection as a means of environmental control, (3) expressive properties that help us to recognize the emotional states and expressive behaviors of other humans, and (4) interpretative experiences that are connected to our ability to manage common life and our overt and covert intentions. These experiences, she concludes, help to achieve goals with evolutionary and social value.

Carroll challenges the disinterested view that an experience only counts as an aesthetic experience if it is pursued in the belief that the experience is valuable for its own sake. Contrarily, she rejects the notion that those who contemplate an artwork, appreciate its formal structures, and track its aesthetic and expressive properties for its instrumental value are not having an aesthetic experience.

Stephen Ross

While accepting of Osborne's disinterestedness of the aesthetic experience, Stephen Ross (1985) is also more cautious and, at the same time, more accepting of the idea that art can have utilitarian value beyond disinterestedness. He cautions that such values are not necessary and sufficient in deciding what is art. He believes that art can have great moral relevance though it is not necessary for it to do so, although there can be an interplay among formal and constructive values and moral and utilitarian values. For him, if something is but a means to certain human ends to be judged by consequences and influences, it is a practical, rather than artistic, object. Art's value lies in what it does, not in what it is. A created work has effects and imposes an influence, but its sovereignty is not separated into its effects and consequences.

Ross believed practical objects are means to certain ends and are to be evaluated by these ends. A work of art, on the other hand, is distinctive, and sovereign in its own sphere, while practical objects are means without any form of sovereignty. Although Ross accepts that works of art have consequences, in his view aesthetic experience is neither necessary nor intrinsic to art or aesthetic value.

When a work of art is interpreted as a cognitive instrument providing information, its sovereignty is diminished. When an artist produces a work that communicates an emotion to an audience, the artistic nature of the work is in its distinctiveness and sovereignty, not its capacity to move an audience. Art may also serve a moral function by which we can learn from art how to consider new possibilities. Nevertheless, the motivated person who appreciates art must also distance him- or herself from these moral consequences.

Chapter 2 The Historical Functions of Art

Art thus can have a double effect. Events can be made more powerful but transformed from a moral to an artistic function in which the sovereignty of the work, and not our actions or experience, dominate.

Utilitarian considerations, however, are in Ross's view, practically inseparable from the artistic features of works of art, although utilitarian ends tend to diminish the sovereignty and distinctiveness of art. This is, as a result, a profound opposition that derives from the fact that the effects of works of art cannot be separated from art itself even when the distinctiveness of individual works impress the observer more as they come to know them better.

POSTMODERNIST THEORIES OF ART

Postmodernist theory is said to begin with the philosophy of G.W.F. Hegel, especially through his theory of thesis and antithesis. Hegel accepted Kant's dualism between mind and body but argued that, in order for us to grow and reason effectively, we need to maintain a continuing dialog between what we think and what it is we learn from the world. This process, he believed, makes the products of intuitive and subjective thought into facts verified through our commerce with the world.

Post-Hegelian philosophers, such as Schopenhauer (1788–1860), Kierkegaard (1813–1855), and Nietzsche (1844–1900), rejected Hegel's belief in reason by claiming that life had no meaning except through accepting the irrational and shaping it in the interest of the individual and the state. Karl Marx accepted Hegel's belief that to be free, we must give up our freedom to the state and also Hegel's belief that it is a knowledge of history that leads us to understand the world. Interestingly, those who followed Nietzsche found themselves supporting Hitler and the Fascists and those following Marx followed Trotsky, Lenin, and Stalin in support of communism.

Postmodernist thought actually begins with social and political theories of Karl Marx and his ideas about the struggle between the workers and the proletariat. Marxists assume that life is a struggle between the rich and the poor, the educated and uneducated, and these struggles throughout history will continue. Although the neo-Marxist or post-Marxists dropped the notion that a violent revolution was the only way to solve such ills, they continue to believe in the struggle; it defines the base of thinking among both postmodern sociologists and political scientists.

Public policy for the political scientist assumes the irrationality of thinking citizens and assumes that governments should think for them; in this view, the electorate is incapable of rational thought and bureaucracy must decide policy for them. Sociologists agree but have more sympathy for the marketplace as a solution than those in public administration, who honestly believe there isn't a government program they can't love.

Postmodernists generally view the artist as a "worker" who is only part of the total production of art that includes the artist, the dealer, the sales agent, the advertiser, the gallery owner, et al. In that sense, the artist has no special aura or is in no way considered as a genius. Art also is not an object but is rather something part of an arts industry, a product like most any other commercial product, either funded by governments in the public interest or a commodified object whose value is determined by the marketplace.

Most postmodern educators view the art object as something socially constructed and useful in order to discuss political and social issues facing society. Art is not, in this view, an object for individual contemplation but rather an event to be discussed in public settings. For postmodern educators, any object that sparks a discussion of a social or political issue is art, and its meaning and utility is subject to the views of those engaged in discussing it. For some postmodernists, art is knowledge; for others, it is a means for educating people to think and take right action. What follows is mention of a number of different philosophers and their theories of postmodern art.

The Institutional Theory of Art

The institutional theory of art, which is still widely debated among art scholars, undertakes to define the nature of the art world itself as a social institution. Opponents of the institutional theory argue instead that art is rather a body of work and cannot be an institution; if it is a workable theory, it needs to show how works of art are embedded in an institutional context. Current institutional theories of art have been championed by philosophers George Dickie, Arthur Danto, Max Wartofsky, and others.

George Dickie

Dickie claims that:

> Works of art are in the classification sense artifacts where a set of aspects conferred upon them gives them the status of candidate for appreciation by some person or persons acting on behalf of the art world. (1981, 411)

Dickie defines the art world as an institution because it meets the definition of an institution by (1) being an established practice and (2) being an established society or corporation. Dickie expands the definition of institutions to go beyond institutions defined only as agents to ones defined by the acts they perform. He believes that the art world is an example of an institutional structure that generates the power to confer status on a work of art. This is accomplished by claiming that art is what is put forward on behalf of the art world. Thus, Dickie's "institutions" are not what we normally think of as institutions, in which the conferring of status occurs within a legal system where procedures and lines of authority are explicitly defined and incorporated into art. Rather, his institutions are found wherever lines of authority are not defined and are incorporated into an art world that carries on its business at the level of customary practice. A social institution thus need not have a formerly established constitution, officers, and bylaws in order to exist and have the capacity to confer status.

Dickie also accepts that the art world as an institution has no clear membership, no one designated to act on its behalf, and no procedure for doing. He believes that anyone who sees him- or herself as an agent of the art world is one. His main claim is that the art world is an institution because it involves an established practice that confers upon objects the status of being art. This process gives art its status through designating it as a candidate of appreciation by the person conferring the status—a person who believed that he or she appreciated it or thought it was worth the attention of others.

The institutional theory does not tell us what art is because it relies on others to tell us. What gives the denizens of the art world authority is that they confer status upon that which they confer status. Membership in the art world is obtained through engaging in the activity of conferring status on objects and by participating in acts, thus self-constituting members' own membership in the art world. They make what is taken to be art something decided by those who view things as art.

Dickie further defines a work of art in a classificatory sense as an artifact of a kind created to be presented to an art-world public. To call something a work of art means that it is worth, or worthy of, contemplation. He also claims that even if art cannot be defined it is still something which can be evaluated. Dickie's scale of evaluation runs from the almost worthless to excellent at the high end of the scale. He also believes that even the worst art will have at least minimal value.

Influenced by Morris Weitz's claim that art cannot be defined (1959), Dickie believes that we must allow for a way to talk about mediocre and bad art because some people talk this way about some art. He is, therefore, in agreement with Weitz that art is both a concept and that, despite its ranking, is worthwhile to engage in dialog about, at least in the evaluative sense. His solution to classifying art is to apply the institutional theory definition in which, "a work of art in the classificationary sense is an *aesthetically good thing*, that is, an artifact of a kind created to be presented to an art world public" (Cometti, 2000). Using this definition, Dickie substitutes an institutional conception of art and a non-institutional schema of a concept of art—both of which he sees as evaluative but distinguishable from efforts that are instead merely classificatory. Dickie, in effect, substitutes the marketplace as the sole evaluator of the work in place of all other schemes that seek to classify art as good and bad. The institutional theory in the evaluative sense can, in his view, have two outcomes: (1) the creation of things that succeed in being aesthetically good and, therefore, art and (2) the creation of things that fail to be aesthetically good and, therefore, fail to be art.

Dickie's institutional theory of art as described by Scholz, includes five general claims:

- The art world is the totality of all art world systems.
- An art world system is a framework for the presentation of an artwork by an artist to an art world public.

- An artist is a person who participates with understanding in making an artwork.
- An artwork is an artifact of a kind created to be presented to an art world public.
- An art world public is a set of persons the membership of which are prepared in some degree to understand an artwork which is presented to them (1994, 310).

Scholz also claims that Dickie's art world is a system where artists, artworks, and art world publics play a role. The system at the secondary level would include museums, galleries, poetry reading groups, concerts, repertory theaters, etc. The bottom level includes artists, poets, composers, playwrights, the artworks and the art world public, including gallery patrons, museum attendees, poetry readers, concert audiences, and theatergoers.

Thus, Dickie's institutional theory describes the art world as a collection of kinds of open classes that are related to each other as positions or roles in a loose framework or structure. As a theory, it does not identify the social roles of those in the art world who confer art status on objects. The theory also does not offer a definition of the term art world, explain why some groups are not part of the art world, nor distinguish gallery and concert frameworks from other events.

Max Wartofsky

The purpose of an institutional theory according to Max Wartofsky (1980) is to decide what can be appropriately taken as a candidate for appreciation or designated for status in the art world and what cannot. The art world is thus self constituting and is just what it takes itself to be as a conferrer or ascriber of the status that makes an artwork an artwork.

Deciding what objects the art world accords artwork status to is not unrelated to Marx's contract theory of price, based on the value of a commodity being determined by its market price. The institutional theory can, therefore, be viewed as a kind of contract theory and thus considered as democratic because decisions are made through a discourse between members of the art world; this in turn requires that these critics be members of an art world in order to be effective in talking about art.

Wartofsky views an institutional theory as essentially uncritical (1980), making the art world that it defines uncriticizable. Moreover, in his view "it elevates whatever the art world does as a matter of descriptive fact, into the going norm by virtue of the fact that it is the going norm" (1980, 241). Whatever the art world establishes as norm is the norm.

The institutional theory is thus seen as a legitimization theory of art. It claims to provide an account of how much status an artwork has achieved or earned. As such, it is not viewed as an aesthetic theory but rather as a theory of the politics of art or as an ideology of the art world. The theory is one that does not define what is art proper but rather as viewing an art world intersecting with non–art worlds.

Supporters of the institutional theory also view it as being universal and essentialist—a theory that hopes to capture within its purview both traditional and non-traditional works. The theory is necessary, supporters believe, because it attempts to legitimize art whose purpose is to challenge all previous standards, an art of protest or an art of the refused and rejected (in which the artist deliberately strives to be rejected).

As a result, Wartofsky claims that the gallery or the salon now develops as a marketplace where the artist becomes a free agent, free to produce whatever sells or does not. In support of his claim he notes:

> Control of the market is a matter of social as well as aesthetic domination and manipulation. The authority of tradition, of the academy, of the gallery owner, the jury of the buyer, and the buyer's agent, becomes a social as well as aesthetic authority in the life of the artist. His work, to exist as an entity in the art market, has to be acceptable as a candidate for exchange, for sale—it has to be a *commodity*. The politics of this art world is a politics of style, of influence, wielded by critics and art entrepreneurs. Style as aesthetic desideratum becomes fashionable as social and economic desideratum. The artist, the free individual creator, the Bohemian figure, the autonomous agent in a world of bourgeois dullness and repression is at the same time at the mercy of this world (1980, 245).

Arthur Danto's aesthetic differs in scope from the institutional theory of Dickie by arguing for the theory of intention, which becomes a basis for deciding the artistic status and identity of artworks. Danto's is essentially a theory of art as communication. His theory of art is that it is not possible that everything we call art can be art at any point in history. Thus, he thinks that it may be possible for something to be defined as an artwork today that would have been impossible to have been an artwork yesterday.

Danto's theory is based on his notion of an art world that is defined as an atmosphere of ideas and theories buttressed by historical developments that enable an audience to recognize some things as art. This concept allows the artist to presume that there is an audience out there prepared to recognize what the artist intends to communicate.

In this view, whether something is art depends upon the historical context, which also offers the audience a historical background useful in recognizing that the object or event being experienced is truly an artwork. Artwork status is then conferred on objects in an art world that provides a constellation of ideas and theories with a certain amount of background history. Artworks, therefore, are about something that can be interpreted through the content the artworks convey.

Danto believes that the identity of the artwork is fixed by its interpretation in an historically rather than economically situated art world (1996). Artworks differ from one another only because different historical situations require different interpretations of their function in a given art historical location; the status and the identity of the work depend on the connections a given work has to its relevant art world, including the art theories, ideas, and histories that constitute the conditions that made the artwork possible. Specific art theories, ideas, and historical understandings are important because of their relevance in the formulation and communication of artistic intentions and their interpretations. In this view, the status of the artwork thus depends in part on what the artist could have intended it to be in light of the historical circumstances in which it was created.

An Ethological Theory of Art

Ellen Dissanayake

Ellen Dissanayake laid out her view of the social utility of the arts from an ethological point of view (1980). She defines ethology as a biology of behavior that accepts man as an animal species who has evolved and whose behaviors, as well as biological organs and systems, have had adaptive value in that evolution. Her ideas are supported by the anthropological theories of Levi Strauss, the biologist Bertalanfy, and the system theories of Jack Burham. Although her writings may not have been addressed widely by the philosophical community, she has been particularly influential in the art education community through one of her most recent works, *What Is Art For?*

Dissanayake argues that human beings universally display certain general features that ethologists have found present in most animal societies. She believes that the history of art as a behavior actually predates what is today considered the history of art; in her view, art is a behavior that enhances the survival of the species whose members possess that behavior and is not limited to a minority of people called artists nor presupposes or means "good art."

Further, she argues that what we call art behavior must be universally applicable to all people and all societies both past and present, that it developed in human evolution from an ability or proclivity that our pre-Paleolithic ancestors might have shown and also had a special status that societies honor. Moreover, she argues that artistic behavior shapes or embellishes everyday life with intention by recognizing what is considered to be another, alternate line of practical life.

She claims that the root activity of art is most likely play and ritual, in part because both use make-believe, illusion, and metaphor; moreover, neither is directly concerned with the primary ends of direct survival. As behavior, ritual and art are similar because they both formalize and shape emotion, they communicate in symbolic language and, for expressive effect, arise from contextual elements of exaggeration and repetition. Dissanayake believes that the closeness of these human activities results from the fact that in evolutionary history they were once indistinguishable.

Art's functional value, she believes, rests on the anthropological claim that art had social benefits in primitive races because it expresses or relieves feelings, reiterates social values, mirrors the social code, and provides an avenue for shared experiences that are all socially useful. The argument for the social utility of art suggests that art has therapeutic value, provides paradigms of order, develops perceptual acuity, and so forth; but these do not, in her view, define what is artistic about art but rather what art shares with play and ritual. She views the meaning of art as being aesthetic only when play and ritual coincide with the aesthetic.

The bioevolutionary view essentially provides a view of art that is universally human but only periodically manifested in the artistic works of all cultures. In this view, art is something that exists in all human societies, but involves more than a taste for beauty, amusement, distraction, or inspiration (Dissanayake 1982). In addition, Dissanayake claimed that not all people need good or great art—a statement she admits cannot be made about our need for pop music, television sitcoms, or magazines on interior decorating.

She uses the analogy of child development in picture making (a recapitulationist theory) to describe the evolution of general behavior in art. She sees today's art as constituting a more mature phase of human development than picture making; it makes things that are special or that can be used functionally or for their own sake.

As a ritual she also views art today as representing an advanced or aesthetic stage where human aesthetic experience can be simply pleasurable, or have novelty, variety, pattern, and intensity that is closely associated with physiological and psychological processes common to all living creatures. The bioevolutionary view does not, in her opinion, aim at radically changing traditional Western aesthetic theory but rather offers a way to deal with non-Western art and with much of the art of the past century in the West.

Dissanayake fleshes out what she believes is a way to deal with changes in traditional values and non-Western art in *What Is Art For?* (1990). What is surprising about her conclusions is her apparent shift from the anthropological argument for art as ritual to an argument for an individual-centered aesthetic. First she claims that in today's western society there are few group values widely shared or transmitted through art. Rather today's values express or transmit individual notions of success, achievement, and power as well as the importance of the self and self expression. This, she notes, is a result of a species learning in an environment for which it was adapted and another one which it then tries to adapt to its own ends. She accounts for this shift by noting the trend from reliance on social authority or group consensus to increasing individualism and privatization. Moreover, she notes this is a change from what can be called a global or prelogical to a highly abstractive and self-conscious mentality. Dissanayake notes:

> For I think it is accurate to point out that both individualism and abstract thought have been extensively promoted by the acquisition of literacy understood as the habits of mind, modes of thought, and patterns of human relationship that a high degree of literacy engenders and encourages (1990, 172).

Literacy, in her view, causes experience to become more abstract and remote and enables us to react to experiences that we never had involving people we do not know. Moreover, it gives us more opportunity for detached, mediated, and isolated experience, thus making us more dependent on amusements and distractions, more interested in the immediate world, and more integrated through socially shared symbols. As the civilization process proceeds, belief has, in general, been increasingly replaced with knowledge and literate readers learn to be persuaded by reason rather than emotion.

The end point of liberalism, in her view, is to acknowledge the simultaneous plurality of truth and realities. This fosters the idea of a distinct and separate self where expression and satisfaction are considered desirable goods. As such, the isolated self no longer looks for a grand scheme by which to live, but rather seeks to find an individual route to spiritual and sensual happiness. Truth is, therefore, replaced by interpretation and universality by point of view. This emphasis on literacy, however, does not require that we burn the libraries or waste our energies on unrealistic yearning for a hunter-gatherer life.

Art is thus an echo of the natural world, an integrator of experience, a therapy, a provider of order, meaning, and significance. In a world now reoccupied with the aesthetic, everyone is, therefore, called upon to be an artist who shapes, imposes meaning, discerns or states what is special about our experience, rather than acting out a communal and confirmatory ceremony.

Art and life today confusedly appropriate one another; avant-garde art today gives art back to life rather than relegating it to the past and to the remote and special worlds of the museum or concert hall. Like Levi Strauss, Dissanayake envisions all art disappearing and reality itself being accepted as a work of art. Art is a way of possessing sacredness and spirituality in a profane world and in everything that is potentially art are ways of imposing coherence on ourselves and upon the experiences that have become fragmenting.

Exemplification Theory

Nelson Goodman

Nelson Goodman holds that something becomes art only when it becomes an act of intelligence (1977). His view is that artworks are symbols like speech, writing, maps, diagrams, cattle brands, and even traffic signals. Goodman argues that there are two kinds of art: one where representational pictures denote things in the world and another where symbols exemplify certain features, properties, or labels. This is similar to Anita Silvers's view that art provides a way to tell us something (1977).

Silvers's view of art also supports Goodman's theory that art is a form of intelligence. She argues, for example, that art is in the cognitive domain even when its products are not reiterative. She believes this is especially true when one uses linguistic or analogic arguments to demonstrate that reiteration occurs in art seen through denotation and exemplification. In her view, art is primarily a mode of telling similar to providing educational models or exemplars that tell children how to make a bed, weed a garden, or learn to iron. She wants art educators to consider art as a mode of exemplification (example) rather than an object of denotation (effect).

Goodman believes that art is a symbol system providing the means for a direct communication of thought between the artist and the viewer. The viewer needs to *read* the art in order to detect the idea the artist intends to communicate; this is seen mostly as an act of communication rather than an opportunity to respond emotionally to it. This suggests that art is more like a road sign communicating a traffic command than an expressive object that has alternative meanings for different viewers.

Goodman claims that artworks either: (1) represent something, (2) express something, or (3) exemplify or tell something. Works of art, he thinks, *can* do all three of these things, but to be art they must do at least one of them. Works of art are also sometimes not works of art; to be works of art, they must function as such works. His theory about "when is art" art is illustrated through his analogy that a stone found in a driveway becomes a work of art when exhibited in an art gallery and a Rembrandt painting, when used as a blanket, is not a work of art.

Goodman also distinguishes between the implementation of a work and the executing of the work. Goodman notes:

> The novel is completed when written, the painting when painted, the play when performed. But the novel left in a drawer, the painting stacked in a storeroom, the play performed in an empty theater does not fulfill its function. In order to work the novel must be published in one way or another, the painting shown publicly or privately, the play presented to an audience. Publication, exhibition, production before an audience are means of implementation and ways that the arts enter into culture. Execution consists of making a work, implementation of making it work (1982, 281).

Goodman further distinguishes execution and implementation by claiming that everything that goes into making the work is execution, but that implementation requires that the work be understood to the extent that we know what and how it symbolizes. He notes, however, the two may overlap, especially where implementation in the form of production, planning, promotion, and ticket sales may begin before execution is complete and may continue though comment and criticism may continue afterward.

Further, Goodman views a work of art as something made. Distancing his ideas from institutional theory, he claims that what counts is functionary rather than any way of effecting it. Implementation is, moreover, not restricted to making a work a work of art but includes making anything work as art.

The question "when is art," in his view, is more fundamental than the question "what is art." The driveway stone, he claims, is not a work of art except under certain circumstances where it functions as art, while the Rembrandt painting used as a blanket, though a work of art, is not functioning in that way.

Goodman's theory is based on a theory of aesthetics that views art as symbolic communication and is essential in his efforts to separate form and content—form being the abstract vessel in which content is conveyed, i.e., the plastic elements. What a picture symbolizes is both external to it and extraneous to the picture as a work of art. Its subject can be subtle or obvious depending on the symbols used, but has nothing to do with its aesthetic or artistic significance or character. What a picture stands for lies outside of it, thereby having no relationship with anything else except what its own intrinsic qualities convey.

Goodman's allegiance, according to his critics, is clearly with the sciences and the scientific view of the world. He admits finding it easier to visualize the process of verifying the truth and/or rightness of the sciences than the arts; the former are concerned primarily with the processing of experimentation and proof. In his view, rightness in an artwork is a feature of the work itself that is tested by the success we have in discovering and applying what is exemplified. These claims are as a result of Goodman's interest in the universal processes of "world making" in which he wants to show that the artists' world is, in many ways, like those of scientists or philosophers.

Goodman is believed to have had a serious commitment to both art and science. As an undergraduate he studied with and was deeply influenced by Paul Sachs, associate director of the Fogg Art Museum. Following his graduation in 1978, Goodman also ran an art gallery in Boston and became an avid collector of art. His commitment to art, according to Gardner, moved him at one point to quip "ask not what the arts can do for you; ask what you can do for the arts" (2000, 248). During his life he also did not think that the arts should play a bit part or supporting role. He believed they deserved to be taken no less seriously than the sciences (Elgin 2000).

According to Elgin, Goodman also believed that works of art perform known cognitive functions and that by attending to them carefully we can identify unrecognized or under-appreciated cog-

41

nitive functions. Works of art, Goodman maintains, belong to symbol systems with determinate syntactic and semantic structures. If we want, therefore, to investigate the cognitive contributions of art, we should concentrate on what its symbols do.

Exemplification as a basic function of art is a mode of reference that, as a sample or example, refers to the features of which it is a sample or example of exemplification. Elgin notes that exemplification has pedestrian functions as well, i.e., as a commercial sample where it highlights, displays, or otherwise points up some of its own features and in so doing affords epistemic access to them. Goodman argues that expression is a mode of metaphorical exemplification whereby the artist and the audience feel what it symbolizes. For him the expression of feeling is not to engender feelings, but rather to refer to them.

Cometti notes that Goodman felt that aesthetics was a field where one could easily fall into conceptual confusion and metaphysical traps (2000). This probably explains his reserve in answering some urgent questions. Cometti also believed that Goodman's functionalism and constructionism led him to assert that works of art exist in relation to some individual or collective subject and that there are no valid or universal standards of taste. For Goodman, subjectivity became the sole arbiter of judgements of taste. What makes Goodman's position powerful, according to Cometti, is that it gives us the means to escape from questions of definition and from both objectivism and subjectivism.

Goodman's theory is not without its critics, including Lopes, who wonders why he fails to answer some questions such as (1) how to define pictures and (2) how to distinguish pictures from other types of symbols (Lopes and McIver 2000). She notes that Goodman is concerned with answering how to distinguish the pictorial from the descriptive and how to distinguish pictures from related symbols, i.e., maps, diagrams, etc. She claims that Goodman refuses to provide an account of depiction, even if he notes that almost any picture may represent almost anything and the choice among systems is free. As a result, she believes Goodman prematurely rules out answers to other questions.

By contrast, Robinson (2000) sees much to praise in Goodman's 1968 *Languages of Art*. She believes that the book offered a powerful new vision of aesthetics grounded in the analytic philosophy of language. She viewed Goodman's effort as reframing many of the questions asked in aesthetics and said that he gave original, ingenious, and often eccentric answers to them. For her, Goodman reconceived works of art as symbols in a symbol system and treated representation and expression as a semantic concept. Because of his book, works of art are now commonly understood as meaningful entities with cognitive value that require interpretation rather than mere appreciation.

Art World Theories of Art

Howard S. Becker

Howard S. Becker, in *Art worlds* (1982), contributed a series of important essays developed from his studies of deviant subcultures as well as from his experiences as a jazz musician and photographer. He viewed the "worlds" in which artists work as more or less institutionalized subcultures isolated from one another. These centers were occupied by four types of artists: integrated professionals, mavericks, folk artists, and naif artists.

Becker views artwork as not being an object or event but rather something made and remade; whenever someone appreciates it, the art audience is thus part of the art object and is undistinguished from the artist who exists in one of four art worlds—each of which is centered on a particular type of artist as worker. He believes art to be socially constructed, carrying the potential of attaining the standing of autonomous artwork instead of just being a useful object. Becker believes that fine artists all too frequently turn craft work into commercial products, thus changing the nature of the end goals of the work. In his view, the decision of whether the work is art or craft is dependent upon the social actors and groups made up of practitioners, spokespeople, and influential members of the public.

Becker's approach is first to demystify art, debunking how high evaluations of art come about and starting with the assumption that, as in all social fields, the regularizing actions of the creative people and their supporting personnel decide how social meanings arise. His particular view of the art world as mixing artists with audiences focuses on how artists live and work within the confines of institutions. If rejected by these institutions, audiences, and patrons, artists may either give up or become liberated from the demands of others in order to become mavericks and innovators free to reject conventions. Becker thus views art, like other social fields, as being regularized interactions among creators and their supporters.

As a musician, Becker believes all artistic work, like any human activity, involves a large number of people in a cooperative relationship. Using the symphony as an illustration, he argues the process as beginning with inventing and making the instruments, and continues with the composing, the training of the musician, ads for the concerts, and even the audience as all being part of the artistic act. He forthrightfully asserts this to be the case for all other artistic activity. This, he believes, presupposes the conditions of there being a civic order, in which people engaged in making art can feel that there are some rules to the game that they are playing and that the rules also justify the state pursuing its own ends (Becker 1982).

He also believes that his view does not support a functionalist theory but rather that the social systems that support art must occur in a particular way in order to survive. While he agrees that a lack of public support will not allow the arts to survive in the same ways as in the past, he feels it would be misleading to suggest that there is any necessity for the arts to survive exactly as they are.

One additional area of concern for Becker is the current belief of both artists and the viewers of art that the making of art requires special talents, gifts, or abilities, which few have. This view, he believes, provides both the artist and the public to believe some artists are more talented than others and that only a very few are good enough to merit the title of *artist.* Becker struggles with this concept throughout *Art worlds* in part because he believes some think that it is important to know who has this gift and who does not in order to bestow upon them special rights and privileges. This view, he believes, supports the romantic myth of the artist and suggests that people with such gifts cannot be subjected to the constraints imposed on other members of society.

The myth of the artist, he believes, permits those merely being part of a production to consider themselves also as artists because they are part of the process (in music) of making art. This includes

44

composers who produce so many bars of music in a day and those who paint so many hours of the day (whether they feel like it or not) being considered as having superhuman talents. He offers examples such as John Cage and Karlheinz Stockhausen providing scores to be played at the discretion of the player, sculptors sending a set of specifications to a machine shop that makes the actual work and the authors of conceptual works never actually embodied in an artifact.

Because the artist's position as an artist depends on the production of artworks, many worry about the authenticity of the art world. They ask questions such as whether the artist who is supposed to have done this work really did it. Becker worried especially about whether the artist who made the work altered it because of a later experience or because of some criticism. He also questions whether, for example, learning that somebody else did it really matters and whether we appreciate and judge the work differently because reputations are established by collating the work they have produced. Should we, he asks, value a work more because it was done by an artist we respect rather than one by an artist whose work we have admired? He concludes that reputations are built on beliefs in the conventions used by the artists and those accepted by the viewer or listener.

Becker believes that art worlds consist of all the people whose activities are necessary to the production of the works that the world defines as art. Further, he believes that works of art are not the products of individual makers called artists who possess a rare and special gift. Moreover, he says that this world exists in the cooperative activity of those people and is not a structure or organization. Art worlds do not have clear boundaries, and, for the sociologist studying them, they need not be concerned with whether the objects or events are really art or whether they are craft, commercial work, folk art, or the expressions of a lunatic. Sociologists, he believes, can solve such problems easier than art world participants. For Becker, the sociologist's unit of analysis is found in an art world where both artness and worldness are problematic.

The sociologist, in his view, needs to understand that the term *art* is honorific and must not limit his analysis to what a society currently defines as art, which leaves out too much that is interesting but denied the name of art. This would allow a definition of art to be made by society, which properly ought to be the subject of the sociologist's study. As a result, sociologists should give equal attention to Sunday painters and quiltmakers as they do to conventionally recognized fine-art painters and sculptors.

Becker's view of public policy in the arts is somewhat benign, believing only that the state should participate in a network of cooperation with the art world and create a framework of property rights within which artists get economic support and make reputations. The state further limits what artists can do and protects people whose rights may have been infringed upon by artists in the course of producing their work. It also should support art and artists when they further national purposes and suppress work that mobilizes citizens to engage in disapproved activities or prevents them from being mobilized for appropriate purposes.

Becker admits that his book, *Art Worlds*, is focused more on the products of artworks rather than on individual artists; he admits this suits the purpose of looking at art from the viewpoint of a sociologist. He also admits that he wishes to challenge the notion that artists have special and rare gifts and that not everything the artist does becomes art. He also believes that the artist's reputation is not based on his or her work but on the collective activity of art worlds that help make reputations and creativity circumstances that favor one or another kind of career or achievement.

As to what kind of art lasts, Becker feels this is too often decided by aestheticians and art analysts who wish to find cultural universals. He admits that their theories may not be incorrect, nor capable of being proven false, but he also notes that neither can one prove them true. Artworks sometimes last for other reasons besides being universally appreciated. This can happen because they are also historically important. One other problem that he notes is that art worlds too often fail to notice work created by others. As a result, the process of selection used by the art world leaves out most of the works that in other situations may be recognized as competent or great art.

Finally, Becker concludes that art is social because it is created by networks of people acting together. He proposes that it needs a framework for the study of differing modes of collective action mediated by accepted or newly developed conventions. These collective actions and events, in his view, produce the basic unit of the sociological investigation in which the world of art mirrors society at large.

Like Becker, Pierre Bourdieu believes that, when it comes to the arts and artists, the creators are acting within a field where production and consumption form the basis for a sociology of artistic culture. He believes the sociology of the cultural worlds involves the totality of relations between the artists and critics, gallery directors, patrons, et al. He also believes that what people call *creation* is found in the uniting of socially constituted *habitus*, its status in cultural production, and what he calls the division of the labor of domination (Bourdieu and Dabel 1969).

He defines the habitus as a feel for the game that encourages people to act and react in special situations in ways that show that art is not always calculated nor consciously obedient to rules. It does rather generate practices and perceptions that go back to childhood and that, over time, become second nature, lasting a lifetime. Habitus accounts for individuals in the same social class adopting objective social conditions. Thus, there is a distinctly different habitus in the working and upper classes.

Habitus is a kind of *present past* that tends to perpetuate itself into the future when governed by social practices. Individuals do not, in bourdieu's view, act in a vacuum but rather in social situations governed by objective social relations. These were, he believed, organized as fields such as economics, education, and culture—each with its own way of functioning. In each field, members engage in competition for control of the interests which are specific to the field. In the cultural field, for example, the competition is among authorities in recognition, consecration, and prestige—which is more a struggle about power than about economics.

Bourdieu offers a mostly pessimistic account of how the arts and lifestyles are used. Taste preferences for him are cultural signs that help perpetuate social inequality so that the dominant classes use their demeanor to exude their superiority. Others not of this class struggle to acquire such status but they soon realize that it is beyond them. Bourdieu says that they have only one recourse, to admit they are not good enough to enjoy what the dominant classes admire.

Some critics characterize Bourdieu's theory of the cultural field as a radical contextualization that takes into account not only the works themselves but also the producers of the works in terms of struggles rooted in their individual and class habitus. His theory also involves an analysis of the field itself, including the positions occupied by the artists. Moreover, it involves an analysis of the position of the field within the broader field of power. His analysis includes a set of social conditions including the production, circulation, and consumption of symbolic goods. The explanation of artistic works for Bourdieu is found not in the object or the history of it but rather in the history and structure of the cultural field. For Bourdieu, the cultural field is based on a particular form of belief regarding what constitutes a cultural or artistic work. Aesthetic value for Bourdieu is socially constituted and is contingent on a constantly changing set of circumstances involving many social and institutional factors. Works of art for him cannot exist independently of the institutional framework that authorizes, enables, empowers, and legitimizes them.

Like Herbert T. Gans (1974), Bourdieu identifies education as the most important mediator for the lower-taste culture and proposes that there should be greater access to it. Bourdieu goes even beyond Gans by claiming that mere knowledge of art and admitting to liking it are not effective criteria for judging arts education. What counts is not how many years of education the student gets but rather how effective the curriculum and teaching are.

The ideal situation in education, for Bourdieu, serves a democratic function available to all on an equal basis, one that provides all students with the same or similar aesthetic disposition. What Bourdieu fears in the education system is its tendency to reinforce rather than diminish social differences and honor talent and superiority of knowledge among students. Bourdieu claims the educational system transforms social hierarchies into academic hierarchies and into hierarchies of merit. Cultural competence, he believes, must be considered a natural talent available to all equally and not be regarded as the result of a process of cultural transmission and training unavailable to some students.

Bourdieu, in the following quote, also attacks popular culture through the sports (football) metaphor by noting:

> The connoisseur has schemes of perception and appreciation which enable him to see what the layman cannot see, to perceive a necessity where the outsider sees only vio-

lence and confusion and so to find in the promptness of a movement, in the unforeseeable insertability of a successful combination of the near miraculous orchestration of a team strategy, a pleasure no less intense and learned than the pleasure a music lover derives from a particularly successful rendering of a favorite work...everything seems to suggest that, in sport as in music, extension of the public beyond the circle helps to reinforce the reign of the pure professional (Bourdieu 1978).

Bourdieu viewed popular sports as an extremely economical means for controlling adolescents, as a symbolic conquest of youth, as a means to maintain political power, and as a form of economic and cultural capital, controlled by economic means. In his analysis he identified a hierarchy of sports which was crowned by mountaineering, an endeavor which he associated with elite secondary and university leaders as means by which they combine aesthetics, health, and social parlor games in order to endow gratuitous and disinterested activities that gain social capital.

Art As Mass and Popular Culture

Both Bourdieu and Becker expand the definition of art to include both mass and popular culture. Mass culture simply defined is popular culture produced by mass production and industrial techniques and marketed for profit to a mass public of consumers (Strinati 1995). Mass culture is considered commercial culture mass-produced for a mass market. Mass culture does not support any culture that cannot make money or be mass-produced, such as art or folk culture. According to these criteria, objects that don't make money cannot be produced and there are no differences between material and cultural products, for example, as seen in the production of films or automobiles (Strinati 1995).

Mass culture, according to its critics, is designed for a mass audience whose emotions and sensibilities are manipulated. It is standardized, formulaic, repetitive, and superficial; lacks intellectual challenge; and creates its own emotional and sentimental responses. Mass culture does, however, break down the barriers of class tradition and taste and cultural distinctions. It produces a homogenized culture that destroys values and value judgements. In the last analysis, it is very democratic because it does not discriminate against anybody or anything and because its greatest effectiveness resides in its capacity to undermine the distinctions between the elite and popular culture by debasing and trivializing what high culture has to offer.

Mass culture is thus considered to be mostly concerned with the process of Americanization—in part, because America is considered to be the capitalist society most closely associated with mass production and the consumption of cultural commodities. European scholars see a threat in this brand of Americanism that challenges European aesthetic standards, cultural values, and national cultures themselves.

Popular Culture

Sociologists like Bourdieu and Becker find refuge, however, in a popular culture that does satisfy their concerns about aesthetic theories that overestimate the past and underestimate the present. By supporting popular culture over high culture, they also are able to alleviate their fear that the high culture of the past, which supports elitist theory, will continue to perpetuate the idealized standards of a culture dominated by an elite to which common people are expected to defer. Likewise, mass culture also affords opportunities for the media giants to engage in the production of a mass culture that can disregard the standards set by intellectuals and provide access to a popular culture outside the bounds of traditional aesthetic hierarchies and the criteria set by the cultural past.

Images of Taste and Style

Sociologists like Bourdieu and Becker also view mass culture as something supported by the public's fascination with taste and style. Style today is considered an incongruous cacophony of images strewn across a social landscape. Style can be borrowed from any source and turn up in a place where it is least expected. As a way of life it is marked by an endless succession of material objects that curiously float beyond the real world. This is the magic of style, a magic that promises that it will lift us out of the dreariness of necessity (Ewen 1999).

Style can be seen as a powerful mode of self expression—the means by which the inner beauty of the individual is expressed. It does, however, come from an external world rather than an inner one and from glamorous images that strike a chord in anyone who has lived in the shadow of what some call the managed image. It is the official idiom of the marketplace and is seen in advertising, packaging, product design, and corporate identity. Moreover, it is considered an intimate component of subjectivity and has emerged as a decisive part of politics and debate over political issues; through the manipulations of image managers, politicians provide the voting public with a telegenic commodity. Style deals in surface impressions and it is difficult to concretize or discern its definitions (Ewen 1999).

Some sociologists believe modern style speaks to a world where change is the order of the day and where one's social place is a matter of perception and made up of diligently assembled emotions. Style is also a manifestation of power, a visible reference point from which we come to understand a life in progress by satisfying the wish to become more powerful than we really are.

Stylists claim technically that style is delivered in reproduced items and images that replace lived experience with images that represent reality better than reality itself. Style is part of the so-called new consumer democracy and is propelled by the mass production of stylish goods designed with the idea that the symbols of the elite can now be made available to the masses. This world of products provides superficially ornate goods linked to widely disseminated images that are less and less associated with workmanship and material quality, but nevertheless provide the illusion of material quality through an abstract and aesthetic appeal.

In this new marriage of art and commerce, culture consists of accumulated understandings through which people's lives are replaced by the industrialization of daily life. Advertising is used to inform people not only about commercially produced goods but also about a restructured perception of the alternatives available to people in pursuit of their everyday lives. Style is an industrialized aesthetic in which the advertising industry can say things that could not be said in words.

Style also is served by being promoted by corporations that have employed social scientific methods for analyzing mass psychology in order to understand the impact of images in the mind of the consumer. The study of beauty and its universal appeal replaces the study of art in order to promote a consumerist response. It was through such means that commercial artists and their employers have learned how to achieve control of unconscious ideas.

Some cultural analysts believe that it is these highly individualized notions of personal distinction and the compulsory consumption of images that form the heart of the American dream—a dream that, according to some sociologists, has left its imprint on the aspirations and discontents of cultures throughout the world. It is a dream that seems to assure each individual access to status and recognition and a sure escape from the anonymity of the commonplace that has shaped the public's understanding of American democracy.

Style is most often connected to conceptions of a middle class defined by a consumptive, rather than productive, lifestyle. It is viewed as an effort of the middle class to avoid being thought poor, and to jockey for status in the pursuit of the opportunity to purchase, construct, and present a viable social self. Style is particularly associated with the yuppie (young urban professional) for whom life is embedded in the trap of credit and debt and where all connections with society or social responsibility are abandoned in favor of individual acquisition and display. Thus is born the so-called *commodity self.*

Style also depends on the perfection of images within an industrial process. The artists, photographers, and writers who function in the arts industry expect to be subjected to the formulaic calculus of the bottom line, sales figures, audience testing, and demographic patterns. The cash value of the creative imagination is the dominant ethic. This is a world composed of Hollywood starlet factories where young actresses are reformed as interchangeable audience-tested ideals, all conforming to a smooth standardized and lifeless modernism to achieve an aesthetic in human form.

Moreover, style is also seen as being associated with the essential quality of a consumer society involved in the continuous cultivation of markets and compulsive shopping. A devotion to following ever-changing style has become a cardinal feature of economic life and popular perception. As a form of information, style creates a consciousness that is at war with real experiences. It addresses deep-seated desires, and promises to release us from subjective conditions. As a form of information, however, it really discourages thought.

As a play on appearances, truth in style is always subject to the forces of the marketplace. The ratings system used by the media assures us that a news program must gauge its informational responsibilities against its potential to attract market share, a conflict that produces the difference between information and infotainment. In the world of politics, advertising agencies package government policies for public scrutiny and consumption. As political media consultants, they attempt to obscure underlying realities and manufacture political fictions. As a result, democracy itself becomes a mere style framed by patterns of spectatorship and consumption.

SUMMARY

This chapter has reviewed a broad number of claims about the utility of art, including both Modernist and postmodernist views of art and the function of the artist. Individuals holding these viewpoints differ with one another with regard to the utility of art as a social experience, suggesting that neither of these points of view shares among its followers a single, agreed-upon definition of art nor of the utility of art as a social enterprise. Both views in their extremes support radically different emphases, where the formalist has an exclusionary emphasis on cultured taste and the postmodernist emphasizes the study of art as a commodified object that would maximize human pleasure and decide community satisfaction by the sum of the satisfaction of all its members.

The chapter also provided a brief review of five different theories or explanations of the aesthetic character of artworks and how they function. These include (1) idealism or functionalism, (2) the institutional theory, (3) the cognitive or reiterative theory, (4) the ethological theory, and (5) the art world theory. Each theory provided some unique distinctions as to what values shape the process of deciding what is and what is not a work of art. In the idealist theory, definitions of art are determined by aesthetic theory; in the institutional theory, art is what the art world and the market decide is art; in the reiterative theory, art functions as education; in the ethological view, everyone and every object has the potential for being a work of art; and in the art world theory, art is determined by an art world. As to how art functions socially, the idealist theory looks to its effects on the behaviors of individuals, institutionalism to how it functions as a commodity in the marketplace, the reiterative theory to what it tells us about the world, the ethological theory to its values as an expressive biological outlet, and the art world theory to how it is manifested in the collective industry of art.

Questions Yet to Be Answered

Although the different theories presented tell us in varying ways how art is identified and the different ways it can be considered instrumental in serving the public, we cannot identify any single issue perspective from which to view them. These aesthetic claims range from Monroe Beardsley's idealistic approach to George Dickie's institutional theory, one requiring at least a standard for what makes something art and the other claiming that something is a work of art if the art world thinks of it as art. Another important question that needs to be asked is whether there is a way to bridge the divide between art definitions that insist on honoring the function of art and art definitions that acknowledge the reality of evolved procedural designation practices.

A review of the theories presented also suggests that each of the adherents, in his or her own way, have developed procedures that successfully confer social status on objects, in some cases without regard for whether these objects serve the ends of art. Further, we should ask whether, if art has a function, how can we also at the same time entertain theories that fail to meet or even subvert its function?

Critics point to a number of factors functionalism may or may not address. These include (1) art created in order to incorporate a subversive function, (2) objects that do not receive aesthetic status until art status is conferred upon them, (3) artworks that need only some aesthetic properties in order to become art, and (4) works that become art only when they function as art. These factors argue against the institutionalist notion that objects only acquire aesthetic properties after art status is conferred upon them. It also suggests that not everything demands a functional explanation and that art status conferral can in itself create the aesthetic properties through the work meeting its function.

There are, therefore, good reasons to both question all past aesthetic norms and recognize that we may attribute art status to objects even in the absence of some precise functional definition. Further, we may also have good reason to assert that art designation practices allow artists, galleries, critics, and museums to make fallible judgements as best they can; also that there may be no valid reasons to exclude the artists from playing a part in determining why a given object may or may not be a work of art. Artists are, after all, people who experience and react to unusually powerful pieces of past art, which helps the artist feel that one needs to find a voice and create a personal standard.

Concerns should also be raised about whether definitions of art really help solve classificatory pursuits to decide what is good or bad art. Classificatory distinctions must, therefore, be understood as being deeply embedded in social circumstances that cannot be resolved without understanding the circumstances and without coming to grips with the reasons that people have for classifying certain objects as art or non-art. It should be admitted, therefore, that aesthetic definitions of art may play only a minor role in resolving the conflicts between what is art or what is good and bad art. Even institutional definitions, whereby someone declares an object to be a work of art, do not, as a matter of fact, help solve classificatory disputes, in part because such declarations refuse to acknowledge the issues that are at stake for those who deny and those who affirm this status.

In conclusion, it may be prudent to assume that definitions of art play little, if any, role in classificatory disputes about art. This may be due in part, as Novitz notes, to the fact that we may be moved to classify a new artifact as a work of art just because it satisfies us in a way that seems unexplainable (1996). This approach accepts the fact that sometimes particular idiosyncratic interests and sometimes the needs of individuals do count, even if we do not always understand why some people choose to classify an object as a work of art. At the same time, it also is necessary to understand that the well- delineated practices, theories, and traditions that surround objects may or may not help determine what is and what is not of artistic significance.

Finally, in spite of these reservations, K–12 American art programs reflect some, if not all, of the claims in these varying definitions of art. As a result, this review will help the policy maker gain the philosophical grounding necessary to both setting the program goals and constraints that help to determine how the policy should be evaluated and developing the fundamental arguments that can be used to provide various policy alternatives.

The next chapter will shift from concerns about the character of art and its sociological value to how art has been used in the past to solve social problems, a process in which artistic values have been advanced in support of the artist as craftsman and the social system. Four historical significant art and education movements will be viewed from a sociological perspective.

REFERENCES

Beardsley, M.C. 1958. *Aesthetic Problems in thePhilosophy of Criticism.* New York: Harcourt Brace.

Becker, H. 1982. *Art Worlds.* Berkeley: University of California Press.

Bourdieu, P. 1978. Sport and Social Class. *Social Science Information* 17 (6): 819-840.

_____. 1993a. "How Can One Be a Sports Fan?" In *The Cultural Studies Reader,* ed. During, S. New York: Routledge.

_____. 1993b. *The Field of Cultural Production.* New York: Columbia University Press.

Bourdieu, P.; and Dabel, A. 1969. *L'Amuride 'art le Muse et son Public.* Paris: Editions de Minuit.

Carroll, N. 2000. Art and the Domain of the Aesthetics. *British Journal of Aesthetics* 40 (2): 191–208.

Cometti, J. P. 2000. Activating Art. *The Journal of Aesthetics and Art Criticism* 58 (3): 237–242.

Danto, A. C. 1996. From Aesthetics to Art Criticism and Back. *The Journal of Aesthetics and Art Criticism* 40 (2): 228–241.

Dickie, G. 1981 in Weiland, J. Can There Be an Institutional Theory of Art? *The Journal of Aesthetics and Art Criticism* XXXIX (4): 409–418.

Dissanayke, E. 1980. Art As Ethological Behavior: Toward an Ethological View of Art. *The Journal of Aesthetics and Art Criticism* XXXVIII (4): 397–406.

_____. 1982. Aesthetic Experience and Human Evolution. *The Journal of Aesthetics and Art Criticism* XII (2): 145–156.

_____. 1990. *What Is Art for?* Seattle: University of Washington Press.

Elgin, C. 2000. Reorienting Aesthetics, Reconceiving Cognition. *The Journal of Aesthetics and Art Criticism* 589 (3): 219–226.

Ewen, S. 1999. *All Consuming Images.* New York: Basic Books.

Gans, H. T. 1974. *Popular Culture and High Culture: An Analysis and Evaluation of Taste.* New York: Basic Books.

Gardner, H. 2000. Project Zero: Nelson Goodman's Legacy in Arts Education. *The Journal of Aesthetics and Arts Criticism* 58 (3): 219–226.

Goodman, N. 1968. *Languages of Art: An Approach to a Theory of Symbols.* Indianapolis: Bobbs-Merrill.

_____. 1977. "When Is Art?" In *The Arts and Cognition,* eds. Perkins, D. and Leondar, B. Baltimore: Johns Hopkins University Press.

_____. 1982. Implementation of the Arts. *The Journal of Aesthetics and Art Criticism* XXXVIII (4): 397–406.

Lopes, O.M.; and McIver 2000. Languages of Art to Art in the Mind. *Journal of Aesthetics and Art Criticism* 58 (3): 237–242.

Mundy, S. 2000. *Cultural Policy: A Short Guide.* Strasburg, Germany: Council of Europe Publishing.

Novitz, D. 1996. Disputes About Art. *The Journal of Aesthetics and Art Criticism* 56 (1): 39–46.

Osborne, Harold. 1986. Aesthetic Experience and Cultural Value. *The Journal of Aesthetics and Art Criticism* XLIV (4): 331–337.

Robinson, J. 2000. Languages of Art at the Turn of the Century. *The Journal of Aesthetics and Art Criticism* 58 (3): 213–218.

Ross, D. R. 1985. The Sovereignty and Unity of a Work of Art. *The Journal of Aesthetics and Art Criticism* XL (2): 145–154.

Scholz, B. 1994. Rescuing the Institutional Theory of Art: Implicit Definitions and Folk Aesthetics. *The Journal of Aesthetics and Art Criticism* 52 (3): 309–325.

Silvers, A. 1977. "Show and Tell: The Arts Cognition and Basic Ways of Knowing." In *Arts, Cognition and Basic Skills,* ed. Madeja, S. St. Louis: CEMREL, 31–51.

Strinati, D. 1995. *An Introduction to Theories of Popular Culture.* New York: Routledge.

Wartofsky, M.W. 1980. Art worlds and Ideology. *The Journal of Aesthetics and Art Criticism* XXXVIII (3): 239–248.

Weitz, M. 1959. "Can Art Be Defined?" In *Problems in Aesthetics,* ed. Weitz, M., Chicago: University of Chicago Press.

Nineteenth- and Twentieth-Century Antecedents to Today's Art Programs

INTRODUCTION

The previous chapter dealt with the various ways that both Modernists and postmodernists interact with and investigate the art world. Examined were the basic assumptions to be used in deciding the goals and restraints guiding policy formation as informed by various theories of art. This chapter will review four major art world movements in the late nineteenth and early twentieth centuries that provide a basis for understanding the ways the arts have changed in order to improve the human condition and serve the public interest. The four major art movements to be reviewed include: the William Morris Arts and Crafts Movement, the U.S. WPA federal art project, the Owatonna Art Education Project, and the German Bauhaus movement.

Choice of Projects

The choice of projects to be reviewed was decided by the need to address (1) the most historically important socially reconstructive programs in the arts, and (2) a range of examples with different approaches to the question of the aims of art that are currently present in the art curriculum of today's schools. The four model projects selected were particularly appropriate to this effort because of the equity and access values of: (1) Morris's program to build a worker-centered program in the crafts industry, (2) Owatonna's goal to build a K–12 school program based on community needs, (3) WPA's effort to provide work for unemployed artists, and (4) the German Bauhaus's curriculum to use arts and crafts in order to improve the aesthetic environment of the common people.

Art education's empirical policy shifts did not officially begin until the 1960s but it also had a long history before then involving differing emphases shaped both by changing conceptions of art and changes in American education. Art education is said to have been introduced in the schools by William Bently Fowle (1821–1850). It is generally agreed, however, that art education as a formalized school program was initially introduced by Walter Smith (1851–1900) who came from England in 1872 to become Massachusetts' state director of art education, scholastic and industrial. There he introduced a drawing manual that was designed to educate students to become industrial artists and designers. It should, therefore, be acknowledged that even from its beginning, art education has always had social goals, which in Smith's time involved serving the needs of the New England textile industry.

American education has always been influenced by the social problems of the times. American schools, even in the beginning, centered on the idea of a common school which was free and open to all children. Art education, like public education, generally has also experienced varying emphases over time, due largely to shifts in national and local economic and social conditions. Thus, from 1851 to 1900 art education in schools was considered as training for industry, from 1901 to 1920 as child-centered creative expression, and from 1927 to 1947 (the Depression era) as art for everyday life. It was not until after World War II that the cognitive emphasis inspired by the work of Viktor Lowenfeld was formally promoted. Even at that time, the major goals of the art program were broad based, including an emphasis on (1) the creative expression of the child; (2) recognition of individual needs, interests, and abilities; (3) the social and cultural uses of the art experience; (4) the relationship of art to the total school program; and (5) the use of art as a means of personality integration.

The shifts of emphasis in art education that occurred from 1850 to 1950 also reflected changes in how the art world viewed itself, including its concern with several key questions. Who is an artist? How does the artist function in society? What is art? And how does art contribute to the public good? Over that time period, the idea of the artist as genius was gradually replaced by the idea of the artist as craftsman-designer. The idea of the artist as commentator on the culture gave way to the artist serving the public good, with art itself being considered a means to improve the home, school, and community environments.

SOCIETY AND ART IN THE TWENTIETH CENTURY

Art and artists around the world became highly political late in the nineteenth century and especially so immediately following World War I. Artists and writers in the late nineteenth century—in particular William Morris, Leo Tolstoy, and Vincent Van Gogh—were visibly disappointed with the indifference and rejection of art by the bourgeoisie and bothered by the widening gulf between the artist and society. Early in the twentieth century, Bauhaus artists started to train artists and craftsmen to participate in the expanding industrial society, and constructivist artists already felt that they were forging a truly revolutionary art for the new world of the masses. (Chipp 1968). Maholy-Nagy, director of the Bauhaus, had set about creating a new guild of craftsmen without class distinctions, and in Mexico, Orozco, Rivera, and Siqueiros issued a new manifesto for "Art with a Social Purpose." Artists such as Andre Breton, the so-called Surrealist Pope, embraced Marxist doctrine and published the periodical, *Le Surrealisme_au-servie de la Revolution*; he and Rivera also signed the *Manifesto Towards a Free Revolutionary Art.*

In America, Stuart Davis, president of the artists' union, viewed the artist as being a have-not and a natural ally of the worker in securing the rights of employment, better wages and social insurance. During the period from 1934 to 1937, the federal art project of the Works Progress Administration (WPA) gave public aid to more than 5,000 artists who felt free to follow the dictates of their own talents and wishes. The WPA project gave artists Milton Avery, William Baziotes, Arshile Gorky, Philip Guston, William de Kooning, Ibram Lassaw, Jackson Pollock, Theodore Roszak, Mark

Rothko, and many others time to create the new modern art movement.

Before and immediately following World War II, a number of other prominent artists both in America and abroad announced their support for the new socialism. In France, Picasso embraced the communist struggle against Fascism and Nazism in Spain, France, and Russia, and joined the communist party. Some historians suggest that in America both Robert Motherwell the painter and the critic Harold Rosenberg were more than sympathetic to the socialist cause.

American socialist art movements from the 1920s to the 1940s, however, were not always in agreement with communist doctrine although they shared some common objectives, including which art forms were to be devalued, which newer forms to admire, which new public uses should be pursued, and which new social goals needed to be achieved. Some of these common goals were set out in the 1922 Manifesto of the Mexican Syndicate of Technical Workers, Painters, and Sculptors. The manifesto supported at least three basic claims:

> We repudiate the so-called easel art and all art which springs from ultra-intellectual circles, for it is essentially aristocratic. We hail the monumental expression of art because such art is public property. We proclaim that this being the moment of social transition from a decrepit to a new order, the makers of beauty must invest their greatest efforts in the aim of materializing an art valuable to the people, and our supreme objective in all art which is today an expression of individual pleasure, is to create beauty for all, beauty that enlightens and stirs to struggle (Chipp 1968, 462).

Leon Trotsky

Artists in both the United States and in Mexico, although agreeing on communism's socialistic goals, overwhelmingly rejected the constraints imposed on artists by the Russian communist state. Even the exiled Leon Trotsky's goals for the new art and the new artist went much too far to the left for the Americans. True, Trotsky had argued that the new personal lyrics of the very smallest scope had an absolute right to exist within the new art. He supported the Marxist conception of objective social dependence and the social utility of art, and denied that art should be produced according to governmental decrees and orders. He felt, however, that the party should protect itself against art that was critical of its political standards. The party, he thought, should repel what he saw as the clearly poisonous and disintegrating tendencies of art and guide it according to strict political standards.

The standard for Trotsky was a political rather than an abstract or cultural one, and one where the standard coincides with culture only in the sense that the revolution creates conditions for that culture. If the Russian revolution had the right to destroy bridges and art monuments whenever necessary, he believed it shouldn't stop short from laying its hand on any art, no matter how great, especially if it threatened to unsettle the revolutionary environment or so excite the internal forces of the revolution that it set the proletariat, the peasantry, and the intelligentsia against one another.

Trotsky was also an advocate of pictorial realism, which he felt gave expression to the feelings and needs of different social groups. Realism had, in his view, a feeling for life as it is, an artistic acceptance of reality and an active interest in the concrete stability and mobility of life. The revolution could not, in his opinion, live together with either mysticism or romanticism. Our age, he believed, cannot have a shy and portable mysticism like a pet dog that is carried along. This age, he felt, wields an ax and needs artists with a single love (Chipp 1968, 464).

Using Lipchitz's sculpture as an example, he rejected the traditional notion of art being "purposeful," arguing that to judge purposefulness art has to have a "real" practical purpose. Trotsky, it is said, could see no purpose or utility in Lipchitz's intersecting planes, pointed forms, and protrusions, and suggested that it would have utility only if used as a hat rack. Then he argued, sarcastically, who wants to recommend that the arts be limited to hat racks?

The primary goal of art in Trotsky's view was achieved when social construction and psycho-physical self-education became one and the same process. All the arts, he believed, would create beautiful forms in which the cultural construction and self education of the communist man could be achieved. Through art, man could become immeasurably stronger, wiser, and subtler; have physically

63

Chapter 3 Nineteenth- and Twentieth-Century Antecedents to Today's Art Programs

more-harmonized movements; become more rhythmic; and acquire a more musical voice.

Stuart Davis

Unlike Trotsky, American artist Stuart Davis rejected government restrictions on the artist, but sided with Trotsky's view of the artist as exploited worker. Davis attacked the capitalistic empowerment of the art dealer, viewing him as having the advantage of a free choice of art from which to select as stock in trade; for the dealer, this costs nothing, except a promise to pay if the work is sold. In some cases, Davis complained that the artists were actually forced to pay for rent, lighting, and catalogues in exchange for mere promises that the dealer would sell their works, meanwhile extracting commissions of a third to a half or more.

This resulted, according to Davis, in only two or three artists emerging as commercial assets to the dealer and providing public evidence of the gallery's success. These artists and other easy sellers were to be used to mount one-man and group exhibitions in which most other artists in the gallery were mere window dressing and served as quantitative filler. Art for profit, in Davis's view, was designed to be a profit for everybody but the artist.

Davis was most proud of the artists' union, which he headed and credited with employing more than 300 teachers, painters, and sculptors in the New York City Municipal Art Projects (Davis 1973). He believed the enemy of the artist was not just the art dealer but also big business, which, in his view, suppressed freedom in the arts. Under the rule of big business, he felt that culture was degraded and forced to serve materialistic ends, crushing the spirit of the creative artist. He also complained in his writings of small right-wing groups with fascist values destroying Rivera and Siqueiros murals and suppressing the Ben Shahn and the Lou Brock mural for the Riker's Penitentiary. No artist, he thought, could afford to remain complacent in the face of these events.

Holger Cahill

Support of Davis's efforts came mostly from the federal art project. According to its director, Holger Cahill, the project was needed because of the failure of an American manufacturing system that produced a clutter of unlovely things and degraded public tastes. Holger saw the need to create a new art, which, for the first time in American art history, would have a direct and sound relationship between the American public and the artist. His belief was that the new art would lead to increasingly larger audiences and greatly expanded public interest. American artists, he felt, should discover that they have work to do in the world, including developing a public awareness of society's need and desire for what they can produce.

Holger did not see art as being merely decorative but rather as useful and interwoven with the very stuff of human experience, intensifying that experience and making it more profound, rich, clear and coherent. Holger envisioned the federal art project as a means of getting artists to participate more in the shaping of social goals, hoping that they would develop a new concept of social loyalty and abandon the romantic concept of nature which had given artists and many others a unifying approach to art.

NINETEENTH- AND TWENTIETH-CENTURY ART SOCIAL EXPERIMENTS

Not all nineteenth- and twentieth-century efforts at integrating the arts into the social system used the same approach or pursued the same goals. This was due in part to the time at which they were pursued, the institutional mechanisms needed to achieve their goals, and the intended beneficiaries of the effort. While, as already indicated, many of these art projects were founded on some of the same political and social values, they were all different, especially in their sense of how the arts could be used in the interest of serving the public good. While it is not possible to review all of the art projects of the period, some of the more important ones can be offered as exemplars or models that typify the broad range of approaches used both here and abroad. These include in chronological order, (1) the William Morris Arts and Crafts

Movement, (2) the WPA federal art project, (3) the Owatonna Art Education Project, and (4) the German and American Bauhaus movement.

These particular projects were selected as exemplars in part because they offer a range of different emphases, including the commercial artist as public taste maker, the fine artist as educator of the public aesthetic, the K–12 art educator as an agent for improved aesthetic living, and the artist as cultural agent in the achieving of a newer and more functional public aesthetic.

ENGLISH ARTS AND CRAFTS MOVEMENT

William Morris (1834–1898)

The industrial revolution in England brought to an end the craftsman/trader concept of the individual as the sole producer of products. Instead, he or she became an assembly-line worker stamping out mass-produced designs made by others. This change had a profound effect on who was to be considered an artist and what was art. As both manufacturer/businessman and designer, Morris introduced the idea of the artist–as–craftsman-designer, which changed not only who was considered an artist but also what was considered art. This advanced both the concept of the artist as a worker and also the notion of art being an object of utility in the home or in the office.

William Morris was, in effect, the model of the Renaissance man: visual artist, poet, political activist, and Marxist theoretician. In addition, he was also considered a designer, writer, businessman, and conservationist. He was a true Victorian, his life spanning much of Queen Victoria's reign. He was born on March 15, 1834 at Elmhouse, Walthamstow, the third child and oldest son of William and Emma Morris. One of nine children, he was born into an affluent family with what the English would call "pretensions."

As a designer, Morris was irritated with the mistakes of contractors manufacturing goods for his firm. This led him to become a social radical and influenced his attitude toward art and its manu-facture—meanwhile exacerbating his frustration at providing shorter hours and increased pay for his workers. He personally viewed himself as a benevolent rather than grasping employer, although perhaps falling short at times of the political ideals that he espoused in his writings and lectures.

Morris's activities as a socialist, political activist, and artist were what made him influential in clarifying the function of art in efforts at social reconstruction. His criticism of nineteenth-century capitalism and the influence on him of Carlyle, Kingsley, and Ruskin helped him decide to become a socialist; his readings in French and German philosophy led him to renounce religion and devote his life to art (Parry 1996). The Turkish suppression of uprisings in the Balkans was what first led him to enter politics. His involvement in the Eastern Question Association and his activism as one of the Association's campaigners—as well as its failure to effect real change—finally convinced him that his liberal radical-ism would never produce genuine change, and that change was made for and by the middle classes as controlled by the rich capi-talists. As a result, he soon rejected involvement in parliamentary politics. Influenced by the ideas of John Stewart Mill and his cri-tique of Francois Fourier's utopian socialism, Morris ultimately became convinced that socialism promised to bring the necessary change and that it was possible to bring it about in his own time. By the summer of 1882 he declared himself ready to join any group who called themselves socialists.

Morris As Politician-Craftsman

Morris's socialism and its connection to art was clearly influenced by his acceptance of Marx's claim that capitalism had destroyed all meaningful connection between the object being manufactured and the satisfaction of the worker making it. Morris saw this dis-connect as a competition between useful work and useless toil. He argued that labor was never something which was good in itself and was deemed to be so by only those who live on the labor of others. Work should hold pleasure in itself, he thought, because it embodies good quality craftsmanship and makes objects good enough to be worth having. In Morris's view, work carries with it the hope of pleasure in rest, in its use, and in the daily exercise of skill. He believed that most worker satisfaction came from the worker making something that he or she feels really exists because he or she is working on it, and in effect wills it into being through exercising the energies of the own mind, soul, and body (Kelvin 1996).

All other work, Morris believed, was worthless and mere slavery to the toil of living and to a life dedicated to toil. Work under capitalism was, he thought, apportioned out unequally amongst the different social classes. First, there was a class of rich people who do no work, and second there was middle class who work but do not produce; they participate only in the distribution of goods. Next were those who spend their lives and energies fighting amongst themselves for their share of the wealth that they extract from the genuine workers who produce the goods. Finally, there came those who were wholly hangers-on, who do not produce anything but seek to gain positions either for themselves or their children, in the hope they will not have to work at all.

Morris viewed modern society as being divided into two classes, one of which is privileged and enriched by the labor of the others and the second consisting of those forced to work. The privileged class takes from this inferior class everything that it can take and uses the wealth taken to keep its own members in a superior position. Through these acts of robbery and waste, it keeps the majority poor. Morris believed that the first step to correct this situation was to abolish the class of privileged men who shirk their duties, and force others to do the work they refuse to do. All, in his view, must work according to their abilities and so produce what they consume. Each man should work as much as he can for his own livelihood, which should also be assured to him; the society should provide for all its members (Morris 1999).

Morris believed a true society was one where all citizens would be treated equally, not just used for the benefit of another; a fair society could establish rules that would benefit all its members equally. He believed that when his hoped-for cultural revolution made it easier to live, all workers would work harmoniously together and there would be no need to go on producing things people don't want. The course to happiness was, in his view, to take a pleasurable interest in all the details of life. This would make all labor reasonable and pleasant, transform the means of making things enjoyable, and turn capital (including the land, machinery, and factories) over to the community. All this was to be used for the good of everyone, supplying the real demands of each and all; no one would work for someone else's profit.

Once this has been achieved, Morris believed, we should begin to think about what is worth sacrificing some idle time for. This requires that we build up the ornamental part of life—its pleasures, bodily and mental, scientific and artistic, social, and individual, to benefit both ourselves and our neighbors. To do this he believed that all labor must be made attractive and directed to some end. The work must also offer a variety of tasks which could be taken over by a system of education towards the goals of fitting people to take their place in the hierarchy of commerce. In such a system, young people would be taught such handicrafts as interested them in order to discipline their minds and bodies. One way to ensure variety would be to teach that art is or should be done by the ordinary worker while he or she is about ordinary work.

Large-scale work performed in the new factories would provide a full social life and be surrounded by other pleasurable activities. These factories he envisioned as being centers of intellectual activity where the tending of machinery might be relegated to a short part of the day's work. This would require that the workers make their factories, buildings, and sheds as decent and convenient as their own homes, thus making them beautiful and true works of architecture. Morris fervently believed that work had to be carried out in an ordered community made attractive by its usefulness; he thought of such a community as displaying intelligence exercised in pleasurable surroundings. Morris admitted his utopian dreams might not be attainable unless some sacrifices were made.

His first socialist effort was carried out with the Democratic Federation where he engaged in propaganda work, gave lectures, regularly attended weekly board meetings, and composed a series of chants to be sung at meetings. Eventually, however, there was a split in the organization, due in part to Morris's supporting an anti-parliamentary stance and focusing on the educating and organizing of the worker. At the federation, he wrote a manifesto for the organization based on Marxist theory, and committed the group to distributing anti-parliamentary propaganda. Morris also helped organize marches by unemployed workers during which a few riots involving local authorities did occur. Morris insisted that the organization not become involved in issues interfering with

69

educating workers in revolutionary socialism; as a result, the organization ousted Morris as a leader, and finally dissolved itself in 1890. This occurred shortly before Bloody Sunday, when London's police banned meetings in Trafalgar Square and ordered 5,000 demonstrators to disperse; the casualties in dead and wounded finally discouraged continuation of the movement.

Over time Morris's views changed from the radicalism of his early activist years to a greater concern for industrial action and specific reforms, i.e., an eight-hour day and minimum pay. Concluding from his early involvement that the working classes could learn how to organize, he decided there were transitional stages in the path to state socialism.

Morris As Designer

Morris was considered a versatile designer. His products ranged from the designing of special, one-of-a-kind products to many that resulted from collaboration with his craft workers and friends. During his early years, he designed one-of-a-kind and small-order production and progressively moved to relatively large-scale productions, as seen in the later days of his factory at Merton Abbey. He also designed products manufactured by other contractors and sold in his firm's showrooms, acting as designer-buyer for his own shop.

As chief designer for his firm, Morris controlled the firm's visual and technical standards in such areas as embroidery, furniture, stained glass, wallpapers, and mural decorations; wood engravings, illumination and calligraphy; printed and woven textiles, and high warp tapestry. In later life he added book design and type design in his own Kelmscott Press operation. His commitment to socialism eventually led him to design whole communities and networks of productive and socially semi-sufficient small country towns, precursors to the early twentieth-century garden cities.

Morris viewed design as a form of visual alertness, and as a basic human function where the shared appreciation of beauty and design in everyday surroundings and ordinary objects became the means for reconciling the artist with society. As a designer, he was particularly noted for his radical approach to materials and processes. Morris admitted to never being happy unless he was either making something or imagining that he was making something. His views on the right way to make something became the credo for the arts and crafts movement. It is said Morris never designed an object he could not produce with his own hands. Making things was both a catharsis for his restlessness and edginess and also a source for theoretical solutions to the intellectual problems he faced as a writer and social revolutionary. His concern for making things began in his early twenties, when he began stone carving, clay modeling, and creating stained glass designs, mural decorations, and painted furniture.

Historians believe that Morris's early efforts in interior decoration and house planning gave him his first real experience in design that included the building up of pattern and the layering of color. This led to his romantic concept of male creative teamwork, consisting of a band of fellow artists who were experts in different disciplines. He felt that it was creative work that gave the most pleasure and that life without rewarding work was mere endurance.

In 1861 Morris established Morris, Marshall, Faulkner and Company, which lasted in much the same form until his death. In addition to financing the company, Morris was also responsible for overall design decisions and quality control. As chief designer he delegated the work to his silk weavers, carpet weavers, dyers, blockers, pattern makers, block cutters, cabinet makers, wood carvers, glass painters, kiln men, laborers, and wallpaper printers.

Morris further considered designing an exercise in fellowship and integration. He worked tirelessly to end class divisions both as a political thinker and sociologist. He believed that a successful pattern provoked thought and feeling, thus generating a shared human experience and one that inspired thinking beyond itself. He was troubled, however, by the inconsistency between his efforts to manufacture luxury goods for the middle class and at the same time being deeply involved in socialist causes.

Morris As Painter

Morris as a painter appeared to be mostly self taught through copying from manuals or prints. His first real drawings from life were two self-portraits. His early efforts at painting were influenced by the ideas of Rossetti and Ruskin. Morris, in time, gave up easel painting and began to create elaborate paintings on furniture. Over the years he made various attempts to return to easel painting but in the end abandoned the effort, considering himself

Panel of tiles. Designed by William Morris.

Chapter 3 Nineteenth- and Twentieth-Century Antecedents to Today's Art Programs

a failure at painting. Historians believe he could have been successful at painting had he abandoned pencil drawings and worked from the model, which most believe was his main interest.

Morris As Stained-Glass Designer

With twelve stained-glass people employed in his workshop, Morris had to familiarize himself with the crafts process and the painting of glass. The design and manufacture of stained-glass windows were separated and supervised at all stages by Morris. He was not considered a technical innovator, nor did he manufacture his own colored glass. Nevertheless, stained glass was the first of the arts that the firm excelled at and later became the mainstay of its business. Most of the partners, including Morris, provided designs.

The early work of the firm focused on medieval glass, where Morris's abilities as a wallpaper and textile designer enriched the backgrounds and drapery motifs of the stained glass. As a designer, Morris is said to have addressed the spirit, rather than the letter, of the medieval window and its simplicity. His concern for process and draftsmanship enabled him to translate this understanding into practice. Morris's designs reformed the then-current tastes for hard, kaleidoscopic colors through the use of the muted blues, rubies, yellows, and greens found in fourteenth-century English glass, using as a base a palette of earth colors like those obtained from the vegetable dyes used in fabrics.

The stained-glass subjects depicted in his work departed from the usual mid-Victorian approach and were selected for their humanistic or visual appeal rather than their liturgical relevance. In the 1860s, most of the religious and secular designs were placed in Gothic Revival buildings. Morris's work was considered quite modern for the times but was largely unrecognized for its real originality and modernity. Morris himself was not well recognized for his glass designs and over time he began to lose business to other glass designers, including some who had worked for him and learned their trade in his workshop.

Morris As Interior Decorator

Morris viewed the home as presenting the most important design problems. All of the decorative patterns and objects Morris designed or helped design were judged by their appropriateness in a home environment, although beauty remained the principal goal. It was the decorations for his own home, nicknamed the "Red House," that most historians believed led to the forming of the firm of Morris, Marshall, Faulkner and Company. Morris viewed his ventures into interior decoration as a crusade to restore the minor arts in England. He viewed house decoration as one of the principal functions of the firm, and at the top of the list of services offered was mural decoration either in pictures or pattern work. The 1862 exhibition established the firm in the minds of the buying public as one of the most exciting new firms in interior decoration.

Late in the 1870s Morris's political awareness began to change his view on house decoration. Although he believed the firm had a responsibility as a manufacturer and retailer to revive an interest in home decoration, he also realized the high prices charged by Morris and the company meant his work was not available to all. As a result of this internal conflict, he decided to supply charity in the form of interior decoration for those who could not afford the prices charged by the firm. This was offered in the belief that his efforts were a contribution to improved public trust and appreciation of the artistic in home decoration. In the process he contributed designs for two wards in Westminster Hospital, London. The designs included ceilings and a wall frieze of fruit in one room. In his effort to improve public taste, Morris also developed a model of a small, working-class home that could be used as a guide for decorating the homes of working- class people. Some historians believe his involvement in such efforts was not altogether altruistic, as he thought the exhibition of the model would also help him establish a start in markets outside London.

Morris As Furniture Designer

Morris advocated the construction of domestic furniture in the average house, solid and well made in workmanship and design, and without extravagance. He divided furniture making into two categories, (1) necessary work-a-day furniture and (2) state furniture, the latter being more elaborate in its carving, inlaying, and painting. Morris himself had learned the trade of wood carving, and his opinions were deemed valuable by others in the firm, so much so that Morris's artistic judgement was used on all furniture designs before sending them out. Morris designed his first furniture for his own home in Red Lion Square. Although he employed others in the firm to actually construct the pieces, this effort provided valuable training for the firm's establishment in 1861.

Morris viewed what he called his good citizens' work as not competing with the more expensive pieces in the furniture market but rather as providing good taste at a price comparable to the cost of ordinary furniture and serving as a model for establishing good taste in the design of ordinary furniture. The designs were both lighter and smaller in scale than the furniture of the day. The introduction of these designs was a good commercial move for the Morris company, in part because it widened the range of choice and at a lowered cost. The longevity and popularity of the designs made them become the standard products of the firm and the ones most copied by other firms. Although it soon became apparent that well-designed furniture suitable for the working class was not profitable, Morris's contemporary attitudes toward furniture design provided clear evidence of his influence over not only his contemporaries but also his successors.

Morris As Textile Designer

Historians claim Morris remained fascinated with textiles throughout his life. He is said to have been particularly interested in pattern and texture. What he most admired were complexities of technique and the visual and practical needs of his own work, which was considered a rare quality for a textile designer of any age. The designing and making of textiles helped Morris solve a number of problems, including developing the means for creating figurative art on an expanded scale. As a designer, his career both began and ended with the design and production of textiles. At first his early, crudely worked panels were attempts to reproduce medieval-looking hangings. His last work focused on tapestries, which he wove shortly before he died. Over the years he was occupied mostly with a long and complex search for perfect pattern colors, textures, and effects for the home. In that effort, Morris is said to have recognized that textiles were an essential part of the decoration and comfort of the home. In the design of his embroideries, Morris included repeating designs of trees, birds, and animals in court scenes based on fifteenth-century illuminated manuscripts that he had studied in the British Museum.

Critics viewed the naïve appearance and structure of his early work as surprising, regarding his first attempts as a reaction against the socially acceptable and very lofty standards set by the professional church embroidery of the time. In addition to his designs, Morris was responsible for the firm's production of all textiles that early on included a series of reproduced designs block-printed in fine woolen grounds that became very popular throughout the life of the firm. They also contributed to his reputation as a major British designer of naturalistic floral chintz patterns.

Morris viewed his greatest success as a practical designer of applied repeating pattern. This was reinforced by the popularity of his commercial work in the production of his wallpaper, his painted interior decoration, and book illumination. His lifetime habit of studying and improving one technique at a time is considered the reason that he became the world's most successful designer, manufacturer, and retailer of printed and woven textiles and machine-made and hand-knotted carpets and tapestries.

Following Morris's death on October 3, 1886, his reputation as an artist and businessman remained unquestioned. Some critics did, however, focus in particular on what might be described as his lack of ethical consistency; his varied practices were perceived as lacking coherence because of the conflict between his intellectual values and practical outcomes. Many of his critics felt that his furniture, socialism, and fascination with old buildings became separated from his public statements, thus contributing to the compartmentalized understandings of the man and his work.

Numerous critics claimed his political life was little more than a foolish preoccupation. During the last half of the century, however, there was a steady reversal of this view. This was especially so following the Second World War, when his political goals were championed by a number of writers. The reality, however, was that his political views about socialism had little or no impact in the political arena of the twentieth century. Morris's influence as theorist and designer in the visual arts, however, was considerable and his efforts were looked upon as widespread and multifarious. In fact, even today people continue to buy Morris goods in larger numbers than ever and the Morris movement still continues, especially in India, Canada, America, Australia, and on the continent.

Because the Morris company regarded his socialist views as incompatible with his artistic ones and lacking economic good sense, the reproduction and derivations of his designs were marketed with little, if any, mention of a political or ethical agenda.

THE WORLD ARTS
AND CRAFTS MOVEMENT

Morris was credited with founding the English arts and crafts movement and also providing the model for it. The movement found its roots, however, in the romantic medievalism of Carlyle, Ruskin, and Morris and the arts and crafts movement that eventually became the epitome of English style. The movement was considered an inspiration to those leading the modern movement, especially among left-wing designers and theorists. Morris's ideas also were an inspiration to a new generation of modernist radicals; he was considered by Nickolaus Peveser as a pioneer of the modern movement and linked to Walter Gropius, founder of the Bauhaus.

Morris, Ruskin, and the arts and crafts movement were also linked to the radical applied arts movement at the turn of the century and were credited with having established the theoretical agenda of the international modernists in Austria, Belgium, Czechoslovakia, Germany, the Netherlands, Hungary, Italy, North America, Poland, and Scandinavia (Parry 1996). The first proclamation of the Weimar Bauhaus in 1919 embraced Morris's idea that there was no essential difference between the artist and the craftsman.

Later in the century Morris and Ruskin continued to be credited with inspiring the modern studio-crafts movement. Modern craft was not considered by the movement as a set of genres, traditions, or techniques, but rather an ethically motivated approach to material culture. Morris's ideals were considered vital to establishing his intellectual foundation for the twentieth-century artist-craftsperson, which has expanded its genres on an international basis, becoming one of the world's most energetic areas of visual culture.

The eagle and palette logo of the Federal Art Project.

Chapter 3 Nineteenth- and Twentieth-Century Antecedents to Today's Art Programs

THE WPA ART PROJECT

The WPA effort reintroduced the easel artist as worker, educator, interior designer, and researcher, as well as a contributing part of the economy. Easel artists painted murals, taught in schools, researched cultural history, and made art for sale to the public. Because this was a national program, it also brought New York artists to live and work in the west, south, and far west, some becoming professors of studio art in midwestern, western, and southern universities. It indirectly encouraged a shift in art from prairie school regionalism to abstract expressionism and firmly implanted the idea that the fine artist was "just like us."

The climate or setting that inspired America's WPA Art Project's creation included such influences as Franklin D. Roosevelt's paternalism and the radicalism that was growing stronger in America throughout the Depression decade (McKinzie 1975). The WPA project carried with it the idea of a mass cultural awareness and of art forms that reflected a radical ideology and served its political purposes.

During the Depression, Americans experienced an upsurge of nationalism and patriotic self-examination. As a result, the American government decided to subsidize American artists through two agencies: (1) The Section of Painting and Sculpture in the Treasury Department and (2) the federal art project in the WPA. These programs were, at that time, justified on the grounds that they stopped the gradual decline in artistic skills among artists in a period when there were few private commissions or sales.

The federal art project (FAP) is said to have been responsible for the creation of 2,500 murals; 17,000 sculptures; 108,000 paintings; 11,000 designs; and a 20,000-piece Index of American Design. The FAP in the end failed to meet the approval of the nation's most conservative legislators, and over time became tainted by association with the more politically radical federal theatre project and the federal writers project. The project's funding actually ended because of the more pressing need to win World War II.

In setting up the program, the Public Works Art Project committee (PWAP) evolved a plan principally to employ artists rather than buy art, even though the idea of government employment of

Beniamino Bufano (in striped trousers) at work in the WPA/FAP sculpture studio in San Francisco.

Chapter 3 Nineteenth- and Twentieth-Century Antecedents to Today's Art Programs

artists was resisted by the arts community. The national committee and the regional committees faced great difficulties, especially in deciding who was an artist, who deserved an award, how to handle the accusations of some art being communist propaganda, and the complaints from artists about regimentation. The PWAP ended in 1934 and was transferred from the Treasury Department as the new Federal Works Project in 1939 (DeNoon 1987).

Aesthetics were always central in the issues argued by the artists and the WPA bureaucrats, in part because creative work was the central element behind the established reputation of the WPA art project and because it engaged forty-eight percent of the project workers. Over the life of the project, reliefers decorated schools, hospitals, and other public buildings with 2,566 murals and created 1,744 pieces of sculpture. In addition, the painters contributed 108,099 works in oil, watercolor, tempera, and pastel, and graphic artists made some 240,000 copies of 11,285 original designs in various print media.

The intention of the FAP, in addition to providing work for artists in a free atmosphere, was to integrate art with daily life by promoting art appreciation and art sales (McKinzie 1975). The assumption was that public appreciation of arts could be achieved through the allocation of art to public institutions and sales through the creation of two national art sales weeks. As to the aesthetics convictions of the 1930s, some artists imitated academic art and some non-representational art, but most were influenced by midwestern regionalists, such as Thomas Hart Benton, Grant Wood, and John Stewart Curry as well as the so-called social realist artists represented in the work of Moses Soyer, Joe Jones, Ben Shahn, Hugo Gilbert, and William Gropper.

Both groups built their art around American themes supported by a countrywide revival of Americanism. This influence certainly engrossed most Americans and was favorably received by the common people, but it also attracted unparalleled criticism from congressional conservatives who understood that some messages the artists had created were connected with the new liberalism. As the decade passed, however, artists turned away from illustrating the American scene to the ideas of Henri Matisse and Pablo Picasso. By 1942 the east coast artists were very heavily influenced by the work of Andre Breton, Max Ernst, Andre Masson, Yves Tanguy, and Jacques Lipschitz.

Federal Murals

The murals that were the mainstay of the FAP, while considered Catholic in taste, also engendered the most critical public responses, in part because the WPA murals were influenced by the Mexican muralists Diego Rivera, David Alfaro Siqueiros, and Jose Clemente Orozco. It was thought that the Mexican muralists inspired many American artists to take an especially negative view of American life, an outlook considered to be the view espoused by leftists. These criticisms included accusations that the WPA art was wasteful, ugly, and communistic and that it would have an alien effect upon children and adults. Accusations of this kind caused some installers to remove murals, and require some specific changes in the work. In spite of the controversies, however, WPA muralists won a good portion of national competitions and prizes. Muralists Philip Guston and Anton Refregier won awards for murals at the 1939 World's Fair. Among the painters, more than 300 who worked on the New York City project won awards. Other artists who were awarded top awards in major museum shows included Ivan LeLorraine Albright, Jack Levine, Marsden Hartley, Philip Evergood, and Mark Tobey.

Art Sales

There is also evidence that, because of the 1940 Art Week sales, five million people attended exhibitions offering opportunities to buy $10,000 sculptures, $2 prints, baby shoes of angora rabbit skin, wrought-iron foot scrapers, little figurines of wood and plaster, Indian blankets, and more. In terms of sales, the artwork shows flopped, with sales that barely exceeded $100,000. A breakdown of the purchases did, however, confirm that the buying public in the middle- and lower-income brackets were reached successfully, with more than ninety percent of all purchases being acquired at a price of $25 or less. The WPA Art Week in 1941 offered 130,000 pieces from 30,000 artists with estimated sales of less than $30,000. By the end of the project, it was rumored that much of the leftover artwork was sold as junk and snapped up by smart dealers who bought works for as little as $5 each, including paintings by Jackson Pollock, Mark Rothko, Adolph Gottlieb, and others. Many of these artists eventually sought to buy back their own work at these prices.

Social Projects

Less frequently mentioned in discussions of the WPA project was that its relief artists were also engaged in numerous socially useful projects. Holger Cahill, director of the project, never defined the artist as simply a creator of murals, sculpture, easel painting, or graphics. Some artists, he thought, only discovered themselves as mural painters because they found themselves on the relief roles. The WPA project was, therefore, not considered a fine arts project but a socially useful one. These FAP practical projects undertook a broad variety of work, including poster-making, photography, recording traditional American designs, craft work, and model making.

The FAP in Schools

The FAP also inaugurated an art teaching program in 1939 where some 465 art teachers were assigned to 180 settlement houses and social agencies. The New York project teachers included mostly long-term art teachers doing what they knew best. New York teachers were offered seminars on subjects such as the therapeutic aspects of art, teaching underprivileged students, art techniques, and pedagogical methods, and some refresher and advance courses.

In the first year eighty percent of the art instruction was directed toward children. Teachers were told that they should first of all become guides and friends to the students. The primary focus of the New York project, according to its director, was to raise a generation sensitive to the visual environment and capable of helping improve it. Classes included trips to the zoo, waterfront parks, and the nearby countryside, and were taught in boys' clubs, girls' service leagues, orphanages, day nurseries, hospitals, churches, and settlements. Art teachers even taught students how to prepare canvases from brown wrapping paper and mix their paints in muffin tins. By the end of the first year it was reported that up to 50,000 children and adults were being reached weekly.

Some other services offered by the New York art teachers included the training of 63 relief artists to teach arts and crafts in traveling workshops conducted in fifty-four Civilian Conservation Corps (CCC) camps. Others prepared exhibits and descriptive literature for public-school teachers, offered artists to conduct workshops for teachers in lithography and silkscreen printing, and led discussions on design. Efforts were also made to conduct evening classes aimed at keeping kids off the streets and thereby reducing juvenile delinquency. It was later reported that the juvenile crime rate did decline around the teaching locations and that the classes in hospitals proved useful in diagnosis and treatment of the mentally disturbed and retarded.

By 1941 the FAP art curriculum comprised twenty-three subjects, including photography, fashion illustration, and ceramics, with adult enrollment increasing from twenty percent to thirty-five percent over a five-year period. It was reported that more than two million students attended classes in 160 locations, with over a half million graduating from the New York City WPA art courses.

Service Projects

Another teaching project involving twenty-five to thirty-five teachers and 300 to 400 students operated as a design laboratory, offering professional courses in industrial design. The curriculum was based on Walter Gropius's program designed at the Bauhaus, and was designed to apply the principles of the fine arts to industrial production. In order to graduate with a three-year diploma in industrial design, textile design, advertising, or photography, requirements included taking courses in the fine arts, both two- and three-dimensional design, and machine/shop taught from the mass-production point of view.

Photo Projects

Another New York project involved photographers on the relief rolls serving in most departments in the New York City government. That effort produced 170,000 prints, photo murals, photo posters, and exhibition prints; publication of Bereniece Abbott's work; organizations of general collections; and also the production of three films.

Home Planning

Another project classified as practical art was conducted by the creative home planning division, involving twenty artists building model apartments. The models were built with interchangeable walls and furniture with various coverings to demonstrate arrangements and color effects. The project offered free instruction on home furnishings and shopping, and classes for making hooked rugs, slipcovers, curtains, and quilts.

Other Services

A similar program was offered in costume design, teaching figure drawing, anatomy, line, form, color, and historical costumes. The project taught girls the elements of contemporary style and taste and their economical application. In 1935, 2,500 girls were enrolled in thirty locations. Model makers and scenic designers were also employed to construct three-dimensional models illustrating flood prevention for the Tennessee Valley Authority and also paint stage curtains at the New York Women's House of Detention. Visual models and dioramas were also made for the New York City museums and for the Federal One Project in New York City. Other projects involved artists illustrating guide books and catalogues for the writers' project as well as special posters programs and brochures for the theatre and music project.

Special practical art and peripheral projects also grew up in many different parts of the country. In New York, FAP artists retouched city-owned art, gave lectures, and conducted tours of city art galleries. One hundred and eighty FAP art teachers provided the first technical art instruction for Negroes. Art instruction was also offered to middle-aged workers in Boston's South End. The WPA conducted poster workshops in Boston, Cleveland, Detroit, Minneapolis, Philadelphia, and St. Paul. Model makers made relief maps and dioramas for local educators, helped establish the American Bauhaus, and produced 495,620 photographs and 15,300 slides. Other projects lent talent to tax-supported museums and created the Index of American Design.

The Index of American Design

The Index of American Design employed 300 individuals for six years. The goal of the project was to find the main types of American decorative art from the colonial period through the gilded age and record them in an Index of American Design. Project artists were expected to examine furniture, household items, quilts, clothing, ship figureheads, cigar-store Indians, weather vanes, toys, tavern signs, baptismal fonts, bootjacks, finger books, and other hand-produced objects.

The project was designed to preserve a rapidly disappearing part of Americana and inspire contemporary design. The project began by employing artists and researchers to survey the local material and selecting items for artists to record and check for their history and authenticity. The artists were expected to review the objects, draw them accurately, and demonstrate clarity in construction, using exact proportions and faithful rendering of material, color, and textures so that each drawing could stand as a surrogate for the object. Project officials argued that drawing the objects instead of photographing them was to ensure accuracy and the spark of life inherent in the original.

After considerable debate between the WPA and several other government agencies, it was decided in 1942 that the index would be housed at the National Gallery of Art. Under the National Gallery's leadership, the purpose of the index remained a project designed to use the diverse skills of the unemployed and provide alternative work to the creative arts projects. In addition, it was the belief of the WPA supporters that, although the pioneers possessed and appreciated the feeling for rhythm, design, and color, this was lost when the novelty of machine-made goods weakened the public's desire for good form.

WPA Art Centers

In general, the WPA supporters believed industrial power prostituted and patronized some artists and left many with native talents

Boy Painting at Phoenix, Arizona, Community Art Center

Chapter 3 Nineteenth- and Twentieth-Century Antecedents to Today's Art Programs

Charles Louff © 1890. Rendered by Henry Tomaszewski, 1939.
Carousel Giraffe

Chapter 3 Nineteenth- and Twentieth-Century Antecedents to Today's Art Programs

completely out of the loop. It was now thought that the creation of FAP art centers would correct the unequal distribution of cultural advantage through their workshops, exhibitions, and other activities. It was hoped that it would return art to the people and correct the condition that had left art a stranger in thousands of communities. The FAP leadership, without the counsel of the artists, even sought to create community art centers whose goals were to awaken social unconsciousness and bridge the gaps between doing and thinking and between theory and practice in education and creative activity (McKinzie 1975, 141).

The FAP art centers that started in 1935 provided frequent exhibitions of local and national art, free lectures and films, free classes, free workshops, and free meeting rooms for clubs as well as political rallies and cultural events. Supporters of the centers believed that they could teach the entire community to discriminate between the kitsch and the authentic and take its message of art in daily life to millions in ten of our largest cities. To support the centers, the WPA furnished the staff, the exhibitions, and some equipment, and the community was expected to donate a building or pay the rent and utilities and help plan the program.

Twenty-five southern and western towns established art centers within the first year of the program. Two years later, forty-seven communities supported art centers. In 1938 and 1939 New York's FAP permitted fifty artists to leave for work in the southern and western centers. Chicago also released about six artists. Although there were cultural clashes between the artists in some of the centers, it did help the program by enhancing the reputation of the existing centers, where some artists remained permanently. Thirty of the sixty-six centers closed in 1939 for lack of federal funding.

In spite of their short-lived existence, the centers received widespread public approval. Buildings were refurbished, children received art instruction, and exhibits were organized. Centers that included up to seventy WPA workers were established at the Walker Art Center in Minneapolis, and Negro art centers were established. Support for the centers came mostly from members of the general public, in part because they felt the centers belonged to the communities they served and were designed with the idea that they would become permanent, as was the case with the famous Minneapolis-based Walker Art Center. Art collections once under WPA center care also helped provide starting collections for the Mobile Museum; the Roswell, New Mexico Museum and Art Centers; the Salem, Oregon Art Center; and the Key West, Florida Art Center.

THE OWATONNA ART EDUCATION PROJECT

Because it was essentially a school project, the Owatonna project had a very direct impact on American art education, especially by introducing the ideas that art education was part of general education for all and that artists no longer needed to be considered creative geniuses. Although the emphasis changed over time, Melvin Haggerty, its creator, saw art education as having utility in improving the home, school, and community environments. In the end, however, Edwin Ziegfeld shifted that emphasis to also include the notion of the creative development of children.

The Owatonna Art Education Project was an attempt to find new materials and methods for art education in the schools. It was predicated on certain basic assumptions about life, art, and education and was designed to test these assumptions in a real school situation. Preliminary studies were made in 1932–33 and the project began in the public schools of Owatonna, Minnesota in September of 1933.

Melvin Haggerty

The project was designed as an experimental study in order to learn how the art needs of the American public could be used as the basis for a school curriculum. The slogan adopted by the project was "Art As a Way of Life", which was coined by project director Melvin E. Haggerty, Dean of Education at the University of Minnesota. He viewed the phrase as reflecting a renewal of the arts, a re-engaging of the arts with the ordinary activities of life, and a removal of it from the hands of art specialists (Haggerty 1935). Haggerty claimed that artists tend to view ordinary folks as

90

ignorant and unappreciative, which emphasizes the artificial and is injurious to, and impoverishing to, life. As an antidote, Haggerty viewed the project as an effort at the public-school level to reclaim the natural relationship that should prevail between art and life, to see life again in its integrity, and to rediscover art as an inseparable aspect of normal living for every human being.

The project viewed art itself as the efforts of human beings to make life more interesting, more pleasing, and more meaningful, especially as a means for increasing human enjoyment. The project also viewed art as the making of all sorts of things in the fittest way in order to discover what activities are characteristic in its making and what kind of art education the schools should offer. The process of the investigation was directed toward discovering how art makes life different from what it otherwise would be, that is, to discover how people live and what they do to make their lives more efficient and more satisfying.

The project assumed that the impulse to improve the appearance of things was a natural human activity. In the typical middle-class home of 1935, art was viewed as having the capacity to enrich life through improving the visual aspect of things in the home, such as the use of color to warm the emotions, the use of pictures on the wall, suitable use of colored tapestry, and the aesthetic choice of furniture. The home thus became one way to learn the role of art in common life and to learn how art is a way of living in the home. Concerns about the uses of art in the home included a focus on its shape and size, the divisions of space, the materials used, the texture and color of the exterior, how the house related to the site, the plantings, and the layouts of walks and steps.

Art was, therefore, not considered something superficial, remote and veneered on life but rather something that arises out of human needs; art was seen as inherent in all the things men make and use. Art also applied to a broad spectrum of other human needs, including clothing, various modes of transportation, advertising design, lettering, printing, the church, the nursery, street layout, and the design of cities and villages.

In Haggerty's view, art is coterminous with man's effort to make things, but is not connected to the aesthetic experiences with nature. As far as the project was concerned, no gulf existed between the simple arts of life and the so-called fine arts. Art was, in effect, viewed as all efforts to create things that increase the comforts, efficiencies, and pleasures of living. As to the difference between good and bad art, the project saw art as succeeding partially or completely, with most efforts falling short of complete satisfaction. Successful art, for Haggerty, involved a persistent and unrelenting search for form, color, and right relationships that express the driving urges of life, the thoughts, the feelings, and the physical needs of active persons and groups of persons.

Haggerty thus embraced a functional view of art that was based on its usefulness in the things men make. The criteria for great art was judged by its relation to the physical components involved, media employed, difficulty of production, rarity of occurrence, and ethical or social value of the purpose leading to production. Art as viewed functionally, however, required that the project understand the functions of family life and all the varied needs and interests of the members of the family. The understanding of life thus became the primary basis for understanding art. This view rejected art as an emotional experience and accepted the notion that some experiences are devoid of an emotional component and are purely intellectual.

Haggerty essentially dodged the issues of creativity and the emotional satisfactions inherent in the creative act. In this regard, he considered creative impulses as being associated with mental images operating wholly within the limits of a mental world. As drives to action and to the movement of the individual, they deal with the modifiable and tangible world of things. What characterizes art is its inclusiveness of both the activity and the product, with the creative impulse satisfied only when the imagined object actually comes into being. Art was not, therefore, considered occupational therapy induced for its own sake and providing its own satisfactions, a plaything for idle hours, or a vehicle for undirected and meaningless expression.

Haggerty's view of the educational program began with his claim that art has everywhere suffered in education. As a result, he said, our cities are unbelievably ugly; our homes are devoid of comfort and beauty, promoting dwarfed and distorted human personalities; our landscapes are marred and disfigured; our manners are crude; and a world of things is far uglier than it needs to be. Further, he argued, education in art is a common need of all young people that addresses the need for its understanding, appreciation, and skillful use as means for elevating taste and the development of sensitive judgement. Haggerty believed that effort by the schools to educate artists was an effort that has gone awry, in part, because the world has little need for the kinds of artists that the schools make—a process that distorts the more important purposes of art instruction. Further, he viewed creative activity as responsible for the widespread trivialities that some schools practice in the name of art.

Shortly before his death in 1937, Haggerty issued a report that was essentially a restatement and expansion of the general philosophy undergirding the project, and to a certain extent a report on the project. His report on the progress of the project was limited to several general claims about the project's efforts and only limited suggestions as to its results. He noted a number of changes, including putting an art teacher in every school, beginning community art classes for adults, and offering art department advice on the decoration of various government institutions, private homes, hotels, churches, public parks, and school buildings (Haggerty 1935).

As to the general progress of the program, Haggerty noted an increase in the arrival of art books in the libraries and a cordial attitude toward the program. He also mentioned the introduction of summer classes for children and adults and classes for teachers of high-school projects and teachers of art.

The Ziegfeld Era

A much more detailed report of the project was prepared by Edwin Ziegfeld and Mary Elinore Smith (1944), eight years after the death of Melvin Haggerty. The report outlines the methods used to gather and report the data collected and describes the programs designed for public outreach and those that funded the art curriculum in the Owatonna schools. The report covers its five years as a project of the Carnegie Foundation for the Advancement of Teaching and the Carnegie Corporation of New York. This report in general follows the original goals outlined by Melvin Haggerty: (1) community needs as the primary basis for determining the Owatonna school art curriculum and (2) the

Chapter 3 Nineteenth- and Twentieth-Century Antecedents to Today's Art Programs

need for greater support of Owatonna's fine arts curriculum. Ziegfeld, in deference to Haggerty, commented on the then-existing curriculum by noting:

> In the schools art had likewise become a matter of painting or drawing or modeling in clay—pleasant unimportant girlish pastimes quite unrelated to anything else the children did. Naturally some few students might attain a high degree of technical skill, might even show a persistent spontaneity despite the rigors of the art curriculum. But the rest, the majority, never found more than a dilettante's satisfaction in the limited list of activities that constituted this curriculum. Whatever they happened to learn about line and color, about spatial relationships, about emphasis and subordination was applied so strictly to the task at hand (say designing a border of creeping nasturtiums) that they could not possibly transfer this knowledge to normal everyday experiences like selecting a neck tie or placing a new piece of furniture in the living room (Ziegfeld and Smith 1944, 3).

In the report, Ziegfeld did note the difficulties in matching the characteristics of a given community, to work out a method of studying art and to use that data in order to draw up a course of study for twelve grades. These issues later influenced Ziegfeld to abandon finding a clear match between the art needs of the community and the design of a K–12 school art curriculum. Owatonna met the originally specified requirement that the experiment should take place in a typical American community with at least 5,000 residents, be relatively close to the University of Minnesota, not have a single large industry, and be neither a boom town nor one experiencing a decline. With respect to the school population, Owatonna enrolled approximately 1500 students in four elementary schools and one single, combined junior-and-senior high.

The general methods employed in the community analysis involved visits to and surveys of the homes, gardens, places of business, public buildings, and the city plan in general. The streets, public buildings, and the exterior of homes and stores were also studied and photographed and the interiors of homes, shops, offices, and gardens were observed through social visits or service calls. No written records were made, but there was an agreement on the method of observation (Figure 3.1)

The underlined scores in Figure 3.1 show the marks received by "House No. 45" using a rating of 5 as highest, 3 as average, and 1 as low. This rating, in comparison with other Owatonna houses, viewed home No. 45 as just average. Ziegfeld also provides an entire page devoted to a narrative description of Home No. 45, much too lengthy to reproduce here. The description does deal with such points as the placement of the house on the lot, plantings, the number of interior rooms, the decorative scheme, the arrangement of furniture, window treatments, the interest of the

Figure 3.1 Interior Design

Exterior

General effect . . . . 1 2 _3_ 4 5
Architecture; relation to
period of construction . . . . . 1 2 _3_ 4 5
Spacings; relation of all
openings and architectural
divisions. . . . . 1 2 3 _4_ 5

Relations to lot . . . . 1 2 _3_ 4 5
Painting and finish . . . . 1 2 3 _4_ 5
Landscaping . . . . 1 2 3 _4_ 5

Interior

General effect . . . . 1 2 _3_ 4 5
Architecture . . . . 1 2 _3_ 4 5
walls; relation to furnishings
and woodwork
  Texture. . . . . 1 2 3 _4_ 5
  Color. . . . . 1 2 _3_ 4 5
  Surface design . . . . 1 2 3 _4_ 5
Floors; quality, color,
finish, etc. . . . . 1 2 _3_ 4 5
Woodwork . . . . 1 2 _3_ 4 5
Furniture
  Arrangement; for
  convenience and effect . . 1 2 3 4 _5_
  Intrinsic value; design,
  construction, workman-
  ship, material . . . . 1 2 _3_ 4 5
  Relation to other
  features; period, design,
  finish, etc . . . . 1 2 3 _4_ 5

Draperies
  Style . . . . 1 2 _3_ 4 5
  Color and Value. . . . . 1 2 3 _4_ 5
  Surface design . . . . 1 2 3 _4_ 5
Floor coverings
  Size and shape . . . . 1 2 _3_ 4 5
  Color and texture . . . . . . 1 2 _3_ 4 5
  Surface design; relation
  to other furnishings. . . . . 1 2 3 _4_ 5
Lights; efficiency, design,
appropriateness
  Wall and ceiling fixtures . 1 2 3 _4_ 5
  Portable lamps. . . . . 1 2 _3_ 4 5
Pictures
  Intrinsic value . . . . 1 2 _3_ 4 5
  Appropriateness. . . . . 1 2 3 _4_ 5
Accessories
  Intrinsic value . . . . 1 2 _3_ 4 5
  Appropriateness. . . . . 1 2 3 _4_ 5

owners in showing art in the home, and other matters. The same general methods were used in studying the uses of art in the business community.

Conversations with people and visits to their homes, gardens, and places of business were reported in the form of personal reports. Questionnaires were administered in the evening art classes and to all the townspeople whom the staff visited. It was because of the varied community responses that it first became apparent that the experiment could not be either a scientific analysis or a statistical survey. In light of the fact that the 7,500 citizens could not be categorized into comparable groups and that they could not delay the start of the schools in order to gather and compile the survey results, it was decided that the staff would build a tentative course of study around the normal activities of school-children.

Program Evaluation

The conclusions drawn on the effectiveness of the art in the community were based on certain generalizations drawn from the community study. These were stated in the form of certain recurring questions: (1) Was art closely related to the lives of the people in Owatonna? (2) What were the people's attitudes toward art? and (3) How much did they know about art? The results of the study suggested the following conclusions: (1) all the people in Owatonna used art; (2) the art problems of the people of Owatonna occurred in all the many areas of living; (3) the art problems arose in the immediate concrete situations; (4) no one person's taste in art was uniformly low; art tastes were in fact compartmentalized; (5) people were often unaware of the beauty in their surroundings; and (6) solving their art problems successfully gave people a sense of satisfaction and well-being. With respect to citizens' attitudes and interests, the report concluded that the people of Owatonna were interested in art, that what most interested them was the art in their surroundings and daily activities and the relationship of art in their own community to that of other American communities. With respect to the art abilities and knowledge of the Owatonna citizens, it was decided that they did not have sufficient ability or knowledge to solve everyday art problems to their own satisfaction and that most did not have sufficient ability or knowledge to utilize materials that were near at hand.

Service Projects

In order to educate the citizenry, the project focused on three areas: service projects, lectures, and summer school. The service projects provided advice to various community institutions and home-owners, including help with interior design and landscaping. The project conducted 250 service projects covering a variety of art problems in shops, stores, public and private buildings, a beauty shop, doctors' and dentists' offices, manufacturing plants, a photographer's studio, a cannery, a factory, a gift shop, clothing stores, a flower shop, the public library, elementary and secondary schools, civic and country clubs, and local parks. A lecture series was also given to local groups, and evening classes for adults and a summer school program were offered in the summers of 1935 and 1936.

Summer Classes

The summer classes included art education instruction for both children and adults. Classes for children were offered to students in the elementary, junior high, and senior high school. Adults in evening classes could select from either lecture or participation groups. Five university courses in art, art education, and educational psychology were offered for college credit.

Community Classes

Both the community classes and the teacher's courses were related to the point of view taken by the project. Classes met in the high school building, where additional rooms were set aside as reading rooms and a library. Exhibits of industrial projects, textiles, wood blocks, and the then-new Carnegie prints of drawings, paintings, and etchings were made available for study.

97

Primary and Intermediate Classes

The primary art classes grades 1–3 met one and a half hours a day, Monday through Thursday. Emphasis was placed on free expression and experimentation in different media. Age-specific activities included outdoor sketching, modeling, finger-painting, simple construction projects, and field trips to areas of local interest. The intermediate art classes grades 4–6 met one and a half hours a day, four days a week. The curriculum provided a variety of activities in different art media and the design and construction of an entire miniature city.

Junior High Classes

The junior high art classes 7–9 met one and a half hours a day, four days a week and included classes in textile design, soap sculpture, finger-painting, and sketching with watercolors, crayons, and chalks, and a final project of designing a summer camp. Art classes in the senior high grades 10–12 were held one and a half hours a day, four days a week and included problems ranging from the designing of labels for a local cannery to pure expression in clay and watercolor. Most of the work focused on such things as house plans, interior designs and models, block-printed textiles, graphic designs for stationery, newspapers, stage designs, and book illustrations.

Adult Classes

The adult art classes designed for people between the ages of 25 and 50 met one and a half hours a day, two days a week. These included classes in art appreciation and creative work where students worked in a variety of media to solve mainly expressive problems. Classes for teachers were organized to observe the actual work done by students of various ages. Credit classes were offered on three topics: (1) principles of design, (2) problems in art education, and (3) educational psychology.

According to Ziegfeld, the art courses offered in the school art program the first year differed little from what the schools had offered in the past. In the elementary schools the classroom teacher conducted such free creative activities as illustration, modeling, and construction. In the junior high and senior high, two art courses were introduced for the first time, one for the eighth grade and one for a group recruited from the senior high. Ziegfeld taught the courses, with the major goal being the development of individual needs, interests, and abilities. In spite of the fact that the project goals specified art was most meaningful when it touches areas connected with daily activities, Ziegfeld felt that the self and its problems constitute the most important area of experience, next the home, and lastly the community as a whole.

The School Curriculum

The curriculum did, therefore, assume a spiral pattern where children in the first grade learned how to arrange their rooms, how to dress, and how to take care of their clothes. In the second grade they also studied their schoolroom and the community stores. In the third grade they continued on these topics but also began the study of the newspaper and the printing industry. The objectives of the entire program, as developed in the report by Ziegfeld and Smith, included:

> to develop a well-adjusted, integrated personality
>
> to experience creative activity in various art fields, using various tools and media
>
> to develop an awareness and an appreciation of art in the environment
>
> to become increasingly interested in improving the environment through the thoughtful solving of art problems
>
> to develop the ability to solve everyday art problems
>
> to become increasingly sensitive to differences of merit in art products;
>
> to acquire such knowledge as will aid in appreciating art objects or in solving art problems
>
> to develop progressive, open-minded attitudes toward art
>
> to develop resourcefulness in leisure-time pursuits and hobbies
>
> to have an opportunity to develop unusual talent (1944, 87)

Activities in support of the program included drawing, painting, sketching, the design of houses, interior design, and color and graphic design. In the elementary grades, where art was taught during the school year five half-hour periods a week, the work centered on decorations for the schoolroom, building a library in each room, making a class newspaper, study of the home, and observing, sketching, and discussing public buildings and parks. In the seventh and eighth grades, art was an elective subject taught in six one-hour periods where students explored the realm of art and its relation to life. Class discussions and activities revolved around community planning, clothing design, printing and commercial design, industrial design, photography, painting, and sculpture. Art in grades 9–12 was also an elective taught five one-hour periods a week, with class discussions and activities focusing on the home and the community. The home design course frequently involved trips to actual homes, discussion and appraisal of the home design, cost factors, and geographic and climate effects.

Overall the art program stressed two important goals: the needs, interests, abilities, and attitudes of the students and the role of art in their own community. The idea was to emphasize neither rugged individualism nor complete conformity but to view art as a part of the total curriculum rather than a series of special skills.

The art program in Owatonna's schools was founded on a set of principles that might govern and direct the purposes, content, and methods of an effective program. Ziegfeld and Smith defined these principles in the following ways:

> An art program should be available to all students at all stages in their educational development.
>
> Methods of art instruction should be sufficiently individualized to offer equal benefits to all students.
>
> As far as practicable the art program should provide experiences in every art field.
>
> To give experiences closely allied to the problems of daily living, the content of the art program should be organized in terms of areas of life.
>
> An art program should place definite emphasis on the forms and expressions of art to be found in the immediate locality.
>
> In an effective art program the relationships among the var-

ious fields of art and the relationships between art and other fields of human endeavor should be made clear and significant. (1944, 101)

Art in the Elementary Grades

The subject matter in these units was varied and expanded in order to keep pace with the children's developmental experiences. The headings listed in Figure 3.2 are not the actual titles of units but are summaries of the information learned in that grade.

Figure 3.2   THE INDIVIDUAL

THE INDIVIDUAL

Grade 1

Clothing: purposes and care; appropriateness for indoor and outdoor wear, for summer and winter; color in dress

Textiles: silk, wool, cotton; sources of each; design and use in clothing

Grade 3

Dress in other lands

Textiles: silk, wool, cotton, linen; their sources; spinning, dyeing, weaving, appropriateness of design to material; textile designs of other lands

Grade 5

Textiles: silk, wool, cotton, linen, rayon; sources of synthetic fibers

Dress: color, line, appropriateness of design; planning a wardrobe

Grade 6

Dress: costume in Greece and Rome in the Middle Ages

THE HOME

Grade 1

Interior: how people's activities determine the use of each room, its furnishings, often its colors; kitchen, dining room, living room, bedrooms, bathroom; tableware and table setting

Grades 3 and 4

Interior: arranging objects on the living-room table and mantle; arrangement of kitchen units; design in tableware and table setting

Homes in other lands

Grade 6

Interior: the whole plan

Exterior: the whole design, as an outgrowth of the interior plan

Grounds: foundation planting

THE SCHOOL

Grade 2

The schoolroom: arrangement of desk, chairs, seats, library corners, maps, etc.; color in stationary elements and in decoration; arrangement of friezes, pictures, pupils' work, bulletin boards

Grade 5

Interior: general plan and circulation; hall decoration, storage space, and other special features

Grounds: lawn and recreational
areas; foundation planting

THE COMMUNITY

Grade 1

The importance of the farmer to the
life of the community

Grade 2

City planning: plan of streets around
the school building; character of
local business and residential streets
Architecture: general exterior design
of stores, factories, homes
Landscape architecture: park design,
front lawns of homes

Grade 3

Trees in the community

Grade 4

City planning: types of plans; design
of residential districts; street planning: location of houses on lots;
street plan of entire city; historical
methods of planning, especially the
American colonial plan

Grade 5

Living in modern American cities

Grade 6

Public architecture: architectural styles;
design of facades; foundation planting
Medieval castles and communities

COMMERCE

Grade 2

Exteriors of local stores

Grade 5

Exterior design of local stores
Advertising in stores: window displays; showcase displays; packaging

INDUSTRY

Grade 2

Transportation: handmade and
machine-made vehicles

Manufacturing: machine processes;
products; manufacture of foods

Grade 5

Development of power machinery
Machine art versus manual art:
importance of the industrial
designer
Machine processes, products, and
materials
Transportation

Grade 6

History of printing
Type faces: classification, old and
new; standard styles; hand lettering;
expressive use in advertising and display matter

RELIGION

Grade 4

Early New England churches
Churches today

Grade 5

Religious architecture contrasted
with public, commercial, and industrial architecture

Grade 6

Churches of other times—Greek and
Roman temples, medieval churches,
and so on—compared with ours today

RECREATION

Grade 1

Circuses
Appropriate decorations and favors
for holidays

Grade 2

Christmas gifts, cards, favors

Grade 3

Newspaper comic strips
Recreation in America and other
lands
Costumes
Christmas gifts and holiday favors
Table setting and decoration for par-
ties and festivities

Recreation pages in magazines
Christmas gifts

Posters for elementary school play-day
Dress designs for sports and recreational activities
Christmas gifts

Greek and Roman athletics and games; adaptation of dress and architecture to these recreational activities
Christmas gifts

Art in the Secondary Schools

The following is a list of all the units taught in Owatonna's junior and senior high schools. The junior high units included Printing and Advertising, Photography, Textiles and Clothing, Interior Design, the House Garden Design, the School, City Planning, Industrial Design, Recreation, Design, Color, Painting, and Sculpture. The senior high units included Interior Design, House Design, Garden Design, the Community, Commercial Architecture, Industrial Design, Painting, Textile Design, Advertising, and Commercial Design and Sculpture.

THE GERMAN AND AMERICAN BAUHAUS

The German Bauhaus 1919–1944

Like Owatonna, the Bauhaus also had a profound effect on the American art education curriculum, primarily through introducing the idea of the artist as craftsman, the Cizek notion of art education through the exploration of materials and processes, and the idea of the "spiritual" in art. As a result, art education in American schools began to emphasize design approaches to materials, let students be free to explore ideas in materials, break down the rigid barriers between fine and industrial arts programs in schools and colleges, and consider the easel artist as a spiritually inspired maker of aesthetic objects.

103

The climate in which the German Bauhaus was created came at a time when the Italian Futurists were disgusted at trying to be artists and when the most admired art came mostly from the hands of "dead men." The Dadaists in Paris were even more vocal on this score than the Futurists, proposing to junk all the aesthetic values of the past. Because of their resentment of the machine, they decided even bathroom plumbing was appropriate for their collages promoting the cause.

At the time there were also influences by the "purist" artists, painting forms based on rectangles, cylinders, and lines. These included artists that later did more work in architecture, typographical design, and design. These artists included LeCorbusier, Leger, Oud, and Mondrian.

In America Bauhaus, ideals were inspired by both the practice of industrial design and the 1929 Depression. At that time, the railroads were in the process of designing the first streamlined, air-conditioned, refurbished coach and sleeper train between the cities. Historians believe America's interest in design for high mass production began with the attempt to find markets during the Depression years.

Building practices were also changing rapidly at that time and architects had to wrestle with how to conceal a cast-iron post in molded Corinthian pillars and how to pin thin casings of marble to a concrete wall. This was done so moldings could hide rectangular window shapes on a flat concrete wall. In short, architects and designers needed to think about rejecting the ancient habits of the past and focusing on the education of future artists, architects, and designers.

It was in this context the Bauhaus was created, first in Weimar, then in Dessau, and later in Berlin and Chicago. Walter Gropius had agreed to take over the old Dessau Crafts and Design School and the fine-arts academy to create a new institution. In 1919 the Duke of Weimar gave him the opportunity to recruit staff and develop a curriculum for what later became known as the New Bauhaus School. Gropius thought that a school where many art forms could be taught together was the best approach to improving the classical academy approach.

In the effort to overcome the traditions of life drawing and painting, he sought in the Bauhaus to establish a revolutionary new concept that would embrace painting, sculpture, architecture, typography, ceramics, metal work, photography, and film. As a result, he created a new kind of beginning course, which in the first year acquainted students with how to work in wood, metal, paper, glass, stone, plastics, and textiles. The approach was for the student to learn first about the inherent qualities of materials, including their flexibility, brittleness, and response to heat and cold, and what tools to use on them. Students were also expected to explore what forms could be created and what combinations of materials were most effective. The first studio course teachers included Josef Albers, Johannes Itten, and Moholy-Nagy, who not only taught the course but also spread the Bauhaus idea throughout the world.

How faculty and students were organized in the new Bauhaus was especially unique for the times. For example, every student was expected upon graduation to qualify for a journeyman's license in his craft and become a first-rate artist. As a result, artist-designers and crafts faculty both had to learn to teach courses in order to provide students with a combined design and craft technical background.

Any attempt to generalize Bauhaus objectives must, however, take into account that there were, in fact, five different schools over the time period from 1919 to 1944. These included the original Bauhaus in Weimar, its reconstruction in somewhat altered forms in Dessau and Berlin, and the two newer versions in America, the School of Design and the Institute of Design. Although all the schools held on to the primary ideals of the original Bauhaus, over the twenty-five years of its existence each school had different leaders and somewhat different emphases.

Bauhaus Origin and History

First and foremost it should be noted that the German Bauhaus was not an isolated phenomenon. It was, in fact, the focus of a complex and multifaceted development that spans from the Romantic period until the present and has important influences, even today. Institutionally, it was an institute for art that emerged as a successor to an art academy and school of arts located in the city of Dessau, Germany. Unlike its predecessors, the Bauhaus assumed an anti-academic attitude from its very beginning. It was considered technically to be a practical educational institution with a strong tendency towards practical and manual training. Over time these goals were gradually replaced with more extensive plans for educating designers to design products for mass production. As time went on, the early Bauhaus moved more toward product development in order to provide a broader economic base in support of the school program.

The Bauhaus in its later years became especially noted for its "new architecture" developed by Bauhaus architects Walter Gropius and Ludwig Mies van der Rohe. It also, over time, developed programs that contributed revolutionary new designs for the home environment and industrial design. It became especially famous for the creative contributions of its painters including Albers, Klee, Feininger, and Kandinski. No less important were its contributions to transforming art teaching methods throughout the world.

Historians also credit the Bauhaus for contributing something more than the sum of the total achievements of its master teachers. This was centered on its human quality that encompassed the whole community, teachers and students alike. Bauhaus students, for example, were not considered mere learners but rather an important part of a community that found expression in the consciousness of a common social responsibility.

The social revolution that the Bauhaus engaged in was triggered by nineteenth-century technological-industrial development that created a gap between artistic conception and realization, i.e., between the "spiritual" and the "materialistic." Conceptually, the Bauhaus followed a path advocated by Gottfried Semper, Sir Henry Cote, John Ruskin, and William Morris. Morris was considered particularly important because of his attempts to break the tendency toward historic style imitation. The Bauhaus curriculum was also influenced by some of the German schools of arts and crafts who were attempting to combine theory and practice by considering craft training as fundamental in art education. Also influential in the curriculum development in the Bauhaus were the new principles of art education developed by Franz Cizek in Vienna.

In general, the intellectual atmosphere in 1919 when the Weimar Bauhaus was created was totally changed from the pre-war years. The peculiar moods of despair and hope were captured in the literature and in the visual arts by the absurdities of the

Dadaists and in the explosiveness of the Expressionists. Historians generally believe the preparatory work for creating the first Bauhaus in Weimar had already been accomplished in Berlin and all director Walter Gropius and his circle had to do was bring these new ideas into the refuge afforded by a confined German provincial town.

Walter Gropius

Gropius was considered as a possible director of the school as early as 1915 but plans for this were delayed until after the war. When Gropius was finally called to head the Bauhaus, the call came from the art academy he was to replace. In his early years in the academy, he had already started to make the changes he later integrated into the new Bauhaus curriculum. The basic components of the early curriculum were established by Gropius in 1919 and were fueled by Holzel and Cizek's fundamental educational concepts, as introduced by Itten and Feininger, who taught in the first term.

The initial emphasis of the new program was on the required synthesis of the crafts and art. In order to support the concept, Gropius avoided the academic title of professor and instead introduced the teaching staff with the craftsman title of "master," a term also given to students upon their graduation. Following completion of the basic course, students were expected to join the Bauhaus workshop of their choice and to work there, first as apprentices and then as journeymen. Following completion of their course work, they were then required to take a journeyman's and master craftsman examination before the apprenticeship board. Because the artists teaching the course had no experiences as practicing craftsmen, they were called the "masters of form," and team- taught the class with the regular "masters of craft."

Frank Cizek

The basic course, which was inspired by Frank Cizek, consisted of studies of materials, i.e., paper, plaster, wood, glass, and cane, in order to develop a feeling for and an understanding of their basic qualities. The solution of a given problem was the student's and was restricted only by the materials being used and the individual's imagination. The process was designed to release the student's hidden creative abilities. Historians credit Johannes Itten as deserving credit for the success of the course. His teaching ability and his capacity to foster and help unfold young personalities were the reasons given for his success.

Itten did, however, also have numerous conflicts with the life-drawing teachers assigned to supplement the basic course. His ideas were in conflict with the ideas of the drawing teachers including Paul Klee, and as a result Itten resigned in 1923 and was replaced by Moholy-Nagy, whose favorite materials were sheet metal, paper, and wood. Joseph Albers, the first Bauhaus student to earn the master title, systematized the teaching of the work-shop, and paper became the principal material because he believed that folding and shaping increased its strength and demonstrated the extraordinary relationship between form and matter. Paper forming helped students to realize how changes in form influence the behavior of material. Another important part of the preliminary courses were the lectures by Klee and Kandinsky, which addressed the fundamental problems of linear and color composition. Klee's *Paul Klee Notebooks Volume 2* (1973) and Kandinski's *Point and Line to Plane* (1979) publications resulted from these lectures.

Despite continuing disagreement among the masters and the administration, the Bauhaus soon found a new goal they could rally around. The new goal was "Art and Technology—A New Unity." This was carried out effectively through the workshop pro-ductions that started in 1922. Some of the workshops and their leaders included the cabinet making workshop led by Gropius, the weaving workshop led by Munche and Helen Borner, the ceramic workshop by master Gerhard Marcks and the printing workshop by Feininger. These workshops produced many fine industrial products that were economical yet solid and contributed respectable furnishings and commodities. Their success encour-aged Gropius to strive even harder to secure financial independ-ence for the Bauhaus. His view was that the teaching of the basic course and the workshops should be financed by the state, while income from private commissions and practical research should be used to pay for further experimentation.

In 1926 the German government gave notice to the Bauhaus masters that for economic reasons they would no longer be able to support them. This turned out to be a fortunate turn of events because the school was given a new home and a new opportunity to work in the city of Dessau. Although the Bauhaus continued successfully for a time in Dessau, the general public began to view the program as being too expensive and a drain on the taxpayers' money. In spite of such pressures, however, the Dessau program continued until the national socialists seized power.

Until its final dissolution in 1933, the Bauhaus continued to retain its academic standing. However, after 1926 a more academic approach was evident in the curriculum. This included conferment of the title of professor to the masters of form, deciding master craftsmen would no longer teach, eliminating dual appointments in the workshop, and requiring that artists and craftsmen teach and work side by side. Under the new title of the Institute of Design, Kandinksy and Klee taught basic instruction and Moholy-Nagy headed the metal workshops. All the other workshops were led by former students, the most famous of whom was Marcel Brewer, who headed the cabinet making workshop. The workshops continued to function well and were supported financially by a functioning corporation selling design products and licenses for the industrial mass production of its prototypes.

At Dessau, Gropius finally exhausted his energies, stopped teaching, and devoted much of his efforts to defending the Bauhaus from both internal and external assaults. As a result, he resigned as director in March 1928. Marcel Brewer, Moholy-Nagy, and Bayer left at the same time. Hannes Meyer became the new director and employed his own socialist ideal of practical work to serve everyone in the community. Meyer was not overly successful, being dismissed only after two years, but he nevertheless saw a trade union school built in Bernau with the cooperation of the school's department of architecture. He also saw the People's Furniture being introduced, the Bauhaus wallpapers developed, and new housing units designed as a solution for economical mass housing.

In the summer of 1930, Ludwig Mies van der Rohe was appointed Bauhaus director. Under his leadership the Bauhaus developed mostly as an academy of architecture. Mies halted the manufacture of commercial goods in order to reduce staffing costs. He also introduced interior decoration to work along with architecture. Under Mies, the artists claimed that they lacked recognition; Paul Klee left for another job. It is said that without the insistence of Kandinsky, even the art class would have disappeared from the curriculum.

In 1931 the national socialists stepped up their campaign of harassment against the Bauhaus and, in the summer of 1932, closed it. As a result, Mies moved the Bauhaus to Berlin where Albers, Engermann, Hilberseimer, Kandinsky, Peterhans, Lilly, Reich, Rudelt, and Scheper joined him. The Berlin Bauhaus began operations in 1932 but remained under constant attack by right-wing extremists. Hitler's seizure of power finally ended all salary payments to the faculty, which meant the Bauhaus had to be financed solely by the royalties from the licenses sold to the manufacturers of Bauhaus wallpaper. On April 11, 1933 storm troopers seized the Bauhaus and subsequently the school was closed.

The closure of the Berlin Bauhaus was the beginning of the emigration of its members both inside and outside Germany. As a consequence, Bauhaus ideas were carried to all parts of the world. Gropius in America introduced Bauhaus methods at Harvard in 1937. Albers developed the preliminary course at Black Mountain College, North Carolina and later at Yale. In Chicago, Moholy-Nagy revived the Bauhaus for a short time but due to financial difficulties, the new Bauhaus closed and was taken over by the School of Design in the Department of Architecture at the Illinois Institute of Technology.

No description of the Bauhaus, however, would be complete without addressing some of the personal views and philosophies of the important artists and designers who led the different programs, designed the curriculum, and taught the classes in the basic courses in drawing and in the workshops. Some of the most important contributions came from Gropius, Itten, Klee, Moholy-Nagy, Mondrian, Albers, and Kandinski.

Course Design and Teaching Philosophies

The Weimar Bauhaus 1919–1923

Walter Gropius: As director in Weimar, Gropius believed that architects, sculptors, and painters must return to the crafts because art was not a profession. For him, there were no essential differences between the artist and the craftsman. The artist is only an exalted craftsman and in rare moments of inspiration will his work become art. Proficiency in a craft, he believed, is essential to every artist. What was needed was a new guild of craftsmen without the class distinctions that raise barriers between the craftsman and the artist. Gropius defined the aims of the Bauhaus in these terms:

> The Bauhaus strives to bring together all creative effort into one whole, to reunify all the disciplines of practical art—sculpture, painting, handicrafts, and the craft—as inseparable components of a new architecture. The ultimate, if distant, aim of the Bauhaus is the unified work of art—the great structure—in which there is no distinction between monumental and decorative art.
>
> The Bauhaus wants to educate architects, painters, and sculptors of all levels, according to their capabilities, to become competent craftsmen or independent creative artists and to form a working community of leading and future artist-craftsmen. These men, of kindred spirit, will know how to design buildings harmoniously in their entirety—structure, finishing, ornamentation, and furnishing (Wingler 1969, 32).

According to Wingler, the principles of the Weimar Bauhaus were based on Gropius's idea that:

- Art rises above all methods; in itself it cannot be taught, but the crafts certainly can be. Architects, painters, and sculptors are craftsmen in the true sense of the word; hence, a thorough training in the crafts, acquired in workshops and in experimental and practical sites, is required of all students as the indispensable basis for all artistic production. Our own workshops are to be gradually built up, and apprenticeship agreements with outside workshops will be concluded.
- The school is the servant of the workshop, and will one day be absorbed in it. Therefore
- There will be no teachers or pupils in the Bauhaus but masters, journeymen, and apprentices.
- The manner of teaching arises from the character of the workshop:

- Organic forms developed from manual skills. Avoidance of all rigidity; priority of creativity; freedom of individuality, but strict study discipline. Master and journeyman examinations, according to the Guild Statutes, held before the Council of Masters of the Bauhaus or before outside masters.
- Collaboration by the students in the work of the masters. Securing of commissions, also for students.
- Mutual planning of extensive, utopian structural designs—public buildings and buildings for worship—aimed at the future.
- Collaboration of all masters and students—architects, painters, sculptors—on these designs with the object of gradually achieving a harmony of all the component elements and parts that make up architecture.
- Constant contact with the leaders of the crafts and industries of the country. Contact with public life, with the people, through exhibitions and other activities. New research into the nature of the exhibitions, to solve the problem of displaying a visual work and sculpture within the framework of architecture.
- Encouragement of friendly relations between masters and students outside of work; therefore plays, lectures, poetry, music, costume parties. Establishment of a cheerful ceremonial at these gatherings. (1969, 32)

Johannes Itten: Johannes Itten's most important contribution to the Weimar Bauhaus was the introduction of the preliminary course where students developed their tactile and visual capabilities and applied them in an aesthetic manner. Instruction included the analysis of old masters in order to recognize the artistic precepts and formal consciousness. For Itten to experience a work of art was to recreate it, which meant to become dependent on the forces of the human mind and soul. Itten believed the ability to represent was dependent on the substance and the physical constitution of the body, including the fingers, hands, arms, and feet. Such ability is dependent on the constitution of all physical substances and organs. Experiencing things was, for him, a faculty of the mind and spirit as seen in the physical and spiritual faculties that produce the experience. To perceive something was to be moved where even the slightest sensation of form radiates movement. For Itten everything that exists was differentiated in the quantity and quality of movement as defined by time and space.

The means of representation, Itten believed, were unteachable. To teach and to learn meant to comprehend, but form and movement could not be taught, as only perception is perceivable. He believed movement gives birth to form, form to movement and every point, line, plane, shadow, light, and color become norms of movement. For Itten there were three differentiated degrees in being moved: (1) the physical degree of being moved, (2) the psychic degree of being moved, and (3) the mental degree of being moved.

The Bauhaus in Dessau 1925–1932

Under the continuing leadership of Walter Gropius, the purpose of the Dessau Bauhaus was revised to include the training of artistically talented people to become creative designers in the fields of the crafts, industry, and architecture (Wingler 1969):

1. **Design instruction**
   Basic instruction
   Craft instruction (goal: journeyman's certificate)
   Architectural instruction

2. **Practical research**
   Production of prototypes for the crafts and industry, buildings and furnishings

3. **Workshops**
   Cabinet making, wall-painting, metal, weaving, printing (typography, commercial art, and art prints)
   Start of the winter semester: October 4, 1925. Admission to the basic course (compulsory for everyone) from age 17 onward—experienced craftsmen, technicians, mechanics, and architects will also be admitted—apply now.

4. **Basic instruction**
   (1 year) per semester: 30 marks, admission fee: 10 marks. Workshop training: free of charge.

5. **Sequence of Instruction**
   Theory and actual work are closely interrelated

6. **Basic practical instruction**
   Becoming acquainted with various types of materials and tools; devising and building of useful objects in the special workshop for the basic course
   Working out original designs and justifying them with respect to the choice of material, economy, and technique
   Independent execution of designs
   Mutual criticism of the finished product with respect to its function and expressiveness and the possibilities for improvements, with respect to form (scale, material, color) material (quantity, value) economy (expenditure, return) and techniques (construction, production)
   Collecting and systematically tabulating samples of materials
   Guided tours through workshops and plants
   Projection and draftsmanship constitute an introduction to the specialized graphic art of the general course

7. **Basic form instruction**
   Theory and practical exercises:
   Analysis of the elements of form (orientation, designation, and terminology)
   Organic and functional relationships (principles, construction, structure)
   Introduction to the principles of abstraction (appearance, nature, scheme)
   Primary and secondary, elementary and mixed application of the means of design
   Design exercises: Drawing, painting, building

8. **Scientific subjects**
   Basic laws of mathematics, physics, mechanics, and chemistry with respect to their practical application and to the logical understanding of the significance of numbers and measurement, substances and form, force and motion, proportion and rhythm for the processes of design.
   The basic course is the indispensable prerequisite for all further work of the Bauhaus and is therefore compulsory for every newly admitted student. (1969, 108–109)

Piet Mondrian

Mondrian contributed to the Dessau Bauhaus literature mostly through seeking to contrast painting and architecture. He believed the distinctions made between architecture judged as practical and painting as social were false distinctions. Pure design was not a reproduction of life but rather the equivalent of representing things that are permanent and transitory. As a result of what he called the "new aesthetics," painting and architecture were consistently executing compositions of counterbalancing and contrasting straight lines, and changing the duality of unchangeable right angles into multiple forms. Architectural education was, therefore, refined through changed requirements, techniques, and materials. This led, of necessity, to a pure design of balanced, refined, and chaste beauty. The new aesthetics of architecture were the same as those used in painting, where a building in the process of clarifying itself was putting into effect the same forms of purification used in futurism and cubism. Because of this unity, buildings and painting constituted one art form and mutually absorbed one another.

Joseph Albers

Joseph Albers, as an instructor in the Dessau preliminary courses, believed creative education came from one's own experience, where experimenting was better than studying and playing, because it developed courage and led to an inventive way of building and discovery. Instruction in professional techniques hampered inventiveness and thus, in the early stages of learning, all tools were taken from the students, forcing them to work without prior instruction, methods, or tools. Albers's approaches to paper without tools required the student to use both sides of the paper in an upright, folded, or sculptural manner with emphasis on the edges. In doing so, the goal for the students was not to create works of art but rather to conduct an experiment in order to search on their own and learn for themselves.

Albers believed the most important act of teaching was inculcating thrift of labor and materials and their best possible use to achieve the desired effect. Learning what emphasized the technical and economical rather than the aesthetic reveals the links between organic and technical properties. It trains spatial imagination, produces agreement on the principles of form, and counteracts exaggerated individualism without trampling individuality. The task of the school was to integrate individuals into society and to engage them in the activities of the time. The cultivation of individuality was the individual's task and not the school's. Individuals should be cultivated not by interfering with their development but rather by helping them achieve a place in a sociological economy based on rejection of the personality cult of current educational systems.

Using the correct methods of instruction was the best way to develop responsibility and self-discipline in the person, the material, and the work. By letting students work with different materials and tools and visit different industries, the students could find the work and the materials that suited them best and assist in their choice of a vocation. This approach, it was thought, trains the students in a non-technical way, as contrasted with vocational school training that stresses manual skills.

Albers's first course was Learn by Doing and the first semester included the following subjects:

- The fundamentals of workshop experimentation
- Use of material with respect to
  a) dimension (volume, space, plane, line, point)
  b) movement (statics—dynamics)
  c) mass (proportion—rhythm, addition—subtraction)
  d) energy (positive—active, negative—passive)
  e) expression (color, light—dark, matter) in projects which either are chosen or given
- Collecting and systematically tabulating materials. Visits to workshops and factories.
- Area:
  Exercises with matter and with materials (repeatedly interchanging)
- Matter:
  The relationship of the external appearance of the materials
  Turning to account of structure, facture, and texture of materials
- Material:
  Construction for the testing of performance and utilization
- Objective:
  To discover and invent independently, the emphasis being placed on economy and responsibility
  Self-discipline and critical ability
  Accuracy and clarity

- For the choice of a vocation:
  Recognition of the area of work and the kind of materials that suit the individual (Wingler 1969, 144)

Wassily Kandinsky

Kandinsky, who also taught at the Dessau Bauhaus, viewed art education as something that could not be taught or learned because it was a matter of pure intuition that could only be energized by force or by instruction. He felt that specialized training devoid of humanistic concepts and without a philosophical foundation was no longer relevant. The goals of education should be directed primarily toward developing the student's capacity to think analytically and synthetically. What was important was not what is being taught but rather how it is being taught.

Kandinsky believed that it was also more productive for the artist to study a field different from his own in order to observe, think, and act simultaneously, analytically, and synthetically. He believed that thinking and creating do not differ in the areas of human activity, be it in art, science, or technology.

The Berlin Bauhaus 1932–1933

As mentioned, the Bauhaus, closed in Weimar as a state school of higher learning, continued its program in Berlin. As a school of design, it remained an independent teaching and research institute under the direction of Ludwig Mies van der Rohe. The curriculum of the Berlin Bauhaus included three levels of instruction covering seven semesters. During the first stage, students with differing levels of education and talent were brought up to a common standard by the beginning of the second stage. Students could now decide what areas of specialized study they wished to pursue, including: (1) architecture and interior design, (2) commercial art, (3) photography, (4) weaving, and (5) fine art.

At the specialized stage students were given the practical, technical, and scientific background necessary for their work in special fields. Theoretical instruction was supplemented by practical experimental work to develop a feeling for design and quality in technical work. Based on acquiring technical knowledge and professional capabilities, the third stage focused on independent design work. In addition to specialized training, special lectures and guest courses were offered to acquaint the student with the issues of the day.

Soon after the break up of the Berlin Bauhaus, Albers moved to the United States and joined the faculty of Black Mountain College and Gropius went on to Harvard. Gropius and Moholy-Nagy soon corresponded as to the possibility of a new Bauhaus opening in Chicago. Moholy-Nagy, as a result, drafted a new program and the Chicago school opened as a non-profit institution supported by the Association of Arts and Industries. Moholy-Nagy was its new director and Gropius acted as an advisor. Named the New Bauhaus with the subtitle of American School of Design, the school had thirty-six students enrolled the first semester.

The New Bauhaus 1937–1938

The New Bauhaus in Chicago was short lived, even with a curriculum that kept most of the principles of the Weimar and Dessau Bauhaus. This was due mostly to Moholy-Nagy's decision to carry over the curriculum from the early years of the Bauhaus. In Chicago he was mostly concerned with providing practical experience in materials and surface effects, in three-dimensional space, and volume. Courses in the natural sciences were offered and staffed by faculty from the University of Chicago. The students now had the choice to take one of six different specialized workshops following completion of the preliminary course. The curriculum finally culminated with students obtaining a degree in architecture.

The main intent of the new Bauhaus was to bring students into contact with the new scientific thought of the times. The school presented a curriculum focused on contemporary science and philosophy as means to reintegrate the artist into daily life. Charles Morris, an associate professor at the University of Chicago, believed that the students needed a simplified and purified language in order to talk about artistic values in the same way scientists talk about the world in scientific terms. Art talk should use the language of scientific philosophy rather than the language of art. Influenced by the ideas of Rudolph Carnap and logical positivism, he adopted

Carnap's belief that all cultural phalanxes at any time moved abreast, though often ignorant of their common cultural front.

In Chicago Moholy-Nagy's fear that contemporary education could easily lead to specialization inspired him to develop a curriculum based on the fundamentals of design as connected with the future tasks of the designer. Independence, for him, was only attainable in an atmosphere of intellectual and artistic freedom where the integration of sensorial and intellectual extremes balanced the development of the student's natural gifts. In order to do this, the program needed to retain the student's child-like sincerity of emotion, truth of observation, fantasy, and creativity.

Moholy-Nagy embraced idealist John Dewey's thesis that every human being possesses creative talent. Dewey and Moholy-Nagy's ideas were that working teams of scholars and students were key to developing a sound student-teacher relationship. Dewey supported him by agreeing to serve as a member of the sponsor's committee of the Chicago School of Design.

In Chicago the basic course continued to emphasize experimentation with tools, machines, and materials including wood, metal, rubber, textiles, papers, and plastics, with no copying permitted. Students working experimentally with materials were expected to gain insights into an object's appearance, structure, texture, and surface treatment. Step by step, each student was expected, through discovering the possibilities of materials, to control the creative process and become more conscious volume and space.

In addition to the basic workshop, the new Bauhaus continued the curriculum in analytical and geometrical drawing, lettering, modeling, and photography. Classes were offered in sound experiments and the building of musical instruments to stimulate the students' auditory senses. The science curriculum included courses in physics, chemistry, biology, physiology, and mathematics. Guest lectures on the history of art, science, philosophy, and psychology were also offered in order to keep students up on contemporary movements in these areas.

Moholy-Nagy believed that the curriculum should not be aimed at developing free artists, in part because there were already too many of them who could not make a living. He felt the Bauhaus should not add to their number but could, as a result of study, cause some students to eventually develop into free artists. First, however, he thought they should learn to see themselves as designers and craftsmen who could make a living at furnishing the community with new and useful ideas.

The School of Design 1939–1940

Although the new Bauhaus was considered successful in reaching its goals, Moholy-Nagy soon received notice from the president of the Association of Arts and Industries that funds for its support were no longer available and that the school would close at the end of the 1938 summer session. In January of 1939, Moholy-Nagy decided to reopen the institute using his own money and the new School of Design continued to offer instruction but with a more limited staff. The school now operated in a somewhat dilapidated building on East Ontario Street, where the teachers furnished their own equipment. In February of 1939, eighteen full-time and twenty-eight evening students enrolled. Unfortunately, on November 24, 1946 Moholy-Nagy died of leukemia at age 51. His death signaled the end of a line of important leaders in the Bauhaus schools. Fortunately, Gropius remained loyal to the institute and continued as its advisor. Moholy-Nagy, as initiator and director of the Institute of Design, was by then considered indispensable, so it was now up to Gropius, his artistic associate, to continue in the Bauhaus.

Serge Chermayeff, who in 1946 succeeded Moholy-Nagy as director, was born in southern Russia and previously worked as chair of the Department of Design at Brooklyn College. Although struggling with controversies over his administration, Chermayeff continued to support the standards that guided the institute since its beginning. He felt the ultimate purpose of all design work was to serve the social totality in a constructive manner. Under his leadership the term visual design was replaced by the term visual communication, which sought to emphasize the social function of architecture as housing for people ranging from single dwellings to communal structures. Under Chermayeff's leadership, enrollments began to decline, yet the school continued on North Dearborn Street and retained its curricular independence. Chermayeff resigned in 1951 and later moved to Massachusetts Institute of Technology, finally assuming a chair at Harvard University.

In 1951 Crombie Taylor assumed the leadership of the institute. The curriculum, developed by Moholy-Nagy and tightened by Chermayeff, aimed mostly at architecture and continued to provide a sound foundation. Taylor consolidated the program and in 1955 introduced Art Education as a special course. The school continued to adhere to the principle that everyone is creative, that education can bring out that creativeness, that creative exercises are the best way to educate creative abilities, and that students should seek solutions through experience. Students were to do this through learning the specific techniques in typography, graphic reproduction, life drawing, film, package design, advertising display, etc. In that atmosphere the school grew, becoming a popular mid-western meeting place for designers, artists, and creative people from throughout the world.

In 1955 Jay Doblin replaced Taylor as director, mainly at the insistence of the Illinois Institute of Technology (IIT) through its influence as legal supervisor of the Institute of Design. As a result, the faculty drafted a manifesto complaining that IIT was leading the Bauhaus down the wrong path. Several faculty members then resigned from the Institute of Design, their departure weakening the Moholy-Nagy faction on the staff.

On April 30, 1956, S.R. Crown Hall, designed by Mies, was dedicated and IIT announced there would be three new departments organized in the new facility. They included the Department of Architecture, the Department of City and Regional Planning, and the Institute of Design, all of which were based on the ideas and the personnel in the Chicago Bauhaus. The major emphasis was placed on the Department of Architecture headed by Mies. In the ensuing decade the School of Design saw a distinct decline in the Bauhaus's influence, which was finally phased out with Mies's retirement in 1959.

SUMMARY

What the arts and crafts movement, the Owatonna project, the WPA project, and the Bauhaus shared in common was an international climate fermenting social change and the belief that the arts could be used as a mechanism for individual and community growth. Although they all somewhat differed in how the arts could be used to improve individual and community life, they all remained committed to the aesthetic and ethical values of art as a form of human expression.

The common political climate of the times included both the desire to relieve the condition of the industrial worker trapped in the exploitation of the late nineteenth-century industrial revolution and the disenchantment of many common people with nationalistic wars that seemed to accomplish nothing but destitution. After the WWI armistice neither the victors nor the vanquished found their destitution less severe. After four years of slaughter and destruction, both sides faced a material destitution and impoverishment severe enough to shake public confidence in the governments that controlled them. It became immediately apparent that government efforts to rectify borders and conquer new ports created a disproportion between ends and means that bordered on madness.

That period also reflected the cynicism of people torn between an old belief in the power of reason, discredited but arrogant, finding solace only in dreams that separated private from public life, the unconscious from the conscious and the dream from logic. Beauty and art were, as a result, considered as the conquest of logic and therefore needed to be destroyed. This led to three important influences in this period: (1) Freud's 1856–1939 contribution to the field of psychoanalysis, (2) Karl Marx's 1818–1833 dialectical materialism and communism, and (3) the influence of Wittgenstein (1889–1951) and Rudolph Carnap (1891) in the development of logical positivism.

These influences led to what is commonly referred to as the New Science and the emergence of new political philosophies of Hegel, Schopenhauer, and Nietzche. In art these events spawned cubist art, which introduced new concepts of space and time, the futurists glorifying the dynamism of the machine, the surrealist violation of custom and convention, and the abstract artists' interest in geometric form as being pure and abstract. These times also created what is commonly referred to as the new spirit in art, which satisfies aesthetic vision through the will to preserve and communicate to others. The artist most closely associated with the spirit movement in art was Wassily Kandinsky, (1866–1944).

The common values of the artists of that period were to welcome changes in the political and artistic universe and bring them closer together in the interest of serving the public good. It was this environment that encouraged Morris to build a worker-centered program in the crafts industry, the Owatonna Project to build a K–12 school arts program to serve community needs, the WPA project to employ artists to serve a public good, and the Bauhaus to view the arts as effectively changing the aesthetic values of citizens and communities alike.

More importantly, all these projects in one way or another continued to support the aesthetic values of the artist, the arts community, and the arts culture. While still attempting to use these values to change the conditions of the work place, the school, and the community, they never sought to use the arts as means to achieving commercial or political ends inconsistent with the expressive values of the art object or its makers. These artistic values became the ends rather than the means by which the arts could demonstrate their value in serving the public interest.

While the social and economic conditions today have radically changed from the industrialized economies of the late eighteenth and early nineteenth centuries, the activities supported in these projects remain socially and artistically viable as they did in those early times. The need for better designed products, more humanely provisioned housing and more sustainable community planning, expanded and greatly improved programs in arts education, and opportunities for the arts to enrich the human condition are all needed as much today as they were a century ago. Though times have changed, the aesthetic values they promoted remain as the instrument of—rather than object for—social and political change.

Questions

From the policy-making viewpoint, especially at the school or district level, these programs include the basic content of much of today's art curriculum, including the crafts, community art, environmental art, taste and style, aesthetics, design, applied arts, creativity, art appreciation, and a varied materials approach to creativity. Because so many of these activities are included in today's school art programs they can be used to form the goals and constraints used to guide the policy-making process and the construction of policy alternatives. As goals the policy makers should, however, address the following questions:

- Are there too many program goals where the curriculum lacks focus and are they too varied to effectively implement?
- Is there a broad enough range of goals to account for individual differences and individual choices or does one single issue dominate the program?
- Are all the goals relevant to the achievement of the program's objectives?
- Do the goals essentially support wisdom thinking rather than struggles to gain power over things?
- Do the goals support the teaching of visual content in ways that produce individual competence and understanding?

The answers to the foregoing questions are necessary for the school art curriculum to have sufficient focus, especially with regard to the central purposes of the art program. Because of time and materials limitations, the art teacher cannot teach everything that is teachable and must provide sufficient time on the central purpose of the art program, perhaps at times neglecting breadth in order to achieve depth in the pursuit of the most fundamental principles of art in the education of the student.

Chapter 4 will focus on what I am calling the nationalization of art education period in which the federal government began to view US school achievement as necessary for the defense of the nation during the time of the so-called cold war. The National Defense Education Act made clear to the nation that schooling was not simply a state concern but a national priority.

REFERENCES

Chipp, H. B. 1968. *Theories of Modern Art.* Berkeley: University of California Press.
Davis, S. 1973 in *Art for the Millions*, ed. O'Connor, F.W. Greenwich: New York Graphic Society. 249–250.
DeNoon, C. 1987. *Posters of the WPA.* Los Angeles: The Wheatley Press.

Haggerty, M.W. 1935. Art As a Way of Life. In *The Owatonna Art Education Project,* Vol. 1–9. Minneapolis: University of Minnesota Press. 5–43.

Hecksher, A. 1963. *The Arts and National Government: A Report to the President.* Washington DC: The US Government Printing Office.

Kandinski, W. 1979. *Point and Line to Plane.* New York: Dover Publications.

Kelvin, N. 1996. "The Morris Who Reads Us." *William Morris,* ed. Parry, L. London: Phillip Wilson Publishers.

Klee, P. 1973. *Paul Klee Notebooks, Vol. 2.: The Nature of Nature.* New York: George Witionborn Inc.

Morris, W.; and Kelvin, N., ed. (1999). *William Morris on art and socialism.* Kelvin, N. (Ed.) Toronto: Dover.

McKinzie, R.D. 1975. *The New Deal for Artists.* Princeton: Princeton University Press.

Parry, L., ed. 1996. *William Morris.* London: Philip Wilson Publisher.

Wingler, H. M., ed. 1969. *The Bauhaus.* Cambridge: MIT Press.

Ziegfeld, E.; and Smith, M. E. 1944. "Art for Daily Living" in *The Owatonna Art Education Project,* Vol. 4. Minneapolis: University of Minnesota Press. 1–155.

The Federalization of American Art Education Policy 1960–1997

INTRODUCTION

Chapter 3 identified a number of important social art experiments conducted around the world in the late nineteenth and early twentieth centuries. These included the arts and crafts movement, the WPA project, the Owatonna Art Education Project, and the German and American Bauhaus. All these efforts profoundly affected American art and industrial arts education programs during the first half of the twentieth century. The influence of these projects firmly established the notion that art was an important component of community life and that its aesthetic impact radically affected both the methods used in art teaching and the content to be studied in the art curriculum.

Prior to 1960, it can generally be noted that the content of art education was largely built upon the Bauhaus creative ideals of materials and process exploration, the arts and crafts movement ideal of the union of the fine and applied arts, the WPA's emphasis on the artist as cultural agent, and the Owatonna ideal of art as a way of life. Although the literature in the first half of the twentieth century reported a number of important empirical research studies in art teaching, including the work of Alschuler and Hattwick (1947), Burt (1921), Goodenough (1928), Harmes (1941), Hevner (1935), Kerschensteiner (1905), Krauss (1930), Lowenfeld (1947), and Rouma (1913). Reported previously in *Mind in Art* (Dorn 1999), prior to 1950 art education had no national professional journals on art teaching and research. only a limited number of texts on how to teach art. There was no national art teachers' organization and art teaching goals and methods were gleaned from only four or five popular art education texts or from the publications of the art materials manufacturers. Art programs of the day, at least in America's big cities, largely reflected the influence of a number of powerful art supervisors in cities like New York, Baltimore, Philadelphia, Boston, Chicago, Minneapolis, Kansas City, Dallas, and Pittsburgh.

THE POST-WAR YEARS

With the end of World War II, the creation of the new United Nations, and the search for world peace, it could be truthfully said that the art world was at peace. The G.I.s who had left the farm and saw the Parisian museums by now were either in art school, cleaning up their lofts in SoHo, teaching in K–12 schools (George Segal), or lecturing in the university. In the American schools that offered art, art teachers were helping kids to creatively integrate their personalities and, in general, to hang loose. Slogans used during that period were "let the child draw," "spontaneity is the key," and "don't let the kids copy or color in the ditto sheets." American education was in its progressive education stage, and experimentation with materials and techniques was the main focus of the art curriculum. That all changed in the late 1950s, however, with the launching of Sputnik I, when the education establishment was heavily criticized for its failure to produce scientists and technologists in either the quantity or the quality to match the Soviet accomplishments.

GOVERNMENT AND THE ARTS

By the time the 1960s came around, the world of education and art were radically different. Education became a matter of national defense in fighting a cold war. Congress, in order to help science and math education in the schools, established a National Science Foundation, enacted the National Defense Education Act, and created President Kennedy's School Science Advisory Committee.

The sum total of these changes was felt in schools mostly through the "new" math and "new" science programs.

The art and education scene in the nation's capitol at that time was also in flux. Kennedy hired August Hecksher as a special art consultant from March 1962 to May of 1963 to work on what Kennedy believed was a growing imbalance in the efforts expended by schools in the teaching of the sciences and the arts. Hecksher was asked to define what ought to be the federal posture in the arts. The United States Office of Education (USOE) was at the same time undergoing changes in order to offer more governmental support for education in the arts and humanities. Arne Randall, Ralph Beelke, and Mayo Bryce, all USOE art advisors, assisted in that effort. The change was to include the kind of across-the-board assistance given to modern languages, mathematics, and science (Hoffa, 1970).

The Players

President Kennedy appointed Frank Keppel, former dean of the Graduate School of Education at Harvard, who in turn named Kathryn Bloom as special advisor in the arts and humanities. By the end of 1965, President Johnson and Congress had created the National Endowment for the Arts and the Humanities and also authorized the construction of the Kennedy Center for the Performing Arts. Roger Stevens, a former arts advisor to President Kennedy, became director of the Kennedy Center.

In my view, the policy shifts in art education in the period from 1962 to 1997 were largely due to the persistent efforts of three progressively minded and politically astute women, including Kathryn Bloom, appointed by Keppel to also head USOE's Arts and Humanities Branch; Nancy Hanks, chair of the National Endowment for the Arts; and Leilani Lattin Duke, who directed the J. Paul Getty Center for Art Education in the 1980s and 1990s. Bloom undoubtedly carried the torch for art as general studies from her early years working at Owatonna (Chapter 3) and from her former league years at the Toledo Museum. Hanks earned her political stripes from working as an assistant to New York governor Nelson Rockefeller from the liberal wing of the Republican party, and Leilani Lattin Duke certainly learned from the ideas and policy decisions of Nancy Hanks when she worked for the National Endowment for the Arts. All three women influenced the art education policy shifts of the period, Kathryn through her efforts at USOE to fund experimental cognitive research and her interdisciplinary education experiments through the JDR III fund; Nancy Hanks through moving the endowment from being an honorific salute to President Kennedy to making art both political and necessary in the public interest; and Leilani Lattin Duke through her fifteen or so years with the Getty and its generous funding of discipline-based art education (DBAE) theory.

The early 1960s was an important time of change in the politics of both American art and education. Pablo Casals played in the White House; Robert Frost read at the Kennedy inauguration ceremony. The Mona Lisa was on display at the National Gallery of Art and was the nation's first blockbuster museum exhibition. The young Kennedys, everyone noted, attended arts events all over the city. In addition, the Heckscher report, *The Arts and the National Government,* was in the works and the new arts and humanities program (then called cultural affairs) was designed to make sure the arts were represented in the world of public policy.

THE EDUCATION COMMUNITY

Art education as a cognate field was not very evident in the 1950s when the G.I.s returned to pursue careers in art teaching in secondary schools and in college art education departments. The college art programs during the WWII years were largely run by women who were former public-school art teachers and in the 1950s were replaced by the new male Ph.D.s and Ed.D.s, coming at a time when doctorates first became the terminal degree for art education teaching at the university. Most of the doctorates being hired had been trained in empirical research long associated with the training of Ph.D.s in education. These graduates also found places for themselves in the so-called research universities, where art education faculty were tenured and promoted not on their artwork but on their output of published research, scholarly papers, and books.

The emergence of the new arts and humanities programs located in USOE's research division also came at the same time as the requirement that the new art education doctorates "publish or perish," which provided a policy window for art education to shift its emphasis from art making to the pursuit and eventual publishing of cognitive studies in student art behavior. In 1962 there were really only three mainstream universities whose art education departments had established cutting-edge doctoral programs. These included New York University (NYU), whose program was headed by Dr. Howard Conant; Pennsylvania State University, headed by Dr. Edward Mattil; and Ohio State University (OSU), headed by Manuel Barkan. By the time the arts and humanities branch opened its program, NYU and OSU both offered doctorates in art education and art and Pennsylvania State had a research-oriented doctorate built on Lowenfeld's interest in cognitive development. Meanwhile, OSU's Manny Barkan was busy reading about Jerome Bruner and sharing ideas with OSU philosopher Morris Weitz.

THE UNITED STATES
OFFICE OF EDUCATION

The Arts and Humanities Program (AHP) under Bloom essentially supported two different initiatives, one called the AHP projects and the other the research conferences. A total of 68 AHP Requests for Proposals (RFPs) were funded. Sixteen were considered research conferences and fifty-two were research projects. Thirty-five, more than half of the fifty-two research studies, focused on the cognitive research in art in schools and the remainder focused on a number of related research projects on assessment, curriculum, and so-called disciplinary studies and/or general education. The disciplinary studies were directed toward establishing the role of the aesthetician, the artist, the critic, and the historian as teachers of art education. Seven studies were funded in aesthetics and seven more in art history, art appreciation, and/or museum studies, accounting for fifty-two of the sixty-eight proposals funded. (See Appendix A.)

The AHP Projects

As already noted, thirty-eight of these projects focused on research studies associated with the cognitive-constructivist view of learning theory and fourteen more with the social cognitive view of learning. The cognitive-constructivist view is associated with the ideas of Bartlett (1932) and Piaget (1970) that conclude the key understanding underlying the mnemonic process involving reconstructing cohesive accounts from underlying schemas and incoming contextual information. The social cognitive view is, on the other hand, associated with the ideas of Bandura (Bandura and Kupers 1964), which focus on the separate but interdependent contributions of personal behavioral and environmental influence. The cognitive-constructivist theory argues that learning is not determined by merely personal (child-centered) processes such as cognition or affect, but is assumed to be influenced by environmental and behavioral events mostly associated with Lockian thought that we discover ourselves only through what we observe about the world in which we live.

AHP Cognitive-Constructivist View

This view is mostly associated with the views of Swiss epistemologist Piaget (1926–1952) who believed that children formed schemas though *assimilation* and *accommodation*. Assimilation refers to children absorbing information, such as sensory qualities, and accommodating them to changes in existing schemas. The schemas are assumed to be flexible and undergo qualitative improvements, but largely reflect the view that the perception of a given object is already present to the mind as a mental set that changes only when the schema or mental set does not accommodate the object seen. In art, this suggests the notion of schema and correction (Lowenfeld 1947), which makes art a largely cognitive or mental function altered through improved mental cognition.

Both Bartlett and Piaget viewed mental schemas as the basis for human learning and recall, and both ascribed a major role to logic and conceptual coherence in the formation of schemas. Constructivists view cognitive functioning as assuming learners play an active personal role during learning and recall and that a human motive is to construct meaning from experience in order to regain cognitive *equilibrium.*

According to Piaget, children's thinking does not become fully *logical* until the children can integrate their perceptions of themselves and the world with those of other people. At the highest level (operational) of self-development, youth are now aware of their own thoughts and can treat them as *hypotheses* to be *tested.* In the process, learners employ strategies in order to attain goals such as processing information as well as managing time, motivations, and emotions. As a result, they become aware of how and when to use procedural and focal or declarative knowledge. What the theory assumes is art making or attending to art is the exercise of mostly cognitive strategies based on the proper use of information and the conscious construction of perception of representational forms.

Constructivists commonly employ discovery-learning procedures, such as viewing the bending of a stick when it is partially submerged in water, and social conflict, such as confronting students with different viewpoints or cognitive levels expected to produce cognitive conflict. Today discovery learning is viewed as reflecting individuality in perception to accommodate mediating constructs with cooperative learning, personal theories, identities, and adaptive actions.

Social Cognitive View

Bandura (1971) argues that people are motivated by the consequences that they expect to receive for behaving, rather than the actual rewards themselves (Zimmerman and Schunk 2003). Bandura believed that outcomes and self-efficacy expectations provide learners with representatives of future consequences and help learners to set goals for themselves. Social cognitive theorists believe that social processes provide a form of modeling or verbal persuasion and various self-regulation processes in addition to environmental factors. Coping modes can be used to overcome adversity, and triumph can increase the students' desire to master a particular activity for themselves.

Social cognitive researchers describe self-regulated learning according to four levels: an *observation* level to learn a model's strategy, an *emulative* level when the learner approximates the model's skill, a *self-control* level when students can perform the skill, and a *self regulation* level when they can adapt their skills as conditions change. Except for limited demonstrations of a skill when needed—i.e., how to mound a ball of clay on a potters wheel—art teachers do seek to inspire student artistic performance by having students model the behavior of other students or adult artists in expressive forming.

The notion that the empirical research findings on learning and cognition alone will necessarily advance the attainment of educational goals, most especially when used to determine the goals of instruction, is indeed questionable. As already noted, the cognitive-constructivist view assumes that art learners, like scientists, establish and test verifiable hypotheses. More appropriately, the social cognitive view assumes we teach art by modeling artistic behaviors that students can imitate.

There are, of course, other cognitive theories including the ideas of Skinner, who believed in what is called *operant behavior,* where behavior depends on the environmental consequences it produces, i.e., a behavior becomes more likely to occur through positive reinforcement (Pavlov's dogs). Also, there is a *phenomenological* view where the individual's personal experience matters; first-hand, subjective accounts are assumed valid through rigorous analysis and careful description and are used for the purpose of identifying the qualitatively different ways in which different people experience, conceptualize, perceive, and understand various kinds of phenomena. Finally, there is also the *information processing* view that assumes that all information is stored in long-term memory with a pattern and an image in that pattern is a network. Each knot in the network, called a mode of information, is linked to several other modes. Without these links, theoretically, there would be no way to retrieve information in long-term memory.

Although some of these theories show a closer connection than others to what we believe occurs in art learning, these cognitive models of behavior supported by research are only *models* of how we *think* the brain functions. No one model is necessary and sufficient in determining the goals of the art program. The goals of art education are essentially what we as artists and teachers value about art and education in art and not something we can claim as a scientific fact.

As to the impact of the AHP projects on the art teaching profession, there is no quantitative way we can know their effect other than to note a major increase in the number of reports published with empirical research in the NAEA's research journal, *Studies in Art Education* and in the number of project reports printed. Due to a sharp decline in the number of empirical studies published since the 1960s and the subsequent increase in the publications of qualitative research on social issues, including issues related to feminism and multiculturalism, it is my view that it was more the social cognitive view which sustained and grew in the art education literature of that period.

The USOE Conferences

USOE sponsored seventeen conferences on art education, beginning with the NYU conference in October 1964, and ending with the Aesthetic Education Conference in 1967. Appendix B provides the title of each of the conferences, its date, the name of the conference coordinator, and the location. Unless otherwise noted, each was supported by the AHP.

Harlan ("Rip") Hoffa has analyzed the content and impact of the conferences in a December 1970 report, entitled *An Analysis of Recent Research Conferences in Art Education* (1970). Hoffa's report, written in his usual irreverent style, provides a very thorough review of the conferences, largely from his own perspective as a former AHP staffer. He viewed the first conference, NYU's Seminar on Elementary and Secondary School Education in the Arts, and the 1966 Next to the Last Conference, A Seminar on the Role of the Arts in Meeting the Social and Educational Needs of the Disadvantaged in Gaithersburg, Maryland, as representing the best models for describing the most important shift in the conference discussions of art education policy. This is, in all probability, due to the fact that the NYU conference began the effort to reform art education through the introduction of various arts disciplines and the Gaithersburg conference focused on the social problems of serving the disadvantaged through art.

NYU Seminar

The NYU conference's hidden agenda was, as Hoffa notes, to consider the role of the artist in art education. Those who gave or responded to papers included New York artists Robert Motherwell, Helen Frankenthaler, and George Segal; college professors of art and art education; architects; art supervisors; art critics including Harold Rosenberg; filmmakers; Roger Stephens (chair and special assistant to the president); and art educators Howard Conant, Ed Mattil, and Fred Logan.

The selection of the participants representing various positions in the art world, government, and academia suggested in advance that the conference dialogue would include a broad range of concerns including the art object, the artist, K–12 schooling, art teacher education, and public policy in the arts. The art educators in attendance were well aware of Jerome Bruner's notion that children could learn anything at any age and Manuel Barkan's notion of art representing the art world of work through the art critic, art historian, and aesthetician (1962). Most of those present were also aware of the NEA 1963 M-3 Study of Art in the Schools, which reported that fewer than fifty percent of the nation's high schools offered art and, in those that did, fewer than fourteen percent of the students in these schools were enrolled in art. What every outsider agreed on was that art education as currently taught was in terrible shape and that art teachers as presently trained were unable to present the world of art to their students accurately or adequately.

The fact that the President's School Science Advisory Committee, who had also been the original advocates of the "new" math and "new" science program in schools, were sponsors of the conference also suggested that a disciplinary and conceptually based program of art would be considered the way to go in art education. Jerrold Zacharias and Sister Jacqueline from that committee essentially controlled the conference.

Hoffa's take on the NYU conference was that everyone arrived with the double intention of pointing out what was wrong with art education, and including the notions "that art was good, and art education was bad; that art educators were the villains; and that artists (who were more actively employed and more sensitively involved in the goodness of art) should take over all of the art instruction in all of the schools (1970, 59).

Hoffa believed that everyone not only arrived with the intention of pointing out what was wrong with art education, but also with the idea that in order to break down the distinction between art and art as an academic subject, art teachers should be artists and students should be directly in touch with genuine artists. Robert Motherwell, a New York abstract expressionist artist, noted:

> In art education, the blind are leading the blind, from the top down. Most art teachers know nothing about modern art. Most art teachers are really quite illiterate. The subject matter is modern art – in any creative epoch!
>
> There is a very deep alienation of art educators, including university art teachers from the principal works of art of modern times. I think there's a real alienation from such artists as Picasso, Matisse, and Brancusi.
>
> Most art teachers are really miserable people because they do not feel what's magical and moving and alive about art. When I hear about what art teachers don't know, and hear about the inadequacies of art education, all the horror of living on the fringe of American culture comes back to me.
>
> From the standpoint of making a picture or responding to it, most of what's talked about is so generalized that it is meaningless and has very little to do with magic of a picture or a sculpture (Conant 1965, 85).

Those in attendance agreed that artists, art scholars, and leaders from other disciplines should serve as teachers, consultants, innovators of curriculum guides, and institute and workshop leaders. The recommendations of the conference were first to bring art students into a continuing relationship with actively producing artists, and second, to have regular and direct confrontations between students and bona fide works of art.

Harold Rosenberg, New York art critic, summed up his view of the need for a new disciplinary approach by noting:

> Nearly everybody in this country, for the last thirty years, has been filled with the notion that you start with activity, that you learn by *doing*. The first idea that occurred was, let's get some stuff and start doing something! To my mind the important thing that's missing is familiarity with certain kinds of experience. If you read, let's say, *Remembrance of Things Past*, you find that Proust, as a young child, found

himself surrounded by theatre, by poetry, by painting. It was just absolutely something that he took for granted as a part of daily life. Now what would prevent kids, I'm talking now about six-year-olds, from having these kinds of experiences?

The art teacher should have a very good knowledge of modern art, very contemporary art, and have a sense, first of all, which is a thing I think we all missed in school, that art is being created *now* by people on *your* block or people in *your* neighborhood or at least in *your* country. One thing I thought to be true when I was a kid, was that poetry was written in the nineteenth century, by Englishmen with beards, and that painting was done by artists such as Rembrandt. The big thing in America today is that artists are able to say "well here I am, and art is here" (Conant 1965, 62).

The conference rhetoric against art education and the proclaimed need to replace art educators in schools with artists, critics, and aestheticians prompted Edward Mattil, then-chair of art education at Pennsylvania State University, to defend the field and the child-centered movement by noting:

I shudder when people think they know the answers to what art is and how art should be taught. I would really be petrified if someone really defined art education and started prescribing precisely what can and should be done. I sincerely believe that this is a diverse field, and what is art to you may not be art to me, and what is art in Africa certainly may not be art in Australia, or in the Antarctic, or in the Arctic. I think we must allow people the privilege of making their own interpretations of what art is to them and to express themselves through art as they see fit. I am not an aesthetician, and I am not a therapist; but I am distressed when I hear people get panicked and say, "Let's rid the schools of art as therapy." I would like to know precisely what people mean by "art as therapy." I was amazed to find people making presentations as though they had discovered something new in art education. Thirty or forty years ago in art education we were doing exactly the same thing with these and different materials and I would venture a guess that, if I could take you into Mrs. Churchill's classes, or Sister Corita's, that all the things that people have been talking about in this seminar were made by others a long time ago in art education. I'm amazed to find people who have so little knowledge about what art education really is in the schools, and what efforts have been made. I'm greatly distressed by dismissing people like Lowenfeld with the rash statement that he was a therapist. If you have ever read his statement about the meaning of aesthetic criteria, you would know it's one of the most profound statements in art education that has ever been written. He was a man who was deeply involved in the aesthetics of art, who was a painter himself, and was an accomplished teacher (Conant 1965, 65).

The true hidden agenda of the conference, in Hoffa's view, was to find out how artists, art scholars, and leaders in other disciplines could serve art education as teachers, consultants, innovators of curriculum, institute guides, and workshop leaders (Hoffa 1970). The agenda was to also break down the distinction between art as an academic subject and art as practiced by artists and to promote the idea that the teacher should be an artist, that children should learn what is practiced by artists, and that art teachers should be remade in the image of artists. In other words, the main thing wrong was the art educators.

Hoffa's view of the agenda, having been both a junior-high art teacher and college art educator, was that the art educators present were engaged in a cat fight with all the other conferees and deeply resented the tone of the meeting that was anti–art education, most especially because of the impression that art currently taught in the schools was more about art therapy than about art.

In retrospect, the NYU seminar signaled to art educators that the art world had declared the child-centered approach to art education a failure and also that the art world was the enemy of art education. It may have, in effect, also helped turn the art education community itself away from the influences of art proper and reject the image of the artist as genius and a proper role model for the education of students in art.

For the art education profession, the Penn State Seminar in Art Education for Research and Curriculum Development in 1965 was perhaps the most meaningful of all the conferences, in part because it was under the control of the art educators themselves. The conference was initially planned by Edward Mattil and Kenneth Beittel of Penn State and later included art educators David Ecker, Jerome Hausman, Robert Burkhart, and Manuel Barkan.

The intentions of the Penn State seminar were to stimulate art education research and curriculum development, identify broad areas of concern in art education, engage the input of professionals outside the field of art education, and design a functional structure which could meet the objectives of the seminar. This included approaching five major problem areas, including (1) the philosophical, (2) the sociological, (3) the content question, (4) teaching and learning, and (5) curriculum. The general objectives of the seminar were:

1. To bring representatives from related disciplines together with art educators to work toward a solution to some basic problems in art education
2. To focus attention on five major problem areas in art education
3. To establish a base of knowledge from which to develop research and curriculum proposals
4. To identify and define specific problem areas which may be effectively studied through research or affected by curriculum change
5. To develop concerted action proposals of research and curriculum development from an interdisciplinary base of knowledge
6. To reformulate basic knowledge in art education
7. To evaluate current basic knowledge in art education
8. To reconsider the goals of art education
9. To identify criteria for determining the content of the art education curricula (Mattil 1966, 2)

The program ran over a ten-day period where up to fifty-eight college art educators listened to prepared papers by David Ecker, Joshua Taylor, Allan Kaprow, Jerome Hausman, Melvin Tumin,

June McFee, Dale Harris, Kenneth Beittel, Elliot Eisner, Manuel Barkan, Nathaniel Champlin, Robert Lathrop, and Arthur Foshay, and heard research proposals from Ralph Beelke, Lambert Brittain, Herbert Burgart, Robert Burkhart, Laura Chapman, Howard Conant, Edmund Feldman, Guy Hubbard, Ivan Johnson, Vincent Lanier, Kenneth Lansing, John Michael, Mary Rouse, Ronald Silverman, Ralph Smith, William Steward, David Templeton, Stanley Wold, and Leon Frankston.

Although this group of presenters and researchers represented only a tiny portion of the number of art educators teaching in the field, nearly everybody who was somebody of importance in art education was there. It can be added that nearly all of the art educators present later became authors of major texts or research studies in art education. As to the question of whether this occurred because those who selected the participants were aware of their potential as authors or whether the conference itself affected their publication output will remain unanswered.

Because the outsiders invited to speak were selected by the art educators, there was certainly less rancor regarding the failures of art educators to properly educate students. The agenda, like the NYU conference agenda, hoped to initiate change in the art education practices of the time to include reformulating basic knowledge, evaluating current knowledge, reconsidering the goals of art education, and revising the basis for determining art education content.

In the course of the conference, June McFee argued for the functions of art and the role of art in culture and society. Elliot Eisner laid out his assumptions about human learning as a basis for deciding the ends of art education, and Manuel Barkan introduced the need for art education to include studies of the art historian, the aesthetician, and the critic, all of whom were key figures in the changes in art education policies during the last half of the twentieth century.

Hoffa's overall evaluation of the conferences was, as expected, somewhat bleak. He often referred to them as "revival meetings" or "meetings of the clan," which indeed reflected his agencies' inside point of view that too few research efforts occurred as a result of the conferences, which he viewed as producing less-than-startling results in promoting research in art education. He also noted that the AHP staff expected a flood of research proposals following the conferences but that no such flood occurred, adding that the federal trough went dry when the maximum payoff might have been expected. He also wondered whether the AHP staff was, at the time, overwhelmingly committed to research as a panacea for all art education ills or it had an unvarnished faith in research. His summary of the results was listed under the title of "non- consequences."

Hoffa's assessment was perhaps unduly harsh, but he was persuasive in believing that the program was mainly designed to encourage research rather than support philosophical values. What he did not see at the time was the total effect of the program's efforts to promote an interdisciplinary and socially focused curricular agenda. The list of the art education conferences and many of the supporting research proposals that resulted do, however, clearly suggest that art education was still too precious to be left in the hands of art educators, especially those who shared the child-as-artist point of view. All the conferences and most of the research proposals supported the need for the artist, museums, art historians, critics, and aestheticians to begin to open the field to provide a humanistic or general education model for the teaching of art in K–12 schools.

KATHRYN BLOOM

JDR III Fund

Kathryn Bloom, director of the JDR III Fund, may have been moved more by the law of unintended consequences than by her lifelong commitments to general and community education. As director of AHP, she influenced the choice of the projects and conferences funded, and also the agendas pursued during her leadership of the JDR III Fund and the Aesthetic Education Project of the Central Midwestern Regional Educational Laboratory (CEMREL) in St. Louis. Although most of the AHP conferences and projects were reviewed by an outside committee, she personally selected the members of the committee and did not always follow the committee's recommendation. And, as Hoffa notes, "Bloom maintained a firm grip on research funds."

Kathryn Bloom officially joined the JDR III Fund in 1969. According to AHP staffer Jack Morrison, the fund was an extension of the mind, body, and spirit of John D. Rockefeller III. Rockefeller created the fund with $500,000 of his own money and convinced Commissioner of Education Harold Howe to allow Kathryn Bloom to commute weekly to New York in order to meet with him to plan the Arts in Education Project. The project began on April 17, 1969, with Bloom as director and Dick Grove, former AHP staff member, as associate director. The office was located on the fifty-sixth floor of 30 Rockefeller Plaza. The first project was Stanley Madeja's Aesthetic Education Program University City Project (Madeja 1992). Forty grants and related forms of support were provided by the JDR III Fund from 1969 to 1979. (See Appendix C.)

Because of the scope of this publication, it is not possible to discuss all these efforts except to note that in general the art policy initiatives Kathryn Bloom supported were framed on her policy ideals, to support public rather than private interests and to advance education in the arts with a view toward providing equity and access for all Americans. In her response to the 1963 NEA M-3 Study of Art in the schools, Bloom could not accept the study findings that only half of American high schools offered art and when they did, less than fourteen percent of the students were enrolled. For Bloom, this was not access and equity but rather art for the privileged few.

Although there were other non-general education projects, such as the grant to the college board, some internships, and one multicultural study grant, all or most of the projects focused on the concept of art as general education rather than art education as the study of art proper. The grant to the University City, Missouri Arts Education Program was the model that she most ardently believed in and, as a result, it was the subject of her first school-based grant.

CEMREL Laboratory

Madeja, as a staff member at CEMREL, believed that Bloom's early efforts in art education and at USOE in the early 1960s were on making and performing in each art form (1992), but the projects and conferences at USOE suggest otherwise. Madeja certainly at the time had an art studio bias, which he argued for over the years he worked with Bloom both at USOE and at CEMREL. By the 1970s, Bloom had clearly bought into Manuel Barkan's bias against the studio, but, as Madeja noted, the schools were not receptive to the idea that the Aesthetic Education Project was actually an integral part of the visual arts (1992, 92). Barkan believed that teaching aesthetics would produce a common curriculum that would embrace all the arts as a general academic discipline. Although Barkan's Aesthetic Education Project was one of the largest single investments made in order to meet the general education needs of all students, the program was never able to produce a consensus among its leaders as to whether it would lead to a single, agreed-upon aesthetic that would unite all of the arts disciplines.

Bloom's support for CEMREL's Arts in General Education Program was, according to Madeja, her second time to support that effort. Madeja personally viewed CEMREL's Aesthetic Education Project as a curriculum development project to be introduced in a school setting for testing and revision. The University City Project that he directed was, as a result, school based, and the goals of the project were focused on ten goals, the last of which were:

> to provide experiences in all the arts for all students at every level in the University City school system
>
> to permeate the general education program with arts concepts in order
>
> to improve the level of arts instruction
>
> to develop instructional units to provide a sequential arts learning
>
> experience for students
>
> to experiment with a behavioral model as a basis for structuring an
>
> art program
>
> to develop generalizable plans which might be used to implement
>
> similar projects in other setting

to involve regular classroom teachers in the process of curriculum

development (Madeja 1992)

According to Madeja, the program faced a multitude of problems, including such issues as the nature of neighborhood schools,
busing, minority concerns, lack of time in the school day, and
growing school dropout rates. In the final report, entitled "All the
Arts for Every Child," the author claimed the project provided a
curriculum design that demonstrated how the arts could be implemented into the liberal arts or general education core of a total
school curriculum.

NANCY HANKS

Nancy Hanks, as chair of the NEA, helped its appropriations
grow exponentially from $8.2 million to over $123.8 million.
Although Hanks herself was strongly committed to the endowment's goal of supporting the artist, she was also very aware of
the political realities of the time. Most credit her with adopting a
political strategy that avoided extremes both in funding and in
programming as well as a commitment to an NEA policy of cultural pluralism. This has been defined as delineation of the arts
capacious enough to allow broadly distributed support for a
diversity of cultural expressions. She was also considered a cultural advocate as opposed to being a cultural zealot; rather than
lecture Congress on its moral obligation to support Western civilization with the taxpayer's money, she would instead remind the
members of the economic benefits the arts brought to their districts.

Although Hanks was not an art educator, she was liberal minded
and, in my view, helped art and art education become considered
as being in the public interest; she made the support of both art
and art education a matter of public policy in which one could
exercise the right of government to interfere with private choice.
Hanks helped art become a part of national politics through advis-

ing members of Congress that NEA grants to individuals and groups supported their constituencies, especially through her efforts to create the NEA Artists in the Schools program, which today is part of the NEA's Arts in Education program and which, in 2002, provided $2,879,400 to state arts agencies in support of art education programs.

Hanks introduced the NEA Artists in the Schools program in 1969, supported by mostly USOE transfer money. The program was pilot tested through a contract with CEMREL and, while not personally guided by Hanks, clearly had her stamp on its structure and function. She insisted, for example, that in the pilot program the artist was not to teach, but was to be given a stipend and an open studio within a school primarily to continue his or her artwork if need be, without interruption from the students. The most feared event was that the artist might become engaged with teaching the students and, as a result, neglect his or her own artwork.

The program, when initiated in the schools, became a lightning rod for art education criticism. Laura Chapman claims it was part of an effort to "de-school" society when at the same time arts teachers were being eliminated in schools (1992, 125). Ralph Smith viewed the program like Chapman and referred to the artists in the schools as temporary schoolmasters, a process he noted as contributing to the politicalization of cultural policy and generating a pervasive welfare state mentality (1992, 138).

In spite of the criticism, the Artists in the Schools program, largely administered today by the state and local arts agencies, remains a valued part of the NEA's Art in Education Project, which attempts to connect community arts organizations' offerings with school arts programs.

Some have argued that Nancy Hanks's political policies may have proven to be more help than she bargained for, especially from Congress, which helped erode at least some of the early arts-centered policies of the NEA. Also, her efforts contributed to the decision to separate museum support from the NEA and to provide increased funding for the states' arts agencies (the little NEAs) and to local arts agencies. But by the end of her administration, local governments and local arts agencies generated more than $600 million a year and the state arts agencies, some $214 million a year.

146

The third key person advocating revision of art education was Leilani Lattin Duke, director of the J. Paul Getty Center for Art Education and the person most intimately associated with the so-called discipline-based art education (DBAE).

Manuel Barkan

DBAE supported a shift from an emphasis on the creative performance of K–12 students as practiced in the 1950s and 1960s to more cognitive forms of knowing *about* art. This emphasis began when Manuel Barkan predicted that a renewed energy would become apparent in the creative development of teaching materials and courses in art history and criticism (1962). Barkan's view was developed in the form of a carefully constructed position, using Jerome Bruner's arguments on the primacy of the discipline as a basis for new curricular conception. Barkan's "prophecy" was the first radically new curricular conception of the field since the 1940s. Unlike Lowenfeld, he proposed "that artistic activity is anywhere the same, whether at the frontier of art or in the third-grade classroom." His 1962 prediction about the growth of courses in art history and art criticism challenged the then-popular notions of creativity and the classroom approach that used a variety of art media. Art education for the first time was presented with the challenge of accepting the notion that the school child, when learning art, is fundamentally only one of many artworkers. Barkan's stress on art education's new cognitive mode gained the attention of his contemporaries throughout the field (Dorn 1999).

In the 1980s the literature in the art education field and the published policies of the arts agencies, schools, and cultural organizations in which art educators function suggested the profession adopt newer curriculum goals. The NEA, for example, in *Toward Civilization*, argued that art is for *all* students and must convey to students the essence of our civilization, the civilizations that have contributed to ours, and even more distant civilizations that enrich global civilization as a whole. Moreover, it claimed that we must give students the tools for creating, communicating and understanding others' communications, and making informed and critical choices. It further said that we must do all of this through *basic* art education by qualified teachers. Basic art education in the field can be interpreted as meaning that art study is valuable as a discipline in itself or that it contributes to the students' general education through energizing experience, enlarging awareness, and contributing understanding.

This new disciplinary approach was aided through the millions of dollars annually spent in the 1980s and 1990s by the J. Paul Getty Trust to advance its DBAE program, which over the years probably spent more than $100 million in school districts and in college and university art education programs throughout the nation. Although the amount of money spent by the Getty Trust did not come close to the amounts that the endowment provided, it was historically the largest contributor to the art education field and as a result has wielded a powerful influence in the field of art education up to today. Although corporate funding is not new (it occurred in the Owatonna project of the 1930s and the JDR III Fund "Art for Every Child" project of the 1960s), the Getty Trust had a greater influence on art education than any previous public or private agency.

Although the Getty Trust was prudent in its publications and did not formally endorse any political goals, it most certainly published, both in print and audiovisual form, the statements of those whose political agendas were consistent with its beliefs about how to influence the conduct of art education at the federal, state, and local levels. Stephen S. Kaagan, as a case in point, was clear in his Getty-published monograph that his study for the trust is about political effectiveness. Kaagan notes:

> This study is about political effectiveness: about making things different, altering social conditions, changing formal policies and actual practice. Its chosen focus is the place of the arts in education. The medium for discussion on political effectiveness is the arts education that takes place almost exclusively in schools. The area in which change is recommended is the composition or configuration of the school curriculum: what students are taught and the way they are taught. A significantly greater place for the arts is sought; "greater place" in this context meaning a

larger allocation of instructional time and energy during the school day directed by teachers and students toward the arts both as subject matter and as a set of skills and capabilities. (1993, i)

Political Agenda

One can also note in Kaagan's remarks about the political agenda that the issues of who gets what, how, and when brought his goals and the Getty Trust's goals parallel to those of the federally based endowment. His recommendations included the following five items:

1. Bring into focus, highlight, and take advantage of the potential of arts education, especially DBAE, to foster students' reasoning and problem-solving abilities.

2. Assume a more aggressive posture with regard to arts education serving students of marked need.

3. Advance arts education, and DBAE in particular, as supportive of attempts to professionalize teaching.

4. Legitimate the arts by advancing efforts to assess student performance and by accounting for progress in expanding the role of the arts.

5. Cause exemplary arts education materials to be developed, taking advantage of state-of-the-art technologies. (1993)

Kaagan politically supported the ideas of both Kathryn Bloom and Leilani Lattin Duke to install the arts as basic education, particularly at the elementary level. Both women knew that art making was so entrenched in the secondary level that there was no hope of initiating change at that level. DBAE, therefore, was designed to educate classroom teachers with no art background in order to offer the elementary school a foothold in art.

The Getty's training institutes were organized around the school principal, with up to ten percent of that school's teachers becoming a school's "leadership team." During training, its members received lectures from specialists in the four disciplines: art, criticism, aesthetics, and art history. They learned to scan and they

149

visited museums. During the second week, they learned art education methodology by visiting classrooms where the DBAE model was already being followed. Each member of the team then selected a lesson from a curriculum such as the Southwestern Regional Educational Laboratory (SWRL), Discover Art, or Art in Action—all of which were commercially available to schools—and teach that lesson to the rest of the team. They also used reproductions from sources such as the National Gallery. During the third week, the group attended planning sessions for implementing the DBAE model in a school. The team then came back the following year for two sessions, on renewal and leadership, after which they returned to their home district and provided in-service training for other teachers.

The pitfalls of using non-art teachers, however, was that in some elementary schools, teachers carefully but incorrectly described the artist' methods. Lining the hallways in some schools were groups of nearly identical artworks by children. In a landscape sponge-painting project, every horizon fell at the same level and each picture contained two trees, one large and one small. In Sarasota, Florida, the school board, in order to save money, temporarily replaced the art teachers with DBAE classroom teachers.

With the help of art education professionals, Duke essentially built the Getty program herself over a fifteen-year period, beginning with the concept that the teaching of art, history, criticism, and aesthetics occurred in good schools. She made the initial case for the program by having the Rand Corporation Fund study schools that incorporated these disciplines and then declared as a result that this was what we ought to do in all American schools (Mclaughlin and Thomas 1984).

The DBAE program clearly had a major impact on the art education literature. As a result, far more publications were made available for teachers to use in teaching art history, criticism, and aesthetics; debates continued between those who favored DBAE and those who did not in our national journals. In the end, however, as Duke claimed, it was a "failed" program in part because it ended in a takeover by the Annenberg Foundation and along with other well-funded outsider programs, in the end "there was silence."

SUMMARY

The foregoing review of what I have called the federalization of art education policy 1960–1997 reviews the early efforts by education scholars to explore the effects of cognition on art teaching and the efforts by government to expand on them at a time when American education became a matter of national defense during the so-called cold war between the Western democracies and the Soviet Union. That particular policy window encouraged the American government to begin to view art education as a policy issue that required interference with popular choice.

As a result, new government-sponsored programs in education and in the arts sought to change the character of art education in the nation's schools from a focus on the development of the individual to the development of students as cognitive thinkers about the arts and their utility in effecting social change. These changes came about through the USOE programs offering funds for cognitive research on learning in art, through conferences on the integration of academic disciplines and general or liberal education, and through private interventions into making the art program into disciplinary study.

Moreover, the nation's art programs began to view the art student as being a participant in an art world made up of artists, aestheticians, art historians and humanists, and artworkers, where the students no longer viewed themselves as artists-creators but rather as consumers of commodified art objects and events. The intended result was to reconstruct a society where the cause of the individual was diminished and individuals were led to sacrifice their individuality, as necessary, in order to be forcefully "freed."

REFERENCES

Alschuler, R.; and Hattwick, L. 1947. *Painting and Personality, A Study of Young Children.* Chicago: University of Chicago Press.

Bandura, A.; and Kupers, C.J. 1964. The Transmission of Patterns of Self-reinforcement through Modeling. *Journal of Abnormal and Social Psychology* 69:1–9.

Bandura, A. 1971. *Social Learning Theory.* New York: General Learning Press.

Bartlett, F.C. 1932. *Remembering.* London: Cambridge University Press.

Barkan, M. 1962. Transition in Art Education: Changing Conceptions of Curriculum and Teaching. *Art Education* 15 (7): 12–18.

Bruner, J.S.; Goodnow, J.J.; and Austin, G.A. 1956. *A Study in Thinking.* New York: Wiley.

Burt, C. 1933. *Mental and Scholastic Tests.* London: P.S. King & Sons.

Chapman, L. 1992. "Art Education As a Political Issue" in *Public Policy and the Aesthetic Interest,* eds., Smith, R.A.; and Berman, R. Urbana: University of Illinois Press.

Conant, H. 1965. *Seminar on Elementary and Secondary School: Education in the Visual Arts.* New York: New York University.

Dorn, C.M. 1999. *Mind in Art: Cognitive Foundations in Art Education.* Mahwah, NJ: Lawrence Erlbaum Associates.

Goodenough, F. L. 1928. *Study in the Psychology of Children's Drawings. Psychological Bulletin* 25: 272–283.

Harmes, E. 1941. Child Art As an Aid in the Diagnosis of Juvenile Neuroses. *American Journal of Orthopsychiatry* 191–200.

Hecksher, A. The Arts and the National Government: A Report to the President. Washington, DC: The US Government Printing Office.

Hevner, K. 1935. Experimental Studies in the Affective Value of Color and Lines. *Journal of Applied Psychology* 19: 385–398.

Hoffa, H. 1970. *An Analysis of Recent Research Conferences in Art Education.* Bloomington: Indiana University Foundation.

Kaagan, S.C. 1993. *Aesthetic Persuasion: Pressing the Cause of Art in American Schools.* Los Angeles: Getty Center for Education in the Arts.

Kerschensteiner. 1905. *The Development of Talent in Drawing.* Munich: Gerber.

Krauss, R. 1930. Graphic Expression: An Experimental Study About the Creation and Interpretation of Lines without Objects. *Beth Z. Angev Psychol* 48: 39.

Lowenfeld, V. 1947. *Creative and Mental Growth.* New York: MacMillan.

Mattill, E. 1966. *A Seminar in Art Education for Research and Curriculum Development.* University Park: The Pennsylvania State University.

Madeja, S., ed. 1992. *Kathryn Bloom Innovation in Arts Education.* DeKalb: Northern Illinois University.

Mclaughlin, M.W.; and Thomas, M. H. 1985. *Art History, Art Criticism, and Art Production.* Vol. 1. Santa Monica, Ca: The Rand Corporation.

Piaget, J. 1970. Piaget's Theory. In *Carmichael's Manual of Child Psychology,* 3rd ed. Vol. 1. ed., Mussen, P.H. New York: Wiley.

Rouma, G. 1913. *The Graphic Language of the Child.* Paris: Mish. Et Thron.

Smith, R.A. 1992. Policy for Arts Education: Whither the Schools Whither the Public and Private Sectors? In *Public Policy in the Aesthetic Interest,* eds., Smith, R.A.; and Berman, R. Urbana: University of Illinois Press. 137–153.

Curriculum Alternatives and Constraints

INTRODUCTION

Policy alternatives as discussed in Chapter 1 should be considered when adopting a public policy at the state, district, school, and classroom levels. Alternatives provide a range of choices to the policy maker, including arguments for maintaining the present policy or adopting policies used in other schools or states, generally agreed-on policies used by all or most agencies, or ones designed uniquely for the situation in a given school, district, or state. Alternatives provide for possible policy shifts listing both pros and cons supporting and criticizing each alternative. Normally policy change is incremental, sometimes described as "tinkering" in order not to radicalize change. A review of well-argued alternatives introduces trade-offs that seek policy approaches that will benefit most stakeholders and cause no harm.

This chapter describes several competing curricular arguments and offers a number of alternatives that policy makers may wish to consider. In all probability, no one point of view will satisfy everyone, so it is reasonable to assume that change will incorporate a number of competing positions, but with the caveat that the central focus of the program will clearly contribute to the health of the discipline.

Sam Hope believes the health of the field is linked to its survival (2004). In order to ensure the continuing health of the field we need to continue efforts to improve what is presented either as an opportunity to build on gains already achieved (the status quo) or as an attempt to correct failures. The first strengthens the conditions for survival; the second weakens them, particularly when the supporting arguments suggest that the arts can be taught by teachers unprepared or barely prepared in the content of the field.

Hope sees the importance of dealing with health issues in a way that analyzes their potential effect on policies related to survival. He argues against the conduct of debates that weaken basic strategic survival positions of the field as a whole. He believes self-discipline and self-regulation within a field are facilitated when every professional has a fundamental understanding of what is at stake.

Art education, Hope notes, interacts with other fields and their interests both within and beyond the arts and education. In a climate of activism, (i.e., single-issue campaigns), it is even more important to understand and act in recognition of fundamental survival issues. Attention to survival and health means entering into all relationships and considering all ideas (alternatives) by asking several strategic policy questions:

1. Will the action we are contemplating cause us to diminish or deny the uniqueness of our field; that is, what can the visual arts do that no other field can do?

2. Will it harm our understanding of what we do and its importance among those who make fundamental decisions about our survival, including parents or students?

3. Will it diminish understanding the need for professionals to conduct the work of our field?

4. Will it damage our ability to recruit, develop, and support future professionals?

5. Will it decrease the number of students we are able to serve with substantive sequential art education?

6. Will it diminish the fundamental resources we must have in order to teach? (Hope 2004, 99)

In specifying policy alternatives in art education it is necessary that we apply Hope's criteria and other criteria related to art (see Chapter 2), which include the need to stimulate creativity and active participation in art, and the curriculum questions posed in Chapter 3, including the curricular focus on individual differences, etc. Policy alternatives also require that we pay attention to how the strategies we use provide for equity, access, and the dignity of all stakeholders in the educational process. These alternatives include consideration of existing policy proposals, policies implemented in other jurisdictions, generic policy solutions, and custom-designed alternatives (Weimer and Vining 1999).

EXISTING POLICY ALTERNATIVES

The choice to first consider the status quo makes sense even if the problem requires new solutions and different outcomes. Today's K–12 art programs vary a good deal from school district to school district. Most agree that the emphasis today is, as in the past, on the process of students making "new things." Although, as mentioned earlier, today's studio offerings provide more attention to historical and critical issues and to different subject matter content including social issues, the environment, and technology, the main emphasis remains on creative expressive learning in a studio context.

School offerings in studio vary from district to district, with smaller school districts emphasizing mostly drawing and painting while others offer a wide array of courses in the crafts, art history, and electronic imagery. Many high schools today also offer art majors where students develop portfolios in order to seek advanced placement and/or admission to art programs in higher education. In the fall of 2002, 29,000 high school art students enrolled as freshmen in higher education. Around 200,000 students today are enrolled in art schools and universities and college at the bachelor's, master's, and doctoral levels (Higher Education Data Services [HEDS] 2003).

Another reason for supporting the status quo is that it is wise to support programs that appear to work and that, over time, have positively contributed to the growth of the school art program and have gained acceptance by the American public over time. For example, in 1962, according to the National Education Association's (NEA) research monograph, 1963 M-3, sixty percent of the elementary schools had time allotted to art. Fifty-one percent had no formal course of study, over half of the schools had no specialists, twelve percent had an art room, and between fifty-eight percent and sixty-three percent had no art specialist (25). At the secondary level only 53.6 percent of the secondary schools offered formal instruction in art and in the schools offering art, only fifteen percent of the students were enrolled (57).

In contrast, in 1993–1994, eighty-five percent of public elementary schools offered art, forty-three percent provided by specialists, twenty-nine percent by specialists and classroom teachers, and twenty-eight percent by classroom teachers alone (Sabol 2004, 26). At the secondary level, more than half (52.7 percent) of all high school graduates earned credit in the visual arts in 1998. In the west, sixty-four percent of the graduates took some art courses (NAEA 2002).

These increases in enrollment, given that in 1962 only sixty percent of the elementary schools offered art, can be compared with today's eighty-five or more percent, and in 1962 only half of the secondary schools offered art where only fourteen percent of the students enrolled, compared with today's figures that suggest 52.7 to 65 percent now graduate with art credits. This suggests that public support for art study has significantly increased over the past forty years. Twenty-eight of the fifty states now even require art study for graduation.

Although these enrollment figures do not verify that all studio art programs are successful, they do in general indicate that the studio emphasis over the past forty years is generally supported. Most all our studio programs today are aimed at the student creating imaginary objects in sense experience, where meanings are reflected in a common cultural agreement or disagreement, made from some tangible material shaped by someone who modifies, alters, shapes, and molds as he or she constructs. As in a previous work, *Thinking in Art*, I am indebted to Harrison (1978) for his ideas on the process of making and thinking in art.

Harrison describes the process of designing while making as one where the artist may have no clear idea of what he or she wants to say, builds forms in the context of what his or her materials will do, and, when questioned about what he or she is trying to achieve, can tell us no more than that the activity is purposive, intentional, and rational. The artist's method is a process in which something is being discovered and where the artist can only show what, if successful, it will look like when it is completed, which is to say what it is to express something. Further, the artist has goals, even if they are only to paint a picture of a certain sort on a specific topic made with certain self-imposed standards, which is to offer a goal or intent based on what the artist is doing in the process of making.

The Intuitive Process

Although Harrison's view may be overly romantic—because not all artists work in such a vague manner—he at least laid out the general nature of the creative artist's intuitive experience, which is certainly the primary form of cognition used in the making of most works of art. This intuitive process, which is a rational one, also makes it possible for the artist to self-reflectively recognize that the work has been successfully completed, what thoughts have led to its accomplishment, and what it is like to make an object in this way and achieve something that is part of a whole in the realization of one component in a total policy.

Harrison's notion of a policy is that which the artist deals with in the work, which may be symbolic, illustrative, or done in a manner in order to tell a story. It is generally found in the arrangement of shapes and colors the artist uses to interest or disturb us and which invites us to pay attention to seeing shapes and colors in ways we have never seen before. How the artist has spread the paint and what conventions are used, modified, or exploited all play a part in how a picture is seen, how it works on us, and how we arrive at an understanding of it. For example, we may observe that the artist began with a random streak of paint and later responded by liking or disliking it, having unconscious associations with shapes of this sort and preserving some favorably received shapes, painting over others that are disliked, and ending such alterations when the result is a satisfactory one. This process may then resume again with some shapes destroying or enhancing others throughout its forming. The result of all this is to invite the viewer to a way of seeing or attending to the picture plane, to see a shape in this way or that, and/or to pay more attention to some shapes rather than others. It tells us more about the degrees of attention paid to certain elements in the picture than its historical or critical contents.

Decision Making

In this process the artist may abandon attempts to preserve, even with modifications, what he or she has already done or made, or attempt to achieve what is not yet done. In this sense, to abandon is, like levels of abstraction, to abandon a goal yet not discard what already is but give up on an attempt to make it otherwise. What the artist pays attention to in this selection process also answers what is being articulated (i.e., what patterns of shapes, colors, and textures are being developed in regard to what already exists and how destroying or enhancing a particular shape or color determines how another shape or color is seen). All these actions involve a number of mental acts that are interesting in their own right, and all are involved with how the artist comes to know what he or she earlier had been concerned with, which also becomes a process of self-discovery. In the end, the artist comes to know not only what it was he or she was concerned with all along, but also something that he or she was previously unaware of and how the choices made did not make nonsense of what had gone on before. It is a process that is not so much about knowing something about the unknown, but rather making that which is already known more vivid.

Not all that is contained in the work is built up through a pattern of activity. The artist's skill in letting the tool do its job, the way things go together to build a pattern of decision making, and the way things are built up reveals the order of the maker's decisions. This permits us to see the object as being designed in a particular way, to see the elements of the design that correspond to how the artist may have seen them, or invite us to do so.

All of the foregoing claims about artistic forming are conceptions that are clearly evident to anyone viewing the artistic object. These are made evident through the patterns of shapes that have been developed and modified through the decision-making process that the artist uses, the natural shapes that are modified in terms of certain goals or abstractions, and what forms of attention the artist has paid to particular details. The object makes us sense these things and respond to them—requiring us to think conceptually.

All works of art by students or mature artists involve the making of abstractions or concepts that vary in their scope and intensity.

To enter the mind of the artist in the process of making requires us to imagine how he or she sees one shape as modifying another or how he or she anticipates future modifications and what past events need to be recalled to make these decisions and anticipate future courses of action.

Thought in Action

This artistic model of conception challenges the conventional wisdom that intelligence is limited to knowing, in advance, exactly what one wants to achieve in creating a concept or abstraction—where thought is, in effect, divorced from action. Artistic thought in action offers a way to react to what one has done, acted on, and reacted to, which is a creation that reveals what one's goals are, what one is concerned about in the world, and what principles need to be observed in the process of its creation. The thought in action process verified that any theory of intelligence should begin with a theory that notes the role of creative activity and acknowledges the critical part it plays in the development of human intelligence.

BORROWING OTHER POLICY ALTERNATIVES/ GENERIC ALTERNATIVES

Borrowing other policies pursued by other school districts or state departments of education in other jurisdictions offers another possibility. Decomposing alternatives into essential components and selecting combinations may be the most promising approach to using borrowed alternatives. In the process of tinkering with other policy choices, we may also end up considering purely generic policy alternatives. Some of these include programs described by Guilfoils (2000); Wheeler (1999); Gregory (1996); Birt, Krug, and Sheridan (1997); and Elliot and Bartley (1998). All use the creative process to explore a variety of social goals, ecology, technology, cultural history, the built environment, academic achievement, and culture.

Generics often involve variations in their approach to the studio, where the studio is used as a tool to study various social goals including ecology, the built environment, and so forth. They may exist as a single specialized course of study or may be organized as a sequence of courses forming a curriculum with a particular social program emphasis.

History through Puppetry

Wheeler (1998) provides a model he used in teaching Alaskan history through puppetry, where students would be cast as Haida Indians, trappers, road builders, mail carriers, soldiers, and architects depicting pivotal moments in Alaskan history. Students were guided in creation of hand puppets using felt bodies and plaster-craft heads. Drawings providing additional information on Alaskan history and supplementary information at the conclusion of each of the puppet enactments. Wheeler concluded that the play and the drawings effectively animated the interaction of humans and their structures.

Architectural Design

Joanne Guilfoils believes we must begin now to teach our young students about art and architectural design as "expression of ideas," and use concepts and skills in art education to instruct and inspire them about: (1) their cultural heritage, including buildings; (2) cultural diversity in architectural styles; (3) related histories and contexts which influence architecture; and (4) influences of change and resulting trends in architectural design (2000). Of course technology, global ecology, and the notion of sustainable architecture are included in any informed discussion of past, present, or future built environments.

She uses as examples two programs, one in Kentucky that required students to solve real people/place problems through discussion, research into the past, systematic observations of the present locations, interviews, and their studio design solutions.

The other example was in the United Kingdom and, during the 1970s and 1980s, linked art, design, and environmental education as a way of seeing and understanding built environments. The purpose was to help students become more appreciative of their surroundings and develop a sense of place. The instruction helped students view buildings and urban spaces with informed and critical eyes, to better understand the influences on design of the built environments. In the United Kingdom program and in the Kentucky project, the point was to "evaluate architectural design" and to understand what was being valued. Students were asked to consider both the content of ideas and the form of expression as two questions: What ideas are being explored? How well are those ideas being communicated to other people? These are *art, architecture,* and *built environment* education questions!

Art As Technology

Diane Gregory sees technology as a savior of art education, stating we don't need more material, but we need to learn how to use wisely the material we already have and consider carefully how we plan to use any new technological tools that become available to us (1996). Gregory describes in particular a site developed by Jane Jalisan, a New Jersey art teacher who invites artists, teachers, and students from all over the world to celebrate the planet's oldest trees by sharing artwork, photos, tree facts, poems, and stories about the oldest tree in their communities. Further, she asks us to imagine that in a regular elementary classroom the children are reading *The Journey of the Red-Eyed Tree Frog,* which tells the story of a brave tree frog who sets out to save his home in a burning rain forest.

Also, she asks us to imagine students discussing a local controversy regarding poisoning one of the area's most famous trees, the Treaty Oak, located near downtown Austin, then deciding to erect a virtual memorial for the Treaty Oak on one student's (Julian's) Web page. For the next several weeks, in their art and regular classrooms, she notes, we can see students are writing poems, talking, and making decisions among themselves, drawing tree pictures with Dabbler or SuperPaint, scanning artwork and photographs, creating a HyperStudio Stack, then putting all these items up on the Web to share with others, moving back and forth between the real world and the mediated world of technology.

Environmental Studies

Birt, Krug, and Sheridan describe an elementary school project entitled Good Education Equals Good Earth (1997). The goal was to help the school community discover the unique natural beauty within its own backyard. The activity that the students chose to implement was construction of a ceramic mural representing their observations and reflections of a wetlands near the school. The activities included a design for the mural collected from the artwork of the students, the making and glazing of ceramic tiles, and the employment of a tile maker to install the mural in the school. The authors emphasize that the students learned to understand the complexity of relationships among art, culture, and nature by immersing themselves artistically in and with their environment.

Ecological Studies

Even in an art curriculum that explores ecology, Elliot and Bartley suggest that students can explore important links between art and technology and develop a wide range of technical skills while still addressing both aesthetic and ecological issues (1998). A successful high school art curriculum, in their view, should be designed to teach each student to explore and view materials, creations, and recreation as part of an ongoing human ecosystem. In the sample program, students are asked to examine old quilts, braided rugs, hooked rugs, and knitted garments. When such objects are brought into the studio, students deconstruct them into parts which are later integrated into specific student works. Students examine the inherent qualities of the material and its potential for art making; the art that emerges is defined by the creative process used on the inherent qualities of the material and by the integrated function of the artwork.

Unlike the behaviors called for in socially constructed art, all these authors, in one way or another, believe in the formal study and production of art objects and events as being instrumental in achieving social goals. Unlike some postmodernists, none recommend the need to deconstruct the art object or avoid the traditional means for the making, study, and analysis of art proper.

UNIQUE ART EDUCATION POLICY ALTERNATIVES

A third approach is to come up with unique or custom-made policy alternative (Weimer and Vining 1999), cautioning, however, that a new policy should not invent a dummy or straw man to make its case more attractive. Also, one should not have a favorite policy to advocate that is mutually exclusive, (i.e., it should offer radically different alternatives to the alternative policies being considered).

What follows are three current unique art education policy alternatives, one supporting a sociological prospective using a structuralist rationalist argument by Arthur Efland (2002). The second is an art education model for social reconstruction based on an argument supported by Kerry Freedman (2003) and others, and the third is a proposal for a socially centered curriculum by Elliot Eisner (2002).

The Structuralist and Post-structuralist Alternative

The structuralist alternative today is an admixture of both structuralist and post-structuralist thought with some concessions to post-Kantian ideals. The methodological assumption of lead theorists such as Efland (2002) is to search through an assortment of cognitive theories that can be used to support a postmodernist argument that art is socially constructed not as an object of aesthetic merit but rather as a motivational agent for inspiring a political dialogue between the student and the art teacher.

What appears to be the common assumption behind Efland's structuralist social theory arts policy argument is the notion that art is mainly a product of intellect and a source for knowledge about what Efland calls a "life world," where the study of art provides occasions for the acquisition of cognitive strategies to carry out interpretive forms of inquiry. Further, he asserts that art is purely an activity of the senses, where human beings find sensorially what it is they look for, feelings and emotions are non-cognitive, and an integrated cognitive theory harmonizes the conflicting policies and practices of art educators. Further, he says that works of art used in instruction should play the role of providing students with landmarks for the cognitive mapping of life worlds and should be used as reference points to reflect important ideas or concerns.

From his point of view, imagination is not useful because it does not come from the senses or from experience. Innate ideas, therefore, cannot exist because they are not empirical and visual images or verbal expressions cannot be literal facts, but are rather embodiments of meaning that only have utility in some other (social) form. As a result, art is a kind of communication in which the expression of an idea requires the learner to interpret its meaning and carry out the appropriate actions dictated by the work.

Perceptions of artistic meanings so constructed are viewed as developing images stored in the student's mind, manipulated by thought, and influenced by behavior when students choose the appropriate responsive action. Learning occurs mainly in a social context and is dependent upon the educational environment that mediates thought where teachers and students view works of art as arbitrary social conventions. In the art class, it is, therefore, the task of the teacher to raise questions that challenge students to examine their presently held beliefs, and where *wrong* student answers are greeted with prompts leading to *right* answers and the understandings sought by the teacher (Efland 2002, 73). Works of art from this perspective are to be viewed as political statements, not as aesthetic objects.

As a result, K–12 art education is primarily centered on the *study* of art objects where teachers must deal with an unspecified number of student hindrances reflecting naïve, undifferentiated, compartmentalized, garbled, or wrong knowledge. These hindrances are caused, according to Efland, by art teachers using conventionalized approaches to the analysis of art objects and providing disoriented research and ritualistic search patterns. Formal analysis in his view is not meaningful, in part because it is too often taught as an autonomous subject where students focus on iconographic similarities among works of art rather than on their political meanings.

Successful art teaching occurs, in Efland's view, when the student agrees with the teacher's interpretation of a recognized artwork or popular culture artifact, thus fulfilling his required methodology for one dialogic goal of art study, which is to teach students how to make feminist or other political statements. For example, he presents one lesson on the evils of McCarthyism through an art teacher's critique of a Jasper Johns painting, Target with Four Faces. Notes Efland:

> The art teacher also prompts the students to discuss the feelings of paranoia, the feeling that evil forces were plotting against America both from outside and from within. "Was this feeling based on fact?" "How did it reflect American society in the mid-twentieth century?" A student asks the art teacher what Hughes meant by the expression, "the McCarthy years." (2002, 126).

As a result, Efland claims the teacher's narrative helps students to link the feelings aroused by the multi-layered narratives of the McCarthy conspiracy with a Jasper Johns painting.

Art As an Art World Construct

The concept "art world" is a term frequently used by postmodernists to explain issues in art such as participation and aesthetic appreciation. Postmodernists generally view an art world as being inhabited by all the people whose activities are necessary to the production of certain kinds of art (see Chapter 1). Moreover, in their view, the art world consists of individuals who play roles that explain the basis for the production, distribution, and utilization of art. Furthermore, art for them represents a social norm not concerned with the evaluation of work but rather something seen within a framework of analysis in which art is assumed to be legitimate art; questions how a work becomes a work of art; and how is it deployed in a struggle for social prestige. These claims have relevance for postmodernists because they believe in the socially constructive nature of art.

Sociological Definitions of Art

Alternatives based on the social value of art encourage definitions of the art that most often use descriptions of the process by which art comes into being and not the object itself. To present a definition of art for the sociologist is beside the point because if art is a social reconstruction, no scientifically valid definition is possible. Moreover, the belief that art is a social institution leads them to include the functions of art as part of the definition, which now includes the features of artworks, features of the art world, and the functions of art as a single concept. This should lead us to question how a sociologist can deal with an art world when he or she doesn't know what art is. For example, how does the sociologist know that art is sociologically constructed or how can the object of study be defined by those who cannot even assess an art world as being an art world?

The Visual Culture Curriculum Model

Visual Culture Art Education (VCAE), as judged by the numer of articles and books written on the subject since the end of the Getty, is one of the most popular policy issues being considered by the field at the time of this writing. Those advocating VCAE include Barrett (2003), Taylor & Ballengee-Morris (2003), Duncum (2001, 2002, 2003), Smith-Shank (2003), Freedman (2000, *TeachingVisual Culture: Curriculum Aesthetics and the Social Life of Art* 2003), Amburgy and Knight, Congdon and Blandy (2003), and Tavin and Anderson (2003). The philosophical base for VCAE advocacy, for example, is also supported by a large number of art educators in the profession today, including Gude (2004), Stewart (2003), Hellman (2003), Taylor (2002), and Diamond and Mullen (2002).

As a curriculum theory, VCAE is based on the premise that art is socially constructed and, therefore, requires that the primary goals of the art program be directed toward the social reconstruction of the society through the art student's focus on the study of social, rather than aesthetic or expressive, outcomes. The underlying reasons given for art students being engaged in the study of mass and popular culture are: (1) students need such study in order to live in a constructed and "climate-controlled" world, (2) art study is for personal and social success, and (3) it is useful as a "corrective" to the idea that the "bright" and "colorful" of contemporary visuals represent the cheap and tacky, while restraint exemplifies the good taste of fine art.

What Are Visual Studies?

Tom Anderson claims that studies of visual culture are needed because we live in a "constructed, climate controlled world" where our waking, sleeping, growing, and living is overwhelmingly constructed by us and the Internet tells us what's real beyond our immediate environment (2003). In addition, he notes we may know more about Ellen DeGeneres or Vanna White than our next-door neighbor and the sound bites and instant replays that keep us from boredom are more appealing and entertaining than real time.

Anderson argues that study of the visual culture is required because people need to be able to "read" the "constructed" environment to interpret and use the visual signs in it (2003). These environments and signs include visual artifacts and performance of all kinds as well as new and emerging technologies that take a consumer's view rather than the artist's view of culture.

The methodology of VCAE according to Anderson would include a postmodern critique of popular media and culture in order to understand the social foundations and ramifications of popular and mass culture and determine the philosophical premises and the impact of these images on individuals and the society. He further notes the goal is not for the sake of appreciation but rather to guide intelligent action along the lines advocated by Walter Benjamin and the Frankfort School.

The study of art in the popular culture sense would be to teach students how to achieve "personal and social success," how art communicates, and what its consumer value is. Its context would be found in the social, economic, and political embeddedness of mass culture objects through a semiotic search for the meaning of signs where meanings are culturally embedded and determined. Art making and visual critiquing of artifacts, Anderson believes, will empower students to explore their own meanings and how different cultures create identity. This they would accomplish through watching the popular arts, including television, movies, video games, design arts, coffee cups, and the Mall of America.

Paul Duncum, like Anderson, supports the notion that VCAE approaches include both making and critique although, like Anderson, Duncum conceives of that art as being "socially constructed" rather than an aesthetic object for individual contemplation (2002). Here, critical understanding and empowerment of popular culture, not artistic expression, are the primary goals of VCAE. Although Duncum cautions us that the critique should not replace making art, his idea of making art is to critique objects that are socially constructed and explore various battles between selective power interests. Critical issues that "informed" *making* activities would include, in Duncum's view, the roles played by imagery in society, audience reception, media ownership, the construction of multiple subjectivities, and the nature of representation. Making in a VCAE curriculum would, therefore, not be about making individual creative and expressive objects of meaning but rather adapting design procedures such as discovering, planning, and doing. How one *makes* such "objects" is not explained. In his criticism of making in today's art education, Duncum notes:

> Mainstream art education begins with the assumption that art is inherently valuable, whereas VCAE assumes that visual representations are sites of ideological struggle that can be as deplorable as they can be praiseworthy. The starting point is not a prescribed, inclusive canon of the *institutionalized* art world but the student's own cultural experience. A major goal is empowerment in relation to the pressures and processes of contemporary image pictures; there is a need to learn how to discuss these images sensibly (2002, 8).

Duncum notes also that VCAE is indebted to DBAE and, like DBAE, it is also profoundly historical. What Duncum refers to as history is likely the Marxist notion of the history of class struggles, not the history of art. As he carefully complains, the sites of global capitalism only appear homogenous and are interpreted differently. Aesthetics, in his view, address social issues in the high and low arts.

Suitable VCAE content, according to Pamela Taylor and Christine Ballengee-Morris (2003), include study of Eminem's music video "Without Me," the TV situation comedy "Everybody Loves Raymond," images on Websites, video, comedy, advertisements, and pop stars such as Elvis. An Elvis study, they suggest, might prompt students to develop a fictional pop star icon, and relate him or her to current celebrities through research, experimentation, identification, and recreation of the various stages of a pop star icon's rise to fame. As a result, they claim, the art teachers would provide a more student-initiated approach to incorporating popular forms of visual culture that would encourage student ownership of their educational experience as well as avoid the appearance of receiving a misguided interpretation.

The Constructed Environment

When VCAE advocates refer to a constructed environment they are using a sociological definition of art that views the art object as a socially constructed event that provides opportunity for discourse related to the social meanings of objects as they relate to certain power interests as manifested in certain political and social struggles between different social and economic classes. These include struggles between the haves and have-nots, rich and poor, educated and uneducated, the privileged and under-privileged as they relate to society.

According to Freedman (2003), the visual arts are expanding not only in their forms but also in their influence through their connections to a range of social issues. As a result, she notes the visual arts have become fundamental to the cultural transformation of political discourse, social interaction, and the cultural identity that has characterized the postmodern condition. In her view, visual culture inherently provides a context for the visual arts in its effects and points out the connections between popular and fine art forms. VCAE includes the fine arts, tribal arts, advertising, popular film and video, folk art, television and other performances, housing and apparel design, computer games, toy design, and other forms of visual production and communication.

Freedman argues that art education is now about visual culture, which includes *all* the visual arts, including fine art, computer games, manga, feature films, toy design, advertising, television

Chapter 5 Curriculum Alternatives and Constraints

programming, dream time paintings, fashion design, and so forth. In Freedman's view, VCAE makes the art curriculum more democratic because VCAE supports the idea that personal freedoms no longer only involve matters of free speech, but also are concerned with freedom of information in a range of visual art forms integral to the creation of individual and group knowledge. Art and art education are, for her, forms of mediation between people in which a range of professional, discursive practice plays an important role and where art mediates both at the level of curriculum development and enactment. Curriculum can be understood, she notes, as an interaction between students and a range of students and a range of people through texts and images.

Freedman views popular media culture as a form of hyper-reality even more real than reality itself; in media culture, in her view, technological images are surrogates for real experiences. Interactivity with a visually complex computer game thus suggests many possible stories and images that spin away from the screen; in her view, even interpretations of seductive and widely distributed images become important for study.

Advertisements in Freedman's view illustrate the process of establishing meaning. One example she provides is a critique on a Calvin Klein ad for the fragrance *Be*, where skin blemishes and the moles of the model have been shown in order to surprise and draw attention to the audience expecting to see the hyper-reality of computer manipulated beauty (2003). Freedman notes:

> The surface of the ad tells each viewer to be yourself—a critical concept to sales in democratic societies—that is, to be a natural individual while convincing us that we should be like the other people who buy the (unnatural) product. (2003, 94).

Frameworks for Teaching

Freedman's frameworks include:

1. PRODUCTION CONTEXTS

   Experience and study the context of production, including cultural purposes of production, visual traditions, artists' personal histories, ethnic backgrounds, artistic intent, use of mass media images, etc. Context includes historical, cultural, political, social, economic, religious, etc. conditions that influenced visual production.

2. EXPLORATION CONTEXTS

Experience and study viewing circumstances, including institutional settings, viewer past experience and prior knowledge, image recycling, influences of culture and tradition on appreciation, etc. Study includes cultural and personal influences on appreciation, such as politics, education, institutional conditions, family, mass media, etc.

3. FUNCTION AND MEANING

Study and articulate multiple perspectives of visual culture(s), including the meaning as interpreted by people in the context of production, student interpretations, and symbolic, metaphoric and other culturally based qualities of interpretation that convey meaning in the context of appreciation. Study includes developing an understanding of consensus building and the acceptance of conflict in interpretation.

4. STRUCTURAL SUPPORT

Study and use elements and principles, technical skills required for production and use (including appreciation), and various media in creating and analyzing visual culture in relation to cultural contexts. (2003, 92)

AESTHETIC FRAMING

Elliot Eisner argues that the arts, like other fields, can be taught in different ways for different ends (2003). He calls this "framing" the world from an aesthetic perspective, which includes the process of socialization where students learn to see the world within a common frame of reference. Seeing, for example, provides practical perceptions of the world that challenge our beliefs, and provokes general questions that lead to productive puzzlement. The function of these frames—that include theories, concepts, images, and narratives—is to appraise the world in particular ways that allow the student to join and participate in a discourse community where meaning is encoded and can be decoded.

Art, in Eisner's view, makes it possible to provide a variety of frames by paying attention to the particular qualities of an object or event, by disregarding labels, and by paying attention to matters of forms and the ways qualities are configured. Formal elements are qualities of the thing experienced, and how these qualities generate expressive content lead to a willingness to allow form to inform the way we feel when we see it.

In his view, works of art should help students grasp general principles regarding cultural influences on the art. These principles are understandable and are powerful heuristic devices for putting art in context. Furthermore, they are teachable, learnable, and conceptual in form. When children's artwork is examined in social rather than individual terms, what they learn about with a given material transfers to what they learn from others as they become members of a community. This comes through sharing one's work with others, carrying with it the potential that students will be able to apply what they have learned; it comes through using language to discuss the arts, sharing common interests, and providing a source of pleasure and a demonstration of competence.

Tiers of Study

Eisner also identifies three levels, or tiers of arts study, that might contribute to academic study through artistic form (1998). These include: (1) arts-based outcomes, (2) arts-related outcomes, and (3) ancillary outcomes, all three of which stress the role of the arts as aesthetic objects or events in achieving instrumental ends. *Arts-based* outcomes suggest that the subject matter the arts teach can help students talk or perform discerningly about the content of a piece of music, architecture, or a cubist painting. *Arts-related* outcomes pertain to the perception and comprehension of formal aesthetic features in the general environment. *Ancillary* outcomes refer to outcomes that transfer skills employed in the perception, creation, and comprehension of the arts to non-art tasks.

SUMMARY

This chapter, which has viewed the thinking involved in supporting the creation of status quo, ancillary, and unique alternatives, is offered as only a partial list of newer and older policy alternatives. The status quo alternative suggests the continuance of the emphasis in studio art currently being offered, lists some ancillary working alternatives that can be added to or infused into the existing curriculum, and suggests some unique alternatives by policy analysis by looking at newer curriculum models uniquely different from the status quo.

The policy maker ideally looks at all three kinds of policy alternatives and offers both pros and cons for choosing which alternative best answers the policy problem. Offering a range of alternatives enhances the chance that newer ideas can be offered and examined as well as the tried and true solutions. Change is inevitable over time, but the review of alternatives offers the possibility of meeting the challenges of change in a rational and systemic way.

Finding suitable answers to the question of whether culture itself exists in order to serve a social need or whether it needs to affect the biological fitness of its citizens is difficult to answer. At least some scholars tend to see that biological and cultural processes have separate mechanisms for producing new information, selecting certain variants, and transmitting them over time. What this suggests is that the evolution of a given culture is not directly related to the way the citizens of that culture behave, at least in a biological sense. Although it can be noted that cultural forms can evolve and grow, they do not in reality enhance the biological fitness of the individuals who produced them. Culture is—in effect—a special kind of information and can be lost, as was the case in Rome and Greece, and in China's cultural revolution where governments sought to eliminate the true cultural information they feared.

Chapter 5 Curriculum Alternatives and Constraints

The Art Experience

Cultural forms depend on an environment of human consciousness. Ideas and artifacts reproduce and grow in the mind, responding to selective pressures that are in principle independent of those that constrain genetic evolution. Csikszentmihalyi notes a cultural evolution can be defined as the different transmission of information contained in artifacts, for example, in objects, concepts, beliefs, symbols, and behavior patterns that exist only because people decided to make them (1994). Further, these artifacts contain implicit instructions on how to behave because they define the reality within which we operate. We like to believe, he notes, that cultural evolution serves the goal of human adaption and enhances the exclusive fitness of the individual who uses it. Artifacts evolve because they help make our lives better, and the growth of artifacts is held in check by human control.

Popular Culture

Csikszentmihalyi argues that the multiplication and diffusion of artifacts follow their own logic, to a large extent independently of the welfare of their carriers. Cultural information, he claims, can kill the environment that made and supports the society, and some of the artifacts we create could well destroy cultural evolution as its own propaganda apparatus, complete with ideology and slogans that people repeat over and over without thinking. Mass cultural forms that on the surface appear benign are being created regardless of how useful they are simply because it is possible to produce them.

In sociocultural evolution, selection is mediated by consciousness and therefore we must consider the evolution's dynamics in order to understand what it is about. Cultural information matters only if we attend to it, but we are also limited in the number of things we can attend to at the same time. The rate of new popular variations produced depends on how much attention free from survival demands is available. Cultural forms depend on the environment of human consciousness. As Csikszentmihalyi noted:

...societies must also have limits on how many works of art, scientific facts, or commercial products they can recognize and assimilate. It is naïve to assume that progress can be enhanced by encouraging more people to be creative. If there is not enough psychic energy available to recognize creative changes they will simply be wasted (1994, 167).

According to Csikszentmihalyi, the amount of cultural transmission retained is dependent upon the investments in attention and social organization that encourage novelty, and the social arrangements that ensure the retention and transmission of new variants. New cultural forms need to be identifiable, which in art means to acquire a consensus of experts who decide whether the artifact is really new. He believes the most universal qualification of positively selected artifacts is that they improve the quality of experience. Enjoyment is, therefore, the main reason to select and retain works of art, in part because the art produces positive states of consciousness. People, in Csikszentmihalyi's view, enjoy most those experiences where they are challenged, although worry and anxiety may result when there are more challenges than skills.

Complexity does not, however, mean that people are constantly motivated to seek higher challenges. Most, in fact, prefer time to relax in front of the TV. Enjoyment that requires developing new skills and greater challenges are relatively rare, yet most people consider such challenges the high point of their lives. Cultural forms that offer increased enjoyment survive because they attract attention, and people who invest attention in such forms acquire more complex forms of consciousness. Culture does not exist to serve our needs, and that realization makes it easier to evaluate cultural forms more objectively and choose on a sounder basis which forms to encourage and which ones to retain.

These alternative social policy approaches to art K–12 instruction will be evaluated in the following chapter, and recommendations as to what direction future art education policy will take during the twenty-first century will be explored. It will be presented as a socially responsive aesthetic art education curriculum for the next century.

Chapter 5 Curriculum Alternatives and Constraints

REFERENCES

Anderson, T. 2003. *Visual Culture Art Education*. Unpublished paper. Tallahassee: Florida State University.

Barrett, T. 2003. Interpreting Visual Culture. *Art education* 56 (2): 6–12.

Birt, D.; Krug, D.H.; and Sheridan, M. 1997. Earthly Matters: Learning Occurs When You Hear the Grass Singing. *Art Education* 50 (6): 7–13.

Congdon, K. G.; and Blandy, D. 2003. Zinesters in the Classroom: Using Zines to Teach About Postmodernism and the Communication of Ideas. *Art Education* 56 (3): 44–52.

Csikszentmihalyi, M. 1994. "NIMES v Genes, Notes from the Culture Wars" in *Changing the World: A Framework for the Study of Creativity*, eds., Feldman, D.H.; Csikzentmihalyi, M.; and Gardner, H. Westport, CT: Praeger Publishers. 160–187.

Diamond, P.; and Mullen, C. 2002. The Postmodern Educator: Arts-Based Inquiries and Teacher Development. Reviewed by Marjo Rasanen. *Studies in Art Education* 43 (2): 175–181. (Book review).

Duncum, P. 2001. Visual Culture: Developments, Definitions, and Directions for Art Education. *Studies in Art Education* 42 (2): 101–112.

_____. 2002. Clarifying Visual Culture Art Education. *Art Education* 55 (3): 8–11.

_____. 2003. Visual Culture in the Classroom. *Art Education* 56 (2): 25–32.

Efland, A.D. 2002. *Art and Cognition: Integrating the Visual Arts in the Curriculum*. New York: Teachers College Press.

Eisner, E.W. 1998. Does Experience in the Arts Boost Academic Achievement. *Art Education* 51 (1): 7–15.

_____. 2002. *The Arts and the Creation of Mind*. New Haven: Yale University Press.

Elliot, S.; and Bartley, S. 1998. Material Arts Design: An Exploration in Creativity, Ecology, and Culture. *Art Education* 51 (3): 53–55.

Freedman, K. 2000. Social Perspectives on Art Education in the U.S.: Teaching Visual Culture in a Democracy. *Studies in Art Education* 41 (4): 314–329.

Freedman, K. 2003a. The Importance of Student Artistic Production to Teaching Visual Culture. *Art Education* 57 (1): 6–14.

_____. 2003b. *Teaching Visual Culture: Curriculum Aesthetics and the Social Life of Art*. New York: Teachers College Press.

Gregory, D.C. 1996. Art Education Reform: Technology As Savior. *Art Education* 49 (6): 49–54.

Gude, O. 2004. Post Modern Principles: In Search of a 21st Century Art Education. *Art Education* 57 (1): 6–14.

Guilfoils, B.K. 2000. Art in American Built Environment Education. *Art Education* 53 (4): 6–12.

Harrison, H. 1978. *Making and Thinking: A Study of Intelligent Activities*. London: The Harveston Press Limited.

Hellman, P. 2003. The Role of Postmodern Picture Books in Art Education. *Art Education* 56 (6): 6–12.

Higher Education Data Services (HEDS). 2003. *Data Summaries, Art and Design, 2002–2003*. Reston, VA: Higher Education Data Services.

Hope, S. 2004. "Art Education in a World of Cross Purposes" in *Handbook of Research on Policy in Art Education*, eds. Eisner, E.W.; and Day, M.D. Mahway, NJ: Lawrence Erlbaum Associates.

Keifer-Boyd, K.; Amburgy, P.M.; and Knight, W.B. 2003. Three Approaches to Teaching Visual Culture in K–12 School Contexts. *Art Education* 56 (2): 44–51.

National Education Association (NEA). 1963. *1963 M-3 Art and Music in the Public Schools*. Washington, DC: Research Division National Education Association.

National Art Education Association (NAEA). 2002. Why Support Improving Arts Education Policy, Update Column. *NAEA News* August 2002.

Sabol, R.F. 2004. "An Overview of Art Teacher Recruitment, Certification, and Retention" in *Handbook of Research and Policy in Art Education*, eds. Eisner, E.W.; and Day, M.D. Mahway, NY: Lawrence Erlbaum Associates.

Smith-Shank, D.L. 2003. Lewis Hine and His Photo Stories: Visual Culture and Social Reform. *Art Education* 56 (2): 33–37.

Stewart, E.O. 2003. The Matrix: A Secondary Postmodern Primer. *Art Education* 56 (2): 33–37.

Taylor, P.G. 2002. Service Learning As Postmodern Art and Pedagogy. *Studies in Art Education* 43 (2): 36–43.

Taylor, P.G.; and Ballengee-Morris, C. 2003. Using Visual Culture to Put a Contemporary Fizz on the Study of Pop Art. *Art Education* 56 (2): 33–38.

Tavin, K.M.; and Anderson, D. 2003. Teaching (Popular) Visual Culture: Deconstructing Disney in the Elementary Art Classroom. *Art Education* 56 (3): 21–24.

Weimer, D.L.; and Vining, A.R. 1999. *Policy Analysis, Concepts, and Practices*. Upper Saddle River, NJ: Prentice Hall.

Wheeler, D. 1999. Sod, Blocks, Lodge Poles, and Cornerstones: On Teaching Cultural History and Structure Through Puppetry Arts. *Art Education* 52 (3): 19–29.

Evaluating Alternatives/ The Future

6

INTRODUCTION

The reader should not expect all this to end with clear predictions of American art education policy in the new millennium. What is certain, however, is: (1) that art education in K–12 American schools will remain largely a socializing enterprise and (2) that its future place in the curriculum will be dependent upon how accountable that enterprise is to the discipline of art and to a concerned American public. The principal question to be addressed in this chapter is, given the current direction of educational policy today, do we have sufficient reason to concur which curricular policies are more consistent with the means and ends of art and education?

Once we have evaluated the relevant criteria and policy alternatives we need to bring them together in order to facilitate choice. Then we face three choices: (1) predicting and forecasting the impacts of the alternatives, (2) valuing the impact of the alternatives, and (3) comparing alternatives across disparate criteria (Weimer and Vining 1999)

PREDICTING AND FORECASTING IMPACTS

Before you can evaluate alternatives in terms of criteria you need to be able to predict within reason what impacts the alternative will have on the art program. Predicting helps pinpoint future congestion levels under current policy. Policies always have multiple impacts so it is wise to use your model, your specification of alternatives, and your common sense to list as many different impacts as you can. Next, you go through your criteria with regard to current policy and make sure you can predict and value the effects of each alternative.

VALUING IMPACTS

Predictions of policy impacts should make impact criteria as comparable as possible without distorting relationships with underlying conflicts. By combining impact criteria that are truly commensurate we may be able to specify a more manageable set of evaluation criteria.

COMPARING
ALTERNATIVES ACROSS
INCOMMENSURABLE CRITERIA

Choosing the best alternative is of little consequence when you have a single criterion or an alternative that ranks highest on all criteria. The policy maker's task is to make explicit the trade-offs among criteria implied by various choices. In addition, you should be explicit about uncertainty because only rarely will you be able to predict value impacts with great certainty.

EVALUATING POLICY ALTERNATIVES

Sam Hope believes that evaluating policy alternatives is critical because it can produce reasonable valuations for losses and gains (2004). In relation to what he calls survival issues, Hope recommends:

- There must be a definition of content and purpose sufficient to distinguish art education from other fields. The field must answer the question, "what is unique about what we do and the content for which we are responsible?"
- A sufficient number of policy makers and/or the public must believe in the work of the field. For these people, the field must answer the question, "why are the unique things we do worthwhile?"
- There must be a group of professionals capable of practicing effectively in the field and advancing it. These individuals must be able to answer questions 1 and 2 as a preface to the question, "what should I/we be doing in this field?"
- There must be a body of people who prepare new professionals. In addition to answering the first three questions, they must answer the questions, "what do future professionals in the field need to know and be able to do?" and "what of this is the most important to teach in the time available?"
- There must be students able and willing to learn.
- There must be basic resources: curriculum, time, materials, and facilities, for example (2004, 98).

Hope's first goal of providing a definition of content and purpose to distinguish art education from other fields suggests we evaluate curriculum policy with the subject discipline in mind.

To evaluate which model is adequate for deciding the alternatives that best meet the goals of the art curriculum, it is necessary that we question them from several viewpoints. These include whether or not any model has psychological validity, social validity, philosophical validity, subject validity, and political feasibility (Thompson 1981). In critiquing a socially centered art curriculum Thompson would ask the questions below.

SUBJECT VALIDITY

Subject validity asks whether the curricular proposal in a given field provides for the accurate and significant representation of

Chapter 6 Evaluating Alternatives/The Future

the products of inquiry as well as the means of inquiry, to the end of serving truth. As to whether the socially constructed art concept model best meets the criterion of subject validity depends on the views of the curriculum maker. This view of art does, however, present a number of difficult problems, including whether or not a socially constructed definition of art or the artist is valid. Given such constraints, it is doubtful that any curriculum maker who does not know what art is can construct a valid *art* curriculum.

For a sociological definition of art to exist, one has to believe that art study tells us something about society and that the purpose of such study would be to reveal more about society than about art. A study of a Turner landscape, for example, might reflectively lead to the conclusion "that his landscape reflects unstable class relationships, most notably through the inclusion of persons of apparent wealth in the foreground of the painting." What such an analysis really implies about art is (1) that paintings embrace norms and values of the society, (2) that art fulfills shared emotional needs and fantasies, (3) that art arises from the collective unconscious and is similar to dream states, and (4) that art reflects the economic conditions of the elite or of the ruling class.

As to whether art truly reveals something about society, one first has to recognize the fact that the art object is, in general, an abstraction and that the events depicted could have been constructed by the artist simply because they were either particularly common or perhaps uncommon. Further, artworks do not reflect an "innocent eye" but are heavily influenced by artistic practices and conventions. A sociologist rediscovering what was the spirit of an age from its art might, in fact, only discover that what art is—*is art*.

Interpretive Methods

We also need to inquire into whether the art teacher should engage students in critiques or dialogs about art, risking injecting the teacher's bias into classroom discussions through explaining to the students what is or what is not the correct interpretation of a work. Certainly such a process suggests the more distinct possibility of introducing a teacher bias rather than eliciting a strictly student point of view. In addition, a content analysis of the subject matter depicted in a work of art or an artifact of popular culture also risks the loss of the context of the data through the process of systematizing it. That process can also lead to generalizations about other social groups than the ones being analyzed. What all this really leads to is the more important question of why the sociologist or the art teacher who wants to know more about society would choose to study art rather than the society itself.

Another question that needs to be asked is whether art really reveals something new about our society and whether the analysis of paintings from another historic period, including our own, really provides a valid reflection of what life is or was like solely on the basis of pictorially analyzed data. Alexander, a sociologist, argues that such reflections are problematic. Indeed she notes, "if art reflects society, then the mirror is one of the distorting kind that is found in a fun fair" (2003, 33). The mirror, she notes, can only reflect one part of reality at any given time and it is systematically distorted. Further, she concludes that such distortions and images have been shaped by a master demon, its creator, and its demon public distributors. Art, she admits, mirrors only those fragments of art that are perceived by audiences who are embedded in a social context and who contribute to the creation of meaning by selectively misperceiving the images they see.

Also, the argument that students should be protected from the harmful effects of exposure to either formalist or popular cultural images wrongfully assumes that students are too ignorant to recognize their true meaning and, further, that all students process images in the same way and receive them with the same impact. The facts are that students rather than teachers are the key to understanding popular culture, where meanings depend on them as consumers and not as creators.

Art, in fact, never stands alone but has to be understood in relation to the feeling states of the students who consume it. The meanings they take from art and the type of art they choose to consume are related mostly to their backgrounds and their social networks. Students have, in fact, a number of ways they can interpret art, including: (1) the dominant hegemonic position where the message is received, (2) an oppositional meaning where the meaning received is not what the maker intended, (3) a middle state, where the student perceives meanings using both the dominant and oppositional meaning, and (4) a confused state in which

Chapter 6 Evaluating Alternatives/The Future

the receiver does not understand what the image is about. Sociologists also agree that students coming from oppositional subcultures create meaning for themselves by actively reworking the arts, fashions, and commodities available from the cultural and consumer industries. Later, as young, working-class men and women, they also symbolically resist both adult culture and middle-class values. As a result, each new generation of youth finally develops its own expressions of resistance which will eventually be captured in a preferred style of response (Willis 1978). The meaning of artworks is thus constructed by students in their use as objects and artifacts that do not have a single valence. It is the act of social engagement with the cultural item that activates social meaning.

Contemporary research in cultural studies also suggests that people take their own meaning from cultural texts, attributing almost full autonomy to receivers in creating meaning (Fiske 1989). Ads, he notes, that intend to dominate either economically or intellectually, are resisted by people through creating messages of their own. In fact, they create their own identities and most often do not accept one offered through the media by dominant elites. Fiske argues further that semiotic resistance supports people in their daily lives. Furthermore, it is a tactic for dealing with subjugation, and a way of making do. Popular images, then, do not as a rule ferment social change or revolution. Young girls buy, but as a result don't necessarily become feminists. Art teachers should, therefore, question whether they should teach art by showing students how to socially interpret images. As reception theory suggests, every student who comes to a "text" will take his or her own unique reading, so that there are, in effect, as many readings as there are readers.

PHILOSOPHICAL VALIDITY

The issue of philosophical validity is focused on the question of whether a curricular proposal possesses internal consistency such that ends and means relate to fundamental premises inspiring the curriculum and whether these premises are explicit to a reasonable conception of the good life. Programs that emphasize the producer's or the consumer's view of knowledge or insist only on general studies or vocational studies may not be philosophically valid. What is needed is a blend into a coherent whole. When art teachers focus their program on social theories that require the student to view the art program principally as means to examine political or social goals or study of the arts as an industry, artistic ends are replaced by political and economic goals.

Shaping Approaches

Art teachers critiquing visual images using a sociological approach may suggest to their students some problematic ways to examine the social values of groups. Art teachers who tell their students that an art object affects society in a certain way are subscribing to what Alexander calls a *shaping approach* (2003). Shaping theories suggest that art can somehow put ideas into peoples' minds and, as a result, claim art forms affect the society in different ways, i.e., that high art or mass art is harmful or beneficial. The agenda most frequently advanced by shaping theorists is that the elites are instrumental in the creation and distribution of cultural products in order to satisfy their own political, social, or economic interests. Marcuse, for example, suggested that the cultural industries create false needs in consumers and cultural industries lull workers into a passive acceptance of capitalism (1972). Frequently cited are the Frankfurt school views that art serving the masses is powerless and that the cultural industries are all-powerful. The Frankfurt approach also emphasizes that the mass audience spends too much time on unedifying mass art and, as a consequence, spends less time in useful educational and productive efforts.

As a result, sociological philosophies can inject the art curriculum with blends of both neo-Marxist and anti-capitalistic values. This is in spite of the fact that there is little or no evidence that students are, in effect, really harmed or positively shaped by images supposedly supporting such values. This also is done knowing that there is no simple, unproblematic mechanism by which art shapes a society. Sociologists know, for example, that there are serious methodological problems in trying to measure the effects of advertising on a society. Also they know that audiences are made up of *thinking* human beings and that they are not drugged automatons. Finally, some sociologists feel that cultural critiques of this order are in themselves elitist. As Abercrombie, et al wrote:

> It is notoriously difficult to say how audiences interpret the output of the media, and many studies avoid it altogether simply by assuming that audiences are affected. There are substantial methodological problems in the way of any empirical investigation of the audience. Even if it is clear that people react to, and are influenced by, television programs in the very short term, it is very difficult to measure long-term changes. Any long-term study will find it awkward to isolate changes in the audience due to the media from those stemming from other social influences. It is not even obvious what is to be measured. For example, is one interested in the influence of the media on the attitudes that people have or on their knowledge? (1994, 432).

Another major problem connected to the shaping theory is that it talks only about the effects of cultural products on society without mentioning the fact that cultural products are consumed by audiences. In fact, injection models suggest that ideas from the arts are injected directly into audiences considered mostly as passive and uncritical and made up of the culturally ignorant.

PSYCHOLOGICAL VALIDITY

The issue of psychological validity raises the question of whether or not the curriculum proposal accounts for human growth and development, learning, individual differences, and the like. It poses the question of *what* can be taught, *when* it can be taught, *how* it can be taught, and *to whom*. Art education scholars who advocate a constructivist cognitive argument supporting a sociocultural model of curriculum should raise serious questions as to whether cognitive psychology alone can be used to establish the *values* that art educators should hold about the goals of the school art curriculum. Cognitive theories, even if supported by empirical research data, cannot be used to determine the goals of the art curriculum because art values are not set by science, and aesthetic interests are not determined by cognitive theory.

Cognitive Models

Further, the effort to base the goals of the art program on a single view of cognition wrongfully assumes there is only one cognitive view and that any one particular view represents some absolute epistemological truth. In fact, as many sociologists note, to interpret art through any particular cognitive style or set of conventions may be futile and may only be useful for sociological research and not determining the means and ends of research. Moreover, no single cognitive learning strategy will work equally well for all students and few, if any, strategies will work optimally on all academic tasks (Schunk and Zimmerman 1997).

There are, indeed, a variety of instructional models one may follow in initiating learning. These include (1) the so-called SRSK model, which organizes interactive learning between teachers and students into metascripts, (2) a transactional strategies research model, (3) a learning to learn model, (4) a self-monitoring model, (5) the *STUDY* instrument tool, (6) a social cognitive model, (7) the strategic content learning (SCL) model, (8) a purposeful learning model, and (9) the verbal task regulation model (Schunk and Zimmerman 1997).

In addition to the notion that there are many different cognitive models one might follow, it should also be noted that the constructivist model itself is not universally supported by all cognitive scientists. There are, as I noted in *Mind in Art* (1999) a number of contending cognitive models which I have described as being top-down and bottom-up theories of the mind and cognition. The study of cognitive theory in the psychological sciences is an empirical science and like all the sciences, as Kuhn notes, they come from scientists studying the same phenomenon using the same scientific methods yet coming to different conclusions (1970).

Lacking assurances that any single learning structure can be associated with the study of mass and popular culture images, it goes without saying that any curriculum sequence and scope based on a single cognitive theory should not be offered. As described by those who include a postmodern dialectic where students engage in group discussions of image meaning, truth seeking becomes irrelevant, art cannot be defined, and aesthetic values are not relevant. What is likely then is that students in different sections of the same class could well decide on totally different interpretations of any set of visual images, especially when the criteria for decision making excludes the use of the principles of design and the study of art history, art criticism, and aesthetics. Even the possibility of considering imagination in visual forming would be rejected for discussion, since imagination is not itself deemed empirical.

Sequence and Scope

Many other questions remain unanswered, especially about what political images should be studied and in what sequence they need to be studied—for example, what knowledges and skills are needed in what order do we need to study them, in what depth do they need to be studied, what cognitive knowledges are required in order to study them, and in what sequence should they be offered? More questions abound, such as which images are most appropriate for the lower or upper grades, etc. As to studio assignments, if offered, one might ask age-appropriate questions such as the following: What age would be appropriate for students to be involved in making commercial illustrations, to address political and social themes, to make signs for political marches and campaigns, or to create graphics advocating a particular presidential candidate, the Green party, or safe sex?

SOCIAL VALIDITY

Social validity implies the degree to which a curricular proposal accounts for the school as a social institution existing in a particular society and for the pupil as an inheritor of mores, social class roles, socialization patterns, technological shifts, and the like. Many curricular proposals do not recognize the social factors necessary to motivate teachers, administrators, and patrons to accept curricular change. The sociological factors to be met include technological change, pressure group power, and philosophical and pedagogical difference among teachers.

Public Accountability

Given the current concerns of parents, legislators, and governments for school accountability, student achievement, graduation rates, employment, and social values respectful of democratic principles, it is appropriate to ask whether art classroom discussions of popular imagery and discourse about sexually explicit film, video, and advertising; displays of public nudity; and discussions of lifestyle choices would meet the Goals 2000 legislation, the national and state performance standards, and the No Child Left Behind Act.

Students critiquing visual images in the form of a spoken or a written dialogue supporting anti-capitalist and political values as part of the art curriculum are not likely to be well received by teachers, administrators, or parents. These critiques would hardly be a suitable substitution for school art study, especially when there are no criteria for deciding the value or truth of the statements or claims that the students produce. How a program of study that overtly rejects democratic values, logical thinking, truth telling, the elements and principles of design, the making of drawings and paintings, the study of art history, criticism, and aesthetics can be supported as being serious and meaningful art study is, to speak bluntly, beyond imagination. Even if our current efforts to establish standards and evaluate school art performance are insufficient, it is still highly unlikely that art classrooms that adopt a political curriculum would be able to pass muster as a school subject without totally abandoning Goals 2000 and the art achievement national and state standards. This does not mean that schools should avoid teaching students to think critically about governments, politicians, and social inequities, but rather it means that the art room may not be the best place to offer such study and that art teachers may be, in the last analysis, some of the least qualified by their training and experience to offer it.

Art Education Policy Formation

No art education policy should ever be based solely on either the social or political goals set by government regulatory agencies or by the politics of social reconstruction, especially as practiced by those who advocate anti-capitalistic and/or Marxist social values. Art education should function as part of an American education system that values democratic principles and requires equal access and equity in benefits to all its citizens through a state-sponsored and locally controlled democratic educational system. The obligation of the American school system is to provide its graduates with both the necessary work skills to survive in a technological society and also the values and skills needed to make living worthwhile. It should aim at helping its future citizens become productive, creative, independent individuals, responsive to the rights, feelings, and beliefs of their fellow citizens.

What the arts contribute to the education process is addressing those education concerns that make living worthwhile, mainly through programs that emphasize the individual as being a unique, creative, imaginative, and feeling human being who is capable, at the same time, of living in harmony with others. This state comes about through the making and contemplation of meaningful objects and events of artistic value; in this process, the artworks students create are meaningful because they contain elements of human motivation and provide an interaction between humans and their environment. The art experience itself is both cognitive and affective, which not only enhances one's enjoyment of art but is also connected to the urge to be creative, the desire to master construction, and eventually to practice it in a fulfilling way. The satisfaction of expressive needs also contributes to the objectification of meaning, which is central to the production of art and its enjoyment. Art has meaning to the individual through providing security and attachment that reveals the relationship between the individual and his or her environment.

As Sam Hope notes, the policy problem is that there are some measures we can control and others which we cannot:

> Like all fields, art education works in a context created by forces over which it has little control. It also has areas of responsibilities where it can exercise significant control. A

third reality is not discussed as much as it should be. This reality can be demarcated by asking several illustrative questions. What choices does the field make about dealing with conditions that appear beyond its control? How does a field delineate and then protect those things that are essential to its survival? How does the field manage the relationship between decisions in areas it cannot control and decisions in areas it can control? How much and what kind of thinking is being done about the short- and long-term ramifications of real or prospective changes? What are the forces influencing areas over which the field has little or no control and areas in which it has control? How are distinctions made between dysfunction and obsolescence? (2004, 94)

MEASURES WE CAN CONTROL

What teachers can control in the policy-making process is found in the setting of goals and constraints that are essential to the policy-making process. This can occur at both the district and school levels through active efforts to support the goals of art thinking and making in the school curriculum. What happens in the art classroom is largely decided by the art teacher who determines how curriculum policy is implemented. The teacher's decisions about external pressures for change versus the steady pursuit of reasonable purpose are revealed through the teacher's leadership. Today in art education there is so much pressure for change on the part of arts advocates and reformers that an illusion of evolving interplays and progression of activisms leads the field. If these views are allowed to dominate our thinking, the pursuit of reasonable and related content is obscured.

Based on the enrollment data reported in Chapter 5 and our observations in several of the nation's school districts (Dorn, Madeja, and Sabol 2004), my colleagues and I believe our art education programs remain solidly committed to art as expressive learning. As previously cited, some 29,000 students enter art programs in higher education each year with approximately 200,000 currently being enrolled in 350 of the 1,200 programs at the bachelor's, master's, and Ph.D. levels (HEDS, 2003). Significant changes have also been noted by those involved over the past five years in K–12 student art portfolio assessment (Dorn, Madeja, and Sabol 2004). Our observations of these events suggest: (1) that studio activity remains the most important part of the school art program and (b) that the subject matter content of the artwork has significantly changed through teachers introducing more art history and more multicultural, environmental, and technological concerns into student art projects. It is, I think, also clear that government efforts to create national and state standards have helped clarify to both teachers and the public what goals the teacher seeks to achieve in the art program. Art teachers today, as evidenced by our national meetings, are better educated and better informed about the importance of having goals and in seeking newer ways to measure them. There is little doubt that we still have a long way to go in strengthening art education in our schools but we also need to recognize that the art education field today is a lot more professional than it was in the '60s. Our concern for the future is to be sure that we continue to improve over the next forty to fifty years.

CHANGING WHAT
WE CANNOT CHANGE

As previously noted, educational policy formation at the federal, state, and local levels all too often fails to open that process to those whose task it is to implement that policy in schools. Art teachers left out of the policy loop are rarely effective in implementing changes they don't own. Reformers traditionally see the teachers as the greatest single obstacle to effecting educational change in part because state departments, legislatures, and special interest groups view themselves as being regulators rather than partners with teachers in the policy-implementing process.

Policy formation at all these levels is also not an exacting science, nor necessarily democratic. Federal educational policy such as the NDEA, inspired by the military's need to defend America from Russian domination in the space race, also produced a policy window that gave an opportunity for educators and special interest groups in math, language, and science education to increase the demands for science, math, and foreign languages in the school curriculum. Policy initiatives propelled by such mixed motives are also subject to the political feasibility of an initiative becoming law, which requires that compromises will be made, as previously noted, brokered by an "iron triangle" composed of special interest groups, legislators, and the educational bureaucrats. As a result, the actual legislation that codifies the education policy will consist of mixed goods brokered through political and economic trade-offs, where everyone gets something and no one gets left out. Political feasibility at the policy formation level is not concerned about policy implementation, but rather about who gets what and how much in the policy-making process.

Deciding on the goals of an art program forms the basis for deciding what policy alternatives to choose. Without agreed-upon goals, successful policy formation is impossible. Unfortunately, the most important educational goals are set by legislators who assume they can enact laws and regulations to be administered by state education agencies. As such, these laws are not open to advocacy except at the stages where policy is adopted and especially where it is implemented in schools. Adoption begins with the formulation of a policy and ends with its formal acceptance as a law, regulation, administrative directive, or other decision decided by rules. Policies, especially laws, rarely specify what is to be done—the place where teachers and school administrators can play their part.

Art teachers can perform the role of actors in the implementation process. They can and do exercise political power when motivated and energized. They also can individually and collectively move the process to focus on other issues, they can find friends in the legislature that work for co-sponsorships of legislation, they can create advisory groups, and they can be actors in compromises that significantly modify policy proposals to be more educationally acceptable. They also can use their influence to remove or modify features of a proposal that are objectionable. They can add features that they find more attractive than the ones being proposed. As an advisory group, they can help make compromises through negotiation, by features known as log rolling, a form of compromise that is characterized by the packaging together of substantially unrelated proposals. Teachers can also form themselves into special interest groups that mobilize other political actors on their behalf and make it politically costly for agenda setters to block proposals.

At the implementation phase, teachers can also participate in coalition building with parents and other interested school groups in finding ways the policy can work in practice. They can, as agents, help legislators develop policies that are politically feasible by helping assure the logic of the policy and the kind of cooperation it requires, and by identifying the skillful and committed people needed to manage its implementation.

To be sure, teachers rarely pursue these ends even when the process is open to them. Art teachers all too frequently are not involved, in part because they have not as yet really agreed on what ends the art education program should pursue. More often, limited by their doubts and divided by their convictions, they are inclined as a profession to pursue many different ends in pursuit of being open to alternatives. We have yet as a profession to agree on the central purpose of schooling in the arts, diluting the resoluteness of our purposes by chasing all the sloganeering bandwagons time has made available to us.

In the future I do not as yet envision a revolution in the art teaching profession to challenge a government policy formation process that is deleterious to the ends of learning in art. I can, however, envision an awakening of a profession to behave professionally in the pursuit of a teaching-learning evaluation process that not only reflects the goals of art but also verifies them in practice so all can see. This can come through a curriculum that is assessable, adaptable to change, and is authentic, one in which we truly know what it is we want children in art to know and be able to do and one in which we show successfully that we can do it.

ART EDUCATION
POLICY IMPLEMENTATION

As already noted, it is highly unlikely that the policy-making process at the federal and state levels will ever be changed merely to accommodate the concerns of teachers who are charged with the responsibility to implement change, yet an active and intelligent lobbying effort by teachers could change that scenario, at least at the district and school policy formation levels. Overall, school standards realistically should be set at the federal, state, and school district levels, but to be really effective in practice they also need to be set by the teacher and the student in the classroom. School art standards must be owned by those who are expected to conform to them, where both teachers and students in art must help determine what standards they will own and implement.

The most critical policy formation and implementation process, therefore, really takes place in the art classroom, in part because all K–12 teachers are independent and self reliant, but in particular because in the art classroom, external forces have no standing in the creative act. As such, no policy of the state can effectively force anyone to be free unless individuals exist in a state where all are free to discover themselves as independent, self-reliant, creative individuals. Art thinking and making is really about fueling consciousness and imagination, which is not likely to come through an educational process that requires students to create according to a legislative fiat.

This point of view is not meant to demean the responsibility of the state to offer educational leadership on matters that maintain and nourish American values which enable us as a nation to remain both secure and free. Federal, state, and local school regulating policies are really needed when in some school districts nearly half of our citizens can't read a ballot or balance a checkbook.

Further, the social, political, and economic achievements that we need in order for America to remain a free, viable, and contributing nation among other world nations must be maintained. Nevertheless, we also need to be aware that national school policies intended to advance learning in math, science, and the social studies do not require that we turn the art room into a science or social studies class.

What is needed are policy implementations that consider what the arts can do to strengthen student achievement both in the arts and in other subject areas of the curriculum. Current school policies that turn the art class into a reading or math class are not effective, and the art teaching profession should make that abundantly clear to any over-zealous and threatened school administrator bent on only meeting regulatory goals. Art education encourages the development of intelligent behavioral skills, but it is not intended to be solely an education in intellect. Art education is also social education where students learn to create form through the use of models provided by the teacher, the artist, and their peers.

Art Classroom Standards

What standards the art teacher decides to use in order to judge student performance is determined both by abilities of the students and the resources that the teacher is provided by the school in order to implement instruction. What standards the student uses to judge his or her artistic achievement must inevitably be set and self monitored by the student. While teachers and schools can provide the environment for creative learning, they do not have the power to give the student the personal goals that he or she needs in order to succeed.

How effective the nation's art teachers will be in implementing educational policies set at the federal, state, and local levels is a matter for speculation, especially given the lack of attention by the art teaching profession to art policy formation and implementation. Only the art teachers are able to decide what offers the most promise for meeting the goals of their art education programs and the broader goals of the schools in serving as a socializing influence in the development of the American character and making schools accountable to the American public. It is up to the art teacher to make the art program serve the interests of both the individual and the public.

THE LIMITS OF POSTMODERNISM

My review of the alternative evaluation policies presented in Chapter 5 suggests that any effort to substitute our current activity-centered studio art program for a socially structured model, making art an academic study dedicated to social reconstruction, may in the long run be counterproductive. Sociological research raises serious questions as to whether the study of images itself tells us much about our society, whether teacher-directed interpretive methods are needed in order to prevent harmful images from influencing student behavior, and whether such approaches can be validated through a single cognitive theory. Most of all we need to question whether any postmodern model would meet our national educational goals and standards for student achievement.

Also deemed questionable were the claims some have made that studio activity makes students more competitive rather than cooperative and that the study of formalist art leads to a rejection of the human condition. Anyone making such claims could not have been a product of the studio or to have seriously practiced it in teaching. Studio teaching, as previously noted, is a social activity where students create objects of meaning using the models shaped by the teacher, the artist, and their peers. As Ernst Gombrich noted, artists learn more from other artists and from the social conditions of the time than they learn from looking. In art, he notes, the conditions of illusions are found in the accepted practices that artists in every society use in order to convey meanings that meet social expectations rather than appearances. As Gombrich also notes, if art was an individual expression of personal form, art could not have had a history. The history of art is, then, a history of style where artists have always used socially accepted conventions for communicating form. The basis for artistic illusion, he notes, come from the schema in the artist's mind and how well that matches the expectations of the viewer.

The Socialization Process

L. S. Vygotsky, frequently cited by postmodernists as a principal advocate of art as a socialization process in education, suggests that in order to understand the learner we need to discover the general relationship between learning and development and how this occurs when children reach school age (1978). This is contrary to the claims of some postmodernists that stage-by-age development is unimportant in learning. As Vygotsky notes,

> A well known and empirically established fact is that learning should be matched in some manner with the child's developmental level (1978, 85).

Also, with respect to the child's mental development, Vygotsky notes,

> Over a decade, even the profoundest thinkers never questioned the assumption; they never entertained the notion that what children can do with the assistance of others might be in some sense more indicative of their mental development than what they can do alone. (1978, 85).

What Vygotsky supports is the need for us to consider the zone of proximal development, which is the distance between the child's actual developmental level in independent problem solving and the potential development that occurs when problem solving occurs under adult guidance or in collaboration with more capable peers. Children, he notes, can imitate a variety of actions that go well beyond their own capabilities. By using imitation, children are capable of doing much more in a collective activity or under the guidance of adults.

SUMMARY

In this effort I have posed a number of questions related to what I perceived as significant policy shifts in education. Moreover, I addressed that over time, art education shifted its emphasis from supporting the child as artist to the study of politics, power struggles, and social reform through socially constructed art. In the interest of explaining the art teaching profession's interest in such reforms, I identified a number of important aesthetic, sociological, political, and philosophical factors fostering this evolution. Discussed were the trend toward an empirical view of art curriculum reform and the effects of government interventions designed to interfere with private choice.

Government Interventions

Government concerns were addressed through the identification of a number of federal government policy interventions in the

198

arts, spurred on by what some critics perceived were the deficiencies in K–12 schooling responsible for the U.S. losing the so-called space race with the Soviet Union. Through taking advantage of the policy window afforded by the National Defense Education Act, Congress was able to create a number of new national arts policy initiatives, including those resulting from the creation of various art education initiatives and the National Endowments for the Arts and Humanities, which, in effect, identified both the market and government failures governments needed in order to justify interventions in the arts. As a result, both the arts and art education begin to be viewed by government as a public good needing support and regulation in the public interest.

With regard to the newly created bureaucracies affecting art education, USOE's Arts and Humanities Program had the greatest impact (1) through its efforts to support empirical research on the student art behaviors needed for policy formation and (2) through offering a number of developmental conferences designed to reconfigure the art teaching profession into a multi-disciplinary study. Following the cessation of USOE funding, two private foundations, as virtual shadow governments, proceeded to influence the curricular shifts that moved art education even further toward the new emphasis on art as general education and interdisciplinary study. These curricular policy shifts resulted in an approach to art curriculum conception as social reconstruction.

Philosophical Shifts

Also addressed were the philosophical shifts that fueled a contest between theorists committed to either the Modernist or postmodernist view of art and the role of the artists. Identified were a number of the Modernist and postmodernist theories most frequently used by art education policy researchers to justify the shift from art being viewed as having the aura of greatness and the artist as genius to a conception of art as a socially constructed object revealing important historical truths about the effects of the economic and social powers of a ruling elite in its suppression of the American working class.

A review of these various theories suggested, however, there may be as many aesthetic theories as there are theorists. Proposals on

Chapter 6 Evaluating Alternatives/The Future

both sides pose concerns that those who oppose their position cause irreparable harm to children exposed to each other's view. Questions as yet unanswered include whether the aesthetic values of any single persuasion can attribute status to art, whether these classificatory distractions really help in deciding what is good or bad art, and finally, whether definitions of art themselves serve any real purpose in deciding what is and what is not art.

Art World Change

Following the review of divergent aesthetic and cognitive theories of art were the descriptions of four major world art movements in the late nineteenth and twentieth centuries, which suggested that the art world itself, even before the 1960s, was undergoing changes in both what was to be considered as art and who actually could be called an artist. The movements analyzed included the William Morris Arts and Crafts Movement, the U.S.-WPA federal arts project, the Owatonna Art Education Project, and the German Bauhaus. Presented also were a number of different approaches to art curriculum conception, new approaches to the teaching of art and design, and newer and broader definitions of the arts. These efforts, it was noted, profoundly affected American art and industrial arts education programs, broadening the base on which educators decided what activities advanced aesthetic growth, what newer methods of staffing were possible, what new creative approaches to art materials and process were available, how to form new unions between fine and applied arts, and how art could be used as a tool for community development and as a way of life.

These newer definitions and newer functions of art as a force for community development, coupled with the felt responsibility of governments to play a part in art education curricular change, clearly made the arts in K–12 schools a product of federal policy— that is, a policy pursued in the public interest and requiring government coerciveness in the shaping of newer art education curriculum policy. These interventions by government came in the form of rules and regulations; direct grants to artists, art educators, and arts institutions in support of empirical research on children's art learning; and support for developmental conferences that broadened the scope of the art activities offered in schools,

200

including the sciences, the humanities, and the social studies. As a result, American art education during the last half of the twentieth century gradually came to be considered a multidisciplinary subject stressing art for cognitive development, audience education, social reconstruction, and political activism. As a consequence, art education in K–12 schooling began to be portrayed in the art education literature as a subject more supportive of a variety of social and economic goals and less as a subject that helped students create new things.

Clearly losing ground were the art education advocates who believed in art as a creative activity, in the importance of studio activities, and in the models provided by the artist, the teacher, and the student's peers. More frequently heard were the claims of art education professionals that studio activity was anti-intellectual, elitist, non-cognitive, lacking in interdisciplinary rigor, and counter-productive in the socialization process. Art education in the last half of the twentieth century thus increasingly became a national priority more concerned with the nation's economic, political, and social development rather than with individual creative activity in service of the life of the mind.

CONCLUSIONS

Finally, socially reconstructive goals were analyzed from the viewpoint of curricular viability. Reviewed in detail were the curricular alternatives offered in the constructivist and deconstructivist curriculum models. Strongly suggested as an alternative was that we support the sociocultural model addressed in Chapter 5. It is this applied art activity approach that comes closest to meeting the curriculum validity issues and the calls for government standards and public accountability.

Art education framed solely as an academic subject is, I think, the best way we can lose the art program in K–12 schooling which may end up as did the industrial arts programs in the 1960s, losing its grounding in active thinking and making and, as a result, being more or less eliminated from the K–12 curriculum. As a field, industrial arts sealed its own doom by first valuing *activity* for its own sake and then not maintaining a hold on its base as a creative activity. What happened in the 1960s to the combined programs in art and industrial art was that the art educators appropriated the metal, wood, and printing shops and redesigned them as jewelry, sculpture, and graphics courses. This left industrial arts with its only base being in the trades or as a general education program, which eventually became obsolete.

Perhaps the lesson to be learned from industrial arts is twofold: (1) that K–12 art activity must continue to emphasize highly creative and inventive forms of expressive meaning and (2) that in order to ensure that our art programs remain that way, we must pay attention to how they can be continuously evaluated. These evaluations should be undertaken by both the art teacher and the art student. The teacher needs to know what he or she expects students to know and be able to do in creative forming; the student needs to engage in self-reflective learning and evaluation, which requires that students claim ownership of their own goals and how they personally can achieve them.

Art education is not, strictly speaking, an academic subject but is rather about creative activity requiring education in imagination, consciousness, thought, and feeling. Both the art teacher and the art student have a personal stake in assuring that the art education program delivers what it promises. Art teachers who disabuse student interest in creative forming may be cutting off their noses to spite their faces.

What students create are objects of meaning that come from understanding first and foremost that the works of art made by humans express meaning and reflect artistic quality. To identify a work of art as such, it must be possible to determine the meaning and artistic quality of the work. Meaning in this sense requires that works of art have content that can be cognitively or affectively experienced and that the artistic quality in artwork refers to specific aesthetic values, aesthetic values that provide sensory perception and that are appreciated. There are, according to Van der Tass, objectified notions linked to artistic values that must be distinguished from other evaluations such as ideals of beauty, or related to natural phenomena such as home decorating or urban design (1999).

Artistic values should predominate in a work of art and eventually become artistic norms, which in time become values. They can be vague and interpreted autonomically and under certain conditions. Meaning and artistic quality may eventually combine in works of art that are defined as created, meaningful objects that function for human beings as individuals and for the society as a whole. They serve socio-psychological, cultural, social, and economic functions because meaningful aesthetic objects functionally relate to elements of human motivation and to the interactions between humans and their environment. The art experience in which the work of art and the human being meet is both cognitive and emotional in nature.

The need to develop and practice one's cognitive and emotional artistic competence can not only enhance the enjoyment of the arts but it is also connected with the urge to be creative and the need to master a particular art until a degree of mastery is achieved. The practice of art is in itself fulfilling, in part because it satisfies certain expressive needs and cultural functions through the objectification of meaning.

A New Theory of Education in the Arts

What is needed is a new theory of education in the arts separate from the art world notion of students as agents with cultural capital (knowledge of art) that they acquire by participating in the objective culture and develop through learning bodies of knowledge that provide the weapons and the rationale to fight the battle in the intellectual field. What is needed is a theory that opposes Bourdieu's idea of inculcating in students an *aesthetic disposition* that is linked to a position in a social class and to cognition rather than emotions, as is practiced in the audience education efforts advocated by general art education.

The Child As Craftsman

David Feldman is particularly critical of educational thinking, blaming the student for a failure to learn (1980). Feldman challenges this claim through arguing that children do learn at varying rates, use capabilities and skills uniquely, and react differently to various materials and to subtleties of teaching. As an alternative, Feldman advocates a framework that would help discrimi-

203

nate among the virtually infinite number of possible futures for a given child and ways to help decide among the tremendous number of tasks, materials, activities, and bodies of knowledge that could be selected as educational at any grade, age, or level of preparation. The image he chooses is that of the child as craftsman.

To view the child as craftsman is, in Feldman's view, to view the child as wanting to be good at something, that is, to take pride in accomplishment and build a sense of integrity about his own work. Feldman argues that the craftsman image is intended to include a more direct link to specific fields of endeavor and to suggest why some activities are so much more compelling to a given child than others. The craftsman view supports that the principal aim of education should be to *engage* the child in the pursuit of mastering a satisfying craft and to find work to do that is likely to bring adult satisfaction, fulfillment, and expression. The craftsman image further suggests that it is a way to think about the child and his relationship to knowledge at any point in his educational life. By thinking of students as actively trying to find satisfying work to do and trying to become good at something, the current aims of the educators and the educational process become somewhat altered. This view extends to all fields of study and to as many kinds of work as society offers, including basket weaving, oration, mathematics, chess, mechanics, and salesmanship.

Learning through Doing

With regard to instruction, Feldman notes how much a child can learn is not a meaningful issue unless considered (1) in relation to a field of endeavor and (b) in relation to the extent to which the child and the field are well matched. This suggests that a child's capability makes sense only after he or she has become engaged in serious attempts at mastery of a domain. With respect to what sorts of mentors or models are most beneficial to the most mature forms of the field, he rejects a novice-master model in favor of a model of apprentice-like quality.

The craftsman notion suggests that all progress be gauged in two important ways: (1) to encourage greater numbers of individuals to find fields to pursue and find work that engages their energies and through which they derive satisfaction, and (2) to require that the student is able to go beyond the limits of the craft, finding yet another problem to be solved, goal to achieve, and idea to be expressed—all of which are the conditions that favor creativity. With respect to the need for creativity and expression, Feldman notes:

> Craftsmanship seems to capture the desire for individual expression that is part of the heritage of every human being. I am not suggesting that the desire for expression implies that young children be given totally free rein to do whatever they please. This is not what I mean by individuality at all. I do believe, however, that those who are responsible for preparing children to enter society should recognize that a substantial challenge lies in being able to help each child acquire the attitudes and skills of craftsmanship in a domain pleasing to them and valuable to their culture (1980, 172).

Choice in Education

The concept of the inequality of art participation discussed earlier cannot be answered by a school art policy that assumes aesthetic preferences are not based on free choice or autonomously developed artistic taste but rather on a social-structural historic condition. Artistic preference, art experience, and judgement of works of art belong, according to this view, to socially determined lifestyles and tastes in art regarded by some as cultural colonialism.

A new educational policy actively supported by art teachers would not be related to formal classification of artwork but rather to the art experience of the individual learner. Further, it could not be based on elements of social reconstruction; the art experience is always more than a social reconstruction and is determined by the way people respond to an artwork. The choices and assessments of individuals are motivated not by social conditions but rather by the variance and regularities caused by the psychological, cultural, and social-structural characteristics of the individual learner.

In general, the art experience is a social-psychological process linking personal characteristics to the artwork. The quality of the art experience is related to the features of the artwork, to the spectator's artistic competence, and to the functions the art experience fulfills for that person. Because the art experience is an interaction between an individual and an art object, it cannot be a categorized object requiring that the school art experience be directed to an optimal art experience for all the students.

Student motivations for learning in the arts cannot be classified as interests that are economic, social, and political, but rather as coming from the satisfaction of needs and the realization of certain ideals and values that have their desirability in common. While it is true that mature artists will not overlook their interests, for example, with gallery owners, their work may also contribute to the sensory and attachment needs in the artistic experience and to one's status and capital interests.

What is needed in art education is a theoretical model for art participation where culturally differentiated experience in art does not contradict some universal features of art and the art experience and where psychological involvement in the work qualifies the relation between the student and the art object. These experiences should contribute to the enrichment of conscious life experiences by giving meaning on a symbolic level, and affectively through feeling that contributes to the enrichment of sensory competence and cognitive enrichment. Valuable artistic achievements and the development of artistic skill are both required for an optimal art experience, and should become the objectives of a sound policy of art participation.

REFERENCES

Abercrombie, V.; Warde, A.; Soothill, K.; Urry, J.; and Walby, S. 1994. *Contemporary British Society*. 2nd ed. Cambridge: Polity Press.

Alexander, V.C. 2003. *Sociology and the Arts: Exploring Fine and Popular Forms*. Malden, MA: Blackwell Publishing.

Dorn, C.M. 1999. *Mind in Art*. Mahway, NJ: Lawrence Erlbaum Associates.

Dorn, C.M.; Madeja, S.S.; and Sabol, F.R. 2004. *Assessing Expressive Learning: A Practical Guide for Teacher-Directed Authentic Assessment in K–12 Visual Arts Education*. Mahway, NJ: Lawrence Erlbaum Associates Publishers.

Efland, A.D. 2003. *Art and Cognition.* New York: Teachers College Press.

Feldman, D. H. 1980. *Beyond Universals in Cognitive Development.* Norwood, NJ: Ablex Publishing Company.

Fiske, J. 1989. *Reading the Popular.* New York: Routledge.

Higher Education Data Service (HEDS) (2003). *Data Summaries, Art, & Design 2002–2003.* Reston, Va: Higher Education Data Services.

Hope, S. 2004. "Art Education in a World of Cross Purposes" in *Handbook of Research on Policy in Art Education,* eds. Eisner, E.W.; and Day, M.D. Mahway, NJ: Lawrence Erlbaum Associates.

Kuhn, T. 1970. *The Structure of Scientific Revolutions.* Chicago: University of Chicago Press.

Marcuse, H. 1972. *One Dimensional Man.* London: Abacus.

National Education Association. 1963. *Research Monograph 1963-M3 Music and Art in the Public Schools.* Washington, DC: Research Division, The National Education Association.

Schunk, D.H.; and Zimmerman, B.J. 1997. Social Origins of Self-regulatory Competence. *Educational Psychologist* 32 (4): 195–208.

Thompson, R. 1981. General Criteria for Curriculum Analysis. In *Foundations for Curriculum Development and Evaluation in Art Education.,* eds. Hardeman, G.N.; and Zernich, T. Urbana: Stipes Publishing Company, 206-213.

Van der Tass, J.M. 1999. *A Theory of the Artworld.* Rotterdam: Erasmus University Press.

Vygotsky, L. S. 1978. *Mind in Society: The Development of Higher Psychological Processes.* Cambridge: Harvard University Press.

Weimer, D.L.; and Vining, A.R. 1999. *Policy Analysis, Concepts, and Practices.* Upper Saddle River, NJ: Prentice Hall.

Willis, P. 1978. *Profane Culture.* London: Routledge.

APPENDIX A

United States Office of Education Projects

The AHP's Projects Listed According to Art Form

Education Number	Final Report	Investigator and Institution
	AESTHETIC EDUCATION	
ED 048315	An Approach to Aesthetic Education, September 1970 (two volumes)	Richard Colwell, University Illinois (Urbana)
ED 071989	Basic Abilities Required for Understanding and Creation in the Arts, September 1972	Nelson Goodman, Harvard University, Cambridge, MA
ED 111751	Basic Research in Esthetic Education, August 1973	Frank Barron, Institute for Personality Assessment and Research, Berkeley, CA
	ART EDUCATION	
ED 002819	A Study of Esthetic Judgement, 1962	Irvin L. Child, Yale University, New Haven, CT

ED 003069	Question Types, Patterns, and Sequenced by Art Teachers in the Classroom, 1964 (University Park)	Robert D. Clements, Pennsylvania State University
ED 003377	Creative Thinking in Art Students: An Exploratory Study, 1964	Jacob W. Getzels, University of Chicago, IL
ED 003483	Development of Sensitivity to Esthetic Values, 1964	Irvin L. Child, Yale University, New Haven, CT
ED 016900	Effect of Self-Reflective Training in Art on the Capacity for Creative Action, 1964	Kenneth R. Beittel, Pennsylvania State University (University Park)
ED 054395	Student and Teacher Interactions During Evaluative Dialogues in Art, University (University Park)	Layman H. Jones, Jr., Pennsylvania State University
ED 003078	Development and Validation of a Descriptive Scale for Measurement of Art Products, 1965	Mary J. Rouse, Indiana State University (Bloomington)
ED 003079	Creative Thinking in Art Students: The Process of Discovery, 1965	Jacob W. Getzels, University of Chicago, IL
ED 003079	Effects of Two Programs and Two Methods of Teaching Upon the Quality of Art Products of Adolescents, 1965	Leon Frankson, Pennsylvania State University (University Park)
ED 010090	The Relationship of Certain Prediction and Self-evaluation Discrepancies to Art Performance and Art Judgement, 1966	Theodore F. Harvey, Jr., Kent State University (Ohio)
ED 010588	Planning Tests to Measure Outcomes of the Research Program, Education through Vision, May 1966	Donald A. Trismen, Educational Testing Service, Princeton, NJ

ED 010417	A Comparative Study of General Art Offerings in University of Wisconsin Extension Centers, State Universities, and Vocational Schools, August 1966	William J. Leffin, University of Wisconsin (Madison)
ED 010416	A Survey of Current Teaching Approaches to Image Making in the Art Schools of Britain, October 1966	Walter M. Askin, California State College at Los Angeles
ED 011063	Improving the Teaching of Art Appreciation in the Secondary School, November 1966	David W. Ecker, Ohio State University (Columbus)
ED 010555	Artists' Ideas About Art and Their Use in Education, December 1966	John A. Michael, Miami University, Oxford, Ohio
ED 012804	Selected Psychological Concepts as Applied to the Teaching of Drawing, December 1966	Kenneth R. Beittel, Pennsylvania State University (University Park)
ED 010415	Testing for Creative Traits of College Students, 1967	Ruby Claire Ball, Southern Connecticut State College (New Haven)
ED 011051	The Effectiveness of Three Motivational Methods in an Art Program in the Elementary Grades, February 1967	Robert D. Clements, Ball State University, Muncie, IN
ED 013368	Criteria for Evaluation of Children's Artistic Creativity, February 1967	Paul Mussen and Hilda Lewis, University of California (Berkeley)

ED 016847	Uses of Symmetry in Design Education March 1967	William S. Huff, Carnegie Institute of Technology, Pittsburgh, PA
ED 055092	Programming Visual Behavior, March 1967	Aatis E. Lillstrom, Columbia University, New York City
ED 012380	Bases of School Children's Esthetic Judgement and Esthetic Preference, June 1967	Irvin L. Child, Yale University, New Haven, CT
ED 017044	Education through Vision, September 1967	Bartlett H. Hayes, Harvard University, Cambridge, MA
ED 023354	The Relationship of Motivation and Evaluation to the Process and Product in the Artwork of College Students, December 1967	Rudy S. Ackerman, Moravian College, Bethlehem, PA
ED 026403	A Study of the Relation of Museum Art Exhibitions to Education, December 1967	Bartlett H. Hayes, Jr., Harvard University, Cambridge, MA
ED 048745	The Application of Programmed Learning and Teaching Systems Procedures for Instruction in a Museum Environment, December 1967	C. G. Screven, University of Wisconsin (Milwaukee)
ED 024181	A Comparison of Group Versus Individual Production of Non-verbal Artistic Creativity, January 1968	Stephen C. Zambito, Eastern Michigan University (Ypsilanti)
ED 022221	Study of Visual Factors in Concept Formation, May 1968	Rudolf Arnheim, Sarah Lawrence College, Bronxville, NY

ED 025529	An Investigation into the Character and Expressive Qualities of Early Adolescent Art, October 1968	W. Lambert Brittain, Cornell University, Ithaca, NY
ED 047652	A Cognitive Approach to the Assessment of Esthetic Responses, December 1970	Arthur D. Efland, Ohio State University (Columbus)
ED 054185	Assessment of Affective Responses Conducive to Esthetic Sensitivity, January 1971	Irvin L. Child, Yale University, New Haven, CT
ED 052219	Evaluation of Trained and Untrained Observers' Affective Responses to Art Objects, March 1971	George W. Hardiman, University of Illinois (Urbana)
ED 013367	An Investigation of the Means for Utilizing Academic and Community Resources to Provide Services to Arts Organizations and through Them to Schools and Colleges, July 1966	Harold Burris-Meyer, Florida Atlantic University (Boca Raton)
ED 045631	An Inquiry into the Education of Non-verbal Communication, July 1970	Harold Burris-Meyer, Florida Atlantic University (Boca Raton)
ED 054188	The Identification and Selection of Creative Artistic Talent by Means of Biographical Information, January 1971	Robert Ellison, Institute of Behavioral Research, Salt Lake City, UT

Appendix A

1. Seminar on Elementary and Secondary School Education in the Visual Arts
   Howard Conant, principal investigator
   New York University
   October 8–11, 1964, at New York University

2. Meeting on Art Education
   Joseph Turner, conference planner
   Harvard University
   Sponsored by the Office of Science and Technology
   December 18–19, 1964, at Harvard University

3. Conference on a Longitudinal Study of Expressive Behavior in the Arts
   Jack Morrison, principal investigator
   University of California at Los Angeles
   February 18–20, 1965, in Santa Monica, California

4. Research and Development Team for the Improvement of Teaching Art
   Appreciation in the Secondary Schools
   David Ecker, principal investigator
   Ohio State University
   June 28–August 27, 1965, at Ohio State University

5. A Seminar in Art Education for Research and Curriculum Development
   Edward Mattil, principal investigator
   Pennsylvania State University
   August 30–September 9, 1965, at Pennsylvania State University

6. Humanities and the Schools
   Richard Miller, conference coordinator
   University of Kentucky
   Sponsored by Westab Incorporated
   December 9–10, 1965, at University of Kentucky

7. Uses of Newer Media in Art Education
   Vincent Lanier, project director
   National Art Education Association
   December 13–17, 1965, in Washington, DC

8. A Developmental Conference to Establish Guidelines for the
   Teaching of Art Appreciation
   Jeanne Orr, principal investigator
   Ohio State University
   January 15–19, 1966, at Ohio State University

9. A Conference on the Role of the Crafts in Education
   Jean Delius, principal investigator
   State University of New York
   March 23–25, 1966, in Niagara Falls, NY

10. Conference on Instructional Television in Art Education
    Edwin Cohen, conference coordinator
    Indiana University
    Sponsored by National Center for School and College
    Television
    May 2–3, 1966, at Indiana University

11. International Leadership Conference in Art Education
    Charles Dorn, principal investigator
    National Art Education Association
    July 27–29, 1966, in Belgrade, Yugoslavia

12. Conference on Museums and Education
    Charles Blitzer, principal investigator
    Smithsonian Institution
    August 21–26, 1966, at the University of Vermont

13. Conference on Curriculum and Instructional Improvement
    in Art Education
    Alice Baumgarner, principal investigator
    National Art Education Association
    September 20–22, 1966, in Washington, DC

14. **A Conference on Advanced Placement in Art**
    Bernard Arnest, principal investigator
    Colorado College
    October 13–15, 1966, in Colorado Springs

15. **A Seminar on the Role of the Arts in Meeting the Social and Educational Needs of the Disadvantaged.**
    Hanna Rose, principal investigator
    Brooklyn Museum
    November 15–19, 1966, in Gaithersburg, Maryland

16. **Aesthetic Education Conferences at the Whitney Museum of American Art and Rhode Island School of Design**
    Harlan Hoffa (in New York) and Manuel Barkan (in Providence), conference coordinators
    Sponsored by U.S. Office of Education (in New York) and Ohio State University and Central Midwestern Regional Educational Laboratory, Inc. (in Providence)
    January 20–21; July 24–25, 1967, respectively

Grant to the School District of University City, Missouri for support of the Arts in General Education Project. This was the first pilot project supported by the JDR III Fund to test the feasibility of making all the arts integral to the education of every child in an entire school system ($346,400 for a five-year period from May 1, 1968 to June 30, 1973).

Grant to the St. Louis Art Museum to develop educational services to complement the University City Arts in General Education Project ($14,000 for a one-year period from August 15, 1968 to August 14, 1969).

Grant to CEMREL (Central Midwestern Regional Educational Laboratory), St. Louis, Missouri, to evaluate the University City Arts in General Education Project ($100,200 for a three-year period from July 1, 1969 to June 30, 1972).

Grant to The Museum of Modern Art to assist with planning and developmental work to create the Children's Art Caravan, a mobile version of the Children's Art Carnival ($35,000 for a year and a half during the period from June 1, 1963 to March 31, 1972).

Grant to the Bank Street College of Education to support the project, The Development of an Integrated Program of the Arts and Humanities for Children in an Urban Community, carried on in Public School 51 in New York City. This was the second pilot project supported by the JDR III Fund (approximately $150,000 for a three-year period from September 1, 1968 to August 31, 1971). A second grant of $23,000 to Bank Street College to evaluate the pilot project during a one-year period from September 4, 1969 to September 4, 1970).

Grant to the Mineola, Long Island, Public Schools for the project, The Improvement and Integration of the Fine Arts Program into the Curriculum of the Mineola Public Schools. This was the third pilot project supported by the fund. ($361,250 for a five-year period from July 1, 1969 to June 30, 1974).

Grant to the Union Free School District No. 5 (Town of Rye), Port Chester, New York for the Project, Developing the Program and Facility for a High School with Special Emphasis in the Arts and Humanities for All Its Students (approximately $113,600 for a three-year period from August 1, 1969 to July 31, 1972).

Grant to Educational System for the Seventies to support a project, Arts Curriculum Development Project for ES '70. (In-kind services in the amount of approximately $31,500 were provided to ES '70 for office space, supplies, and equipment for a one-year period from October 15, 1969 to October 14, 1970).

Grant to the College Entrance Examination Board to inaugurate Advanced Placement in Studio Art, Art History, and Music ($200,000 for a two–and–one-half year period from March 1, 1970 to August 31, 1972).

Grant of $7,500 to New York University to support a graduate internship in the JDR III Fund office ($7,500 for a one-year period from September 1, 1969 to August 31, 1970).

Grant to Carnegie-Mellon University for a graduate internship at CEMREL in St. Louis to assist with the University City Arts in General Education Project ($6,000 for a one-year period from June 1, 1970 to May 31, 1971).

Grant to the Lane Intermediate Education District, Eugene, Oregon to support A Program for the Improvement of Art Education in the Elementary Schools of Lane County ($16,000 for a one-year period from May 15, 1970 to May 31, 1971).

Grant to the University of Oregon to continue the project in the Elementary Schools of Lane County ($12,000 for a one-year period from July 1, 1971 to June 30, 1972).

Grant to John Adams High School, Portland, Oregon for developing the arts in general education in an experimental high school ($54,500 for approximately three years during a period from February 15, 1971 to June 30, 1974).

Grant to Baldwin School of Puerto Rico to develop an integrated arts curriculum ($36,000 for a year and a half from February 1, 1972 to June 30, 1973).

Grant to the Jefferson County Public Schools, Lakewood, Colorado to incorporate the arts in general education into an interdisciplinary curriculum (approximately $282,500 for a five-year period from October 15, 1972 to August 31, 1976).

Grant to the New York City Board of Education-Community District 2 to assist in the development of a new experimental elementary school, Public School 3-M, in which the arts were to be made central to the school curriculum (approximately $50,750 for a two-year period from September 1, 1971 to August 31, 1973).

Grant to the Arts Council of Oklahoma City to implement the Creative Education Program and, particularly, Opening Doors, in the Oklahoma City Public Schools ($113,400 for a four–and–one-half year period from February 1, 1972 to July 31, 1976).

Grant to assist the New York State Department of Education in implementing Project SEARCH, which was initiated to establish an integrated humanities and arts program in six public school districts and one parochial school ($194,000 during approximately five years from June 1, 1972 to April 30, 1977).

Grant to the Pennsylvania Department of Education to assist with the planning and implementation of a state-wide arts in basic education program ($62,000 during a three–and–one-half year period from June 1, 1972 to October 14, 1976).

Grant jointly to the Asia Society and CEMREL for a pilot project to develop teaching materials in Asian arts for classroom use ($17,000 for a six-month period from February 1, 1973 to July 31, 1973).

Grant to the Education Development Center, Newton, Massachusetts to plan to develop educational television programming based on concepts common to science, technology, mathematics, and the arts that led to the educational television series, "The Infinity Factory." ($13,700 for a three-month period from February 1, 1973 to April 30, 1973).

Grant to the Research Division of the Institute for the Development of Educational Activities, Los Angeles, California to support A Study of the Arts in Precollegiate Education (approximately $80,200 for a four-year period from September 1, 1973 to August 31, 1977).

Grant to the Ridgewood, New Jersey, Public Schools to develop a project in aesthetic education ($12,000 for a period from June 1, 1973 to October 14, 1974).

Grant to the Boston Metropolitan Cultural Alliance to assist in planning for an arts in education program for the Boston Public Schools ($12,500 for a one-year period from October 15, 1973 to October 14, 1974).

Grant to the National Association of State Boards of Education to conduct a Survey of Arts in Education Policies of State Boards of Education ($5,500 for a six-month period from October 5, 1977 to April 15, 1978).

Grants to each of the six school districts in the League of Cities and the nine state education departments in the Ad Hoc Coalition of States for the Arts in Education to support the JDR III Fund Administrative Fellowship Training Program ($5,000 each, or a total of $75,000 was appropriated for five-month fellowships beginning January 3, 1978 and ending August 31, 1978, and $6,000 each, or a total of $90,000 was awarded for fellowships ranging up to one year beginning July 1, 1978 and ending September 1, 1979) (Madeja 1992).

Reference

Madeja, S., ed. 1992. *Kathryn Bloom Innovation in Arts Education.* DeKalb: Northern Illinois University.

INDEX

225

INDEX

228

INDEX